LESLEY RIDDOCH is an award-winning broadcaster, writer, journalist, independence campaigner, podcaster and land reform activist. She writes weekly columns for *The National* and is a contributor to *The Guardian*, BBC *Question Time*, *Scotland Tonight* and *Any Questions*. She is founder and Director of Nordic Horizons, a policy group that brings Nordic experts to the Scottish Parliament and produces a popular weekly podcast. Lesley has presented *You and Yours* on BBC Radio 4, *The Midnight Hour* on BBC2 and *The People's Parliament* and *Powerhouse* on Channel 4, and has been a columnist for the *Herald* and *Scotsman* newspapers. She founded the Scottish feminist magazine *Harpies and Quines*, won two Sony awards for her daily Radio Scotland show and edited *The Scotswoman* – a 1995 edition of *The Scotsman* written by its female staff. She was a trustee of the Isle of Eigg Trust that pioneered the successful community buyout in 1997. She has presented and co-produced films about the Faroes, Iceland, Estonia and Norway. Lesley was awarded a PhD, the Fletcher of Saltoun Award for her contribution to Scotland's civic life and Independence Campaigner of the Year award in 2020. She lives near the sea in north Fife.

By the same author:

Riddoch on the Outer Hebrides, Luath Press, 2007
Blossom: What Scotland Needs to Flourish, Luath Press, 2013
Wee White Blossom: What Post-Referendum Scotland Needs to Flourish, Luath Press, 2015
McSmörgåsbord: What post-Brexit Scotland can learn from the Nordics, Luath Press, 2017
Huts, a Place Beyond: How to End Our Exile from Nature, Luath Press, 2020

Thrive
The Freedom to Flourish

LESLEY RIDDOCH

Luath Press Limited

EDINBURGH

www.luath.co.uk

First published 2023
Reprinted 2023

ISBN: 978-1-80425-081-5

The author's right to be identified as author of this book under the
Copyright, Designs and Patents Act 1988 has been asserted.

The paper used in this book is recyclable. It is made from totally
chlorine-free pulp produced in a low-energy, low-emission manner
from renewable forests.

MIX
Paper from
responsible sources
FSC® C117931

Printed and bound by
MBM, East Kilbride

Typeset in 10.5 point Sabon LT

Contents

6

Acknowledgments

I'm grateful to the Luath team, including Tom Bee who cut through a flurry of indecision about the best name for this book in classic Gordian-knot-cutting style, Amy Turnbull who co-designed the breezy, cheery cover with Tom, Kira Dowie who organised a mini tour of Thive events and Luath publisher, Gavin MacDougall who delivered constant, patient encouragement. Thanks to Professor Alan Riach for his kind permission to quote from *Praise of Ben Dorain*. The Scottish Independence Foundation financed a month without journalistic work in January 2023 to let me focus on writing and the *Herald* and the *National* have kindly given permission to use extracts from columns. Finally, I'm almost grateful to Nicola Sturgeon for resigning when she did, so I had the chance to consider whether her departure terminally damages the case for independence.

The answer, with all respect to her legacy is, no.

Scotland has bigger fish to fry.

Preface

Independence.

For those who crave it, for those who dread it and for those utterly bored by the whole debate – we are living together through deeply frustrating times.

In late 2022, the Supreme Court dismayed the half of Scotland that favours independence by announcing 'the world's most powerfully devolved parliament' cannot consult its own people in a lawful referendum. But the half of Scotland against independence was dealt an equally forceful blow – Yessers showed no signs of giving up, even though their democratic path was blocked. So it's deadlock, Groundhog Day and – if you chuck in the sudden departure of Nicola Sturgeon and the fractious contest to replace her – the winter of 2022/23 has produced the perfect, political storm. And a big departure from Scotland's own status quo.

Most Scots under the age of 30 can't recall a Scottish Parliament without one of Britain's two most formidable politicians at the helm – Alex Salmond and Nicola Sturgeon. He saw an 'Executive' become a 'Government', pioneered a massive expansion of wind energy using only devolved planning powers, 'broke' the proportional voting system to win an absolute majority in 2011, extracted the Edinburgh Agreement from David Cameron and nearly won the 2014 indyref. She saw a divided country through the indyref's aftermath, developed Scotland's own welfare state to mitigate cruel Whitehall benefit sanctions, reached out to Europeans after the sudden shock of Brexit and reassured people with well-researched, empathetically delivered, daily briefings during the Covid pandemic – in stark contrast to the largely absent, un-briefed, King of the crony contracts and VIP 'fast lanes', Boris Johnson.

Salmond and Sturgeon have been massive political figures, recognisable across the world and despite their fierce falling out, history and public opinion may view them as sharing a legacy – together they normalised independence for Scotland over 16 short years, even though neither actually delivered it.

Scottish Labour has had 10 leaders since the Scottish Parliament resumed in 1999.

The SNP has had five. So the recent SNP leadership contest saw a generational change – none of the candidates vying to become the fifth SNP leader had even left school when Alex Salmond took over in 1990. Yip, that includes the (still young to me) Ash Regan.

A leadership election was always going to be a shock to the system for SNP members and a chance for long stifled, though perfectly natural differences about independence strategy, domestic policy and party democracy to surface. Still, the campaign was surprisingly bruising and left winner Humza Yousaf elected by a slender majority, but making history as Scotland's first Muslim leader.

So, Scotland's political world suddenly feels very unsettled.

In many ways, that's a good thing. It lets things be said that have needed saying – and hearing – by the SNP leadership. Things like the need to build a distinctive wellbeing economy – as championed by the policy group Believe in Scotland with more long-term planning effort than just slapping new headings on old press releases. And things like getting the corporate sector out of Scotland's public institutions, as advocated by Common Weal whose challenging slogan, 'appoint no-one, elect everyone' suddenly has renewed resonance.

Some Yessers fear that without such truly fresh thinking, Scotland will be forever Britain's 'mini me' and lack of tangible progress to reduce inequality and improve governance will hobble the drive for independence.

And yet, all of this is also just weather – albeit a particularly gusty version of the airborne turbulence for which Scotland is famed. The climate still suggests independence will happen, thanks to strong, sustained support amongst voters under the age of 50. And even if some of them grow cautious with age and others grow disillusioned – there's still a majority for change, someday soon.

But why hasn't the dial shifted further and faster towards breaking free from a United Kingdom that's never been more discredited, disorientated and economically deflated? What is it that gets so many people to the edge of the diving board, only to hesitate, shiver and climb back down again?

Is it the absence of a totally watertight, unanimously backed economic case – if such can ever exist in an uncertain world? Or does the demand for certainty mask deeper performance anxieties that must be tackled whether Scotland moves towards independence? This book tries to shine some light on longstanding myths about Scotland which dampen confidence and enthusiasm, and to survey what's changed since 2014 for the nation of Scotland, the kingdom of Britain and the small, successful neighbours whose examples beckon us onwards.

So this isn't a book about the history, prospects or failures of the SNP, a collection of Frequently Asked Questions about independence or facts and figures about Scotland's strengths in life sciences, creative industries, chemical sciences, food and drink, higher education and renewables. Excellent books and online resources exist on all these subjects and there's no point duplicating them. Similarly, *Thrive* is a companion volume to *Blossom*, first published ten years ago, which described the origins of disempowerment in Scotland and the distinctive aspects of culture, language, history and housing that have kept solidarity and nationhood alive. So, I'm hoping not to repeat those arguments either. Well, not much.

I'm well aware that relating some less-told stories about Scotland invites the charge of creating a selective history that underplays uncomfortable home truths. I'm hoping for Scotland's last Not Proven verdict on that one. Accounts of Scottish failings and inadequacies are so oft retold and exaggerated as to require little repetition, while other very real sticking points remain undiscussed – along with remedies deployed by more equal and successful northern neighbours. Scots hyper know the received wisdom about Scotland and its downsides. So, *Thrive* is an attempted corrective, which will doubtless be read in conjunction with the gloomy, contrary opinions produced by a sceptical mainstream world. Having said that, it's not my intention to pretend Scotland or Scots are a cut above. We are an ordinary country with our own strengths, assets, problems and demons. Indeed, the mark of readiness to proceed is an unsentimental, clear-eyed recognition of our own national character – flawed but entirely good enough to construct a new, independent country. Just like all the other ones.

Introduction

The new case for Scottish independence

What is it?

It's not which currency Scotland would adopt, if or how quickly we would rejoin the EU or whether the SNP would fade away or rule forever. Important questions that are all we talk about. But not the case for independence.

It's not whether the Gender Recognition Reform Act, late delivery of Hebridean ferries, success or failure in shrinking the attainment gap, running the NHS or mitigating poverty reflect well or badly on the current Scottish government. These are relevant debates – but the SNP's performance as a Scottish government isn't the same as the case for independence, which pre-dates the SNP's ascendancy and the Scottish Parliament itself.

It's not the identity or personality of the First Minister – though Nicola Sturgeon's time at the top was eventful and her resignation unsettling – a condition compounded by the resignation, arrest and release of her husband as Chief Executive.

It's not even evidence that Westminster is a busted flush, Brexit is a disaster and Scotland-sized countries out-perform the UK. All these statements are true. But they do not – by themselves – make the case for independence. Just as a recipe – by itself – doth not a clootie dumpling make. (Google it.)

It's not the vexed issue of borders and how much hardware, delays or queues would or wouldn't exist when Scotland's back in the EU and England's still stubbornly outside, watching its economy fall apart, on its lonesome. There's no question that managing a Schengen border would take energy on both sides and a level of 'can do' that's generally in short supply at Westminster. But happily, the Irish border is trialling a solution. Yet even this sizeable and important discussion is not the case for independence.

Since the day Alex Salmond kicked off the first independence referendum campaign in 2012, the most important decision facing Scots has seen a media and professional class focus only on the problems of independence.

We rarely hear them weighed against the problems of the status quo or the advantages of independence. Why not?

Imagine a set of constitutional scales with indy difficulties on one side and advantages on the other. That's the kind of debate I always imagined we'd have – eventually. The kind you construct yourself when facing a big decision – a list of pluses, minuses and then a long ponder.

But instead, the plus side of the scales is totally empty whilst the minus side is overflowing – and that's no fair reflection of reality. Yet the more Yessers dutifully engage with real and imagined concerns, the more PROBLEM becomes wedded to the very IDEA of independence. Which may well be the intention. The most succinct, well-researched responses only subtract a few grammes from this consciously constructed, minor mountain of negativity. They don't expand the positive argument or fix the underlying imbalance in the one-sided independence debate.

I suspect no-one really backs or rejects independence because of currency, borders or deficits. These are secondary issues which beg a big, fat primary question. Can independence improve Scotland?

Consider. Scotland is trying to decide whether to move home, based on the probable cost of the removals van. It's crazy. If a move is deemed necessary, then a vehicle will be found. But instead of tackling the big, important question of the move, we are getting stuck on particulars of the van hire. And, if there's ANY disagreement about the speed of EU accession or which currency to use, Scottish independence is deemed impossible. That's a strange logic. Like sticking with oil and gas indefinitely because renewable energy has storage issues.

In fact, it's stranger.

The need to make big choices about currency is regarded as terminal for independence, whereas big choices about energy storage are just challenges for clever Scots to fix. Why the difference?

Well, no government or political party has chosen to weaponise the difficulties that inevitably lie ahead as we transform a fossil-fuel-powered world into a sustainable one. Yip, big difficulties do exist. Nope, they aren't getting talked about. Because not even Tories fancy sounding like climate-change deniers these days.

The things we worry about, talk about, the facts and figures that lodge stubbornly in our brains, the expenditure that looks unjustifiable, the problems that seem insurmountable are all the things raised day-in, day-out by status quo-supporting papers, media and vested interests. It's a carefully crafted Selection Box of worry.

Thus, the cost of the 2014 indyref was £15.85m. That's either outrageously wasteful or a real bargain. £15.85 is twice the cost of enlarging the main door into the House of Lords (£15.85m v £7m) and one hundredth of the price-tag for restoring the whole Palace of Westminster (£14bn).

Now, I'm not saying the crumbling Commons is a satisfactory place for MPs or staff to work. I am saying a successful exercise in popular democracy (85 per cent turnout) conducted for twice the price of a door into the world's second largest unelected chamber sounds like a pretty good deal to me. Value and waste depend on how the argument's framed.

So, this book takes a wee tilt at frames which generate a pervasive gloom and negativity before any rational argument about independence has even begun. We'll also hook up with our collective inner child – the one that desperately wants to believe some option for the future is relatively problem-free, and that confident-sounding entitled people really do know best – even when our collective inner adult knows that just ain't so.

But God love that tired, scared, demoralised inner child.

Who would be any kind of bairn in this fractious world and broken, loadsamoney UK? The presumption is that bad times, corruption and utter incompetence hasten change. And up to a point, they do. But petrified passengers often hesitate to abandon a sinking ship – and exhausted voters may also shun better directions that involve disruption, anxiety and choice between competing risks. The new path always looks daunting, and folk always fear the new boss will strongly resemble the old one. These worries form a deep-seated block to independence which cannot be countered by a stunning new take on the Scottish Pound. It's a bit like worrying about the quality of seed, when the ground is already waterlogged. So first things first.

Until Scots decide themselves that muddling along isn't enough, they will ignore pamphlets, leaflets, articles and deny the existence of problems with the status quo, in the same way reasonable, intelligent people prevaricate before tackling big health problems. It's hard to face up to challenge and change.

I quite understand why many folk cross the road or leave by the rear exit (looking at you Boris) when independence comes their way. It's relentlessly portrayed as an expensive, disruptive, fuss over nothing, that interests no-one save the bampots and diehards. If an alternative portrayal of independence existed, as the only truly safe bet for our children's future, its associated problems might seem like the problems facing renewables. Challenges to be overcome.

In short, let's hear the blinking case for independence. And just for once, let's hear the case for the union – if someone actually wants to make it. Then, finally, we can properly gauge the risks and advantages of one possible future against the other. Because risk exists in every constitutional scenario and is never totally eliminated by any 'foolproof' plan. During the last campaign, Better Together demanded complete certainty from the Yes campaign – a call echoed so strongly by a hostile media that hard-to-keep guarantees about the shape of a new country were made by SNP leaders.

I understand why.

In a world where big false promises written on the sides of buses get you an 80-seat Commons majority or four years in the White House, it's hard to sell shades of grey.

But we've watched the 'oven-ready' trade deals of Brexit fail to materialise. We've watched President Trump fail to make America great again and President Putin's 'special operation' in Ukraine grind to a halt. Those who live by certainty tend to (politically) die by it too.

Yet the desire for certainty thrives in uncertain times. What are the odds-on Rishi Sunak still being Prime Minister by the time this book is published? I was going to ask about Nadim (tax dodger) Zahawi, but a mere week after this sentence began, he was toast. Meanwhile, what about you? Will you retire at 64, 66, 68 or never?

Life is becoming increasingly random and uncertain – especially for folk without heating this crisis-strewn winter. But the more old certainties dwindle, the more we crave them. No wonder politicians choose undeliverable promises over coming clean with the electorate, every time – even though madness lies therein and disillusioned voters end up wishing a plague on all party political houses.

The truth is we don't live our lives by certainty but by probability and trust. Yet this reality-defying demand – that the future be 100 per cent predictable – is applied to just one side of the constitutional debate. That doesn't mean a detailed prospectus isn't needed. Just that its absence right now may not be a bigger obstacle for independence than this impossible-to-satisfy thirst for absolute certainty.

Let's drop the independence bar to the same height louped by every other proposition for Scotland's future, including the status quo, and consider briefly here – and at length later on – what's highly probable after a Yes vote.

EU membership – yes, we will doubtless rejoin though I'd fully suspect the 'halfway house' trade group EFTA to start a bidding war. Why not? Scots have been good EU members for 40 years, we subscribe to the green, progressive, cooperative tilt of European politics, possess vast renewable energy resources, friendly people, and a vital geopolitical location. In short, we are a bit of a catch. And, fears of a Spanish veto – always exaggerated – have retreated still further since Brexit.

Border – yes, there will be one, but as IT arrangements around the Irish border will soon demonstrate, future trade everywhere will be managed more by technology and less by physical searches or wadges of paperwork. As for having to change money, most personal transactions in any country these days are by card not cash. Thanks to Brexit and the sea that divides us from mainland Europe, citizens of the British Isles don't cross international borders often enough to see how easy that is – even borders shared with grumpy ex-partners. In truth, despite negative headlines, the average border is very quiet. Ironically, it's the problematic British/EU border that gives national boundaries a bad name. Brexit aimed to keep all forms of immigration down – from asylum seekers in small boats crossing the Channel to seasonal workers and skilled migrants. The terrible irony is that desperate 'boat people' keep coming, whilst the workers who once staffed every sector from the NHS to hospitality are moving freely within the EU instead. Meanwhile, the Prime Minister of Luxemburg has summed up Britain's situation: 'They were in with a load of opt-outs. Now they are out, and want a load of opt-ins.'

Quite. Brexit has failed and public opinion has shifted – even in Brexit-mad England. Two large opinion polls suggest Leave voters, searching in vain for the 'sunlit uplands', have changed their minds, with 54 per cent now saying it was wrong to leave, and that was early 2023, before day-long queues to cross the Channel developed again at Dover. Who could have guessed that ending free movement for Europeans might also end free movement for Brits?

So where does that leave us politically? It may be impossible for the Tories and pre-election Labour to state the bleedin' obvious. But a U-turn is likely in the medium term, regaining single market access if not full membership. Such a volte face is too embarrassing to contemplate right now, since Britain will forfeit all the opt-outs negotiated upon entry in 1973, but gain nothing in return except self-inflicted economic and reputational damage. Even partial re-entry though will help create a smoother iScotland/rUK border experience.

Which might prompt some to ask, why bother about independence? Well, the scary thing is that a governing party, electorate and craven opposition south of the border combined with ease to stoke a 'culture war' against Europe, simply to avoid facing the fact that Britain's problems are caused by Britain and its near-ideological unwillingness to embrace empathy, equality and honest self-examination. Even if the weather eases up under a new Labour government, the underlying trend will continue. Scotland beware.

So, will independence be disruptive – yes. The better question is whether it will be more disruptive and damaging in the medium to long run than the 'erratic' and damaging behaviour of the UK.

The London School of Economics predicted in 2021 that independence would cut incomes by 4.5-6.7 per cent. That is scary looking but also unknowable and should be set against losses incurred continuing on our present path.

The same LSE report estimated Brexit losses to be 2 per cent of GDP per capita, while the Office of Budget Responsibility put them at 4 per cent. Last year, 49 days of Liz Truss left the economy 2 per cent smaller than it was before her disastrous budget. Then an energy crisis triggered by Russia's invasion of Ukraine caused unprepared, gas-dependent countries like Britain (energy is reserved to Westminster) to treble energy bills. Right now, food price inflation is 17.6 per cent – the highest since 1977 – and workers are £11,000 worse off per year due to 15 years of wage stagnation. According to the Resolution Foundation, the gap between British and German household income was £500 per annum in 2008 – and £4,000 today.

If that's stability, I'm a trampoline.

So, there is disruption either way and the basic question

remains. Life is full of choppy water. Is it best navigated by Holyrood or Westminster?

Meanwhile, back to the big questions.

Trade will also continue in an independent Scotland, which already outperforms all the other UK nations in international exports and has done since records began which means Brexit hit Scotland relatively harder than the rest of the UK, and that's prompted former No voters in the farming, food and drink, business and fishing sectors to ponder how access to the vital EU market will be restored without independence. As Gordon MacIntyre Kemp points out in *Scotland the Brief*:

> Scotland's exporting success is nothing to do with being part of the UK – it's our reputation for quality, natural resources and brand image that spans energy expertise, whisky, beef, salmon and seafood.

And that won't change.

Nor will demand for vital goods currently subsumed within the UK's internal market – like energy. There is no way England will not want energy supplies from Scotland post-independence. Otherwise, the lights will simply go out. Meanwhile an iScotland will have to develop new routes and trading partners, just as Ireland has done since Brexit to achieve the highest growth rate in the EU today. Stephen Kinsella, associate professor of economics at Limerick University says Scotland will likely experience a 'short shock' after leaving the UK, but quickly adjust to change:

> In 1920, the UK made up 95 per cent of exports from Ireland – it's 12 per cent now. Looking at the north of Ireland [compared to] the south – it's an economic experiment in the costs and benefits of colonialism over a century, and there's no doubt which group has fared better.

Much more on this later.

Currency – yes, there will be one. No nation became independent in order to have a new currency. None failed to jump ship for the want of one. And none facing difficulty, went back to the currency they had left. Why would Scotland be different?

Deficits – I cite my guys, you cite yours. Does any argument completely satisfy? Deficits have accumulated on Westminster's watch – they won't disappear in an independent Scotland and they exist in almost every economy. Why the mere whiff of indebtedness seems to immobilise Scots is a good question worth asking. But for a discussion of THE ACTUAL NUMBERS read Professor Richard Murphy.

Economic viability then?

C'mon.

With plentiful supplies of the world's major assets – water and renewable energy – plus whisky, tourism, life sciences, music and friendly people, Scotland is unquestionably 'investable'. To squander these natural assets, Scots would have to be a different species to every small country around. And we're not.

In summary – currency, borders, deficits and economic viability are important. And fear of the unknown is a big factor. But let's put the big rocks in first – and these are still not the big rocks.

If Scots voted No in 2014 because we were frightened of losing the pound – a currency that has since tanked courtesy of HMG – we were a world first. If we voted No for fear of losing the developed world's worst pension – ditto. If we worried about losing the high governance standards of Britain, we weren't paying attention – and to be fair, hadn't yet witnessed the effects of Brexit and crony Covid contracts which together sent the UK plummeting down World Bank governance rankings. In 2020 the UK was 19th, behind all the Nordic nations. Scotland can do better.

What about losing our nuclear weapons at a time of heightened threat from Russia? Expert opinion agrees there is nowhere else in Britain to put the Trident submarines based on the Clyde. But the war in Ukraine means those nuclear warheads don't just create local jobs, they make the west of Scotland a prime target for attack. Modelling suggests the detonation of a 100 kiloton nuclear bomb in Glasgow city centre would deliver potentially fatal doses of radiation and third degree burns to anyone within a 50 kilometre radius. Over 73,000 people could be killed and twice that number injured. In short, there's a reason places like Milford Haven, Falmouth and Devonport don't want Trident. They don't want to become Britain's biggest nuclear target.

Back in the pre-Holyrood 1960s, Scotland could not object. That will change if we become an independent state and can finally do what nuclear Britain will not – move in the opposite direction to de-escalate the nuclear arms race, because advances in peacekeeping and disarmament often happen in the wake of armed conflict.

After WW1, the League of Nations – set up to solve international disputes peacefully – morphed into the United Nations. After Cold War hostilities produced the Cuban Missile Crisis in 1962, a partial Nuclear Test Ban Treaty was signed, prohibiting test detonations in the atmosphere, space and underwater. Six years later, a non-proliferation treaty forced the Soviet Union and United States to reduce their nuclear arsenals. The end of Russia's illegal invasion of Ukraine could provide another opportunity for progress with more states signing up to the Treaty on the Prohibition of Nuclear Weapons 2021 (TPNW) which prompted billions to be disinvested from nuclear weapons by the Bank of Ireland, Allied Irish Bank when Ireland and 84 other states signed up.

But not Scottish banks, since Westminster refused to join them and plans instead to spend billions on a new system of nuclear weapons for the Clyde, opposed by 70 per cent of Scots.

The future for the planet can be very different. Why would an independent Scotland not want to be working within that progressive vanguard?

What about losing the monarchy? The latest poll suggests 55 per cent of Scots would be quite happy with that outcome, but it's odd (and characteristically British) that big constitutional issues are considered piecemeal. We need a written constitution like every other normal independent country and a cross-section of the population drafting it. If such a Citizens Assembly suggests a president within a whole, new, written (at last) constitution, which is endorsed in a referendum by the people – then we'll have a president. Andy Murray, you have been warned. Joke. Mebbe.

What about folk who work across the British Isles and fear tighter borders and even Visa restrictions? If Britain didn't close borders when the Irish Free State seceded in 1923, why would it shut Scotland out today? Yip, just six months after that monumental blow to British authority, common sense somehow prevailed with the creation of the Common Travel Area (CTA) between Britain, Ireland, Jersey, Guernsey and the Isle of Man.

Today,

> Irish and British citizens can move freely within the CTA with access to employment, healthcare, all levels of education, and social benefits on the same basis as citizens of the other State, as well as the right to vote in local and national parliamentary elections.

Why on earth would an independent Scotland be treated any differently?

It's the same story across the North Sea where the Nordic Passport Union (modelled on the CTA) began in 1953, four decades before Schengen, and lets citizens of Norway, Sweden, Finland, Denmark, Iceland and the Faroes live and work in one another's countries without passport checks, residence or work permits. The UK actually created the gold standard in close neighbour cooperation. That will continue.

What about watching the BBC?

Well, wherever you live these days, what's stopping you? Subscription channel viewing is the new normal, especially for under 24s, 90 per cent of whom head straight for Netflix or a streaming service and watch traditional broadcast TV for just one hour daily – a fall of two-thirds since 2014, according to media regulator Ofcom.

That suggests the broadcasting issue might look quite different next time around. Once again, Ireland's experience is instructive – BBC channels are widely available in Ireland though there's no access to the iPlayer. But money not given to Aunty in licence fees funds RTÉ's TV and radio stations. Are they any good? Well, in 2016, RTÉ TV broadcast all of Ireland's 20 most popular programmes and 19 of its 20 most popular sports programmes. Doubtless, using that model, citizens of an independent Scotland might finally get to watch our own national men's team beat Spain again (you've got to dream) on state TV.

Last time around, the SNP proposed a Scottish Broadcasting Corporation (SBC). A new indy government might want to negotiate a continuing supply of SBC programming to the BBC in exchange for iPlayer access. But meantime, BBC hit series are watched across the world, and again – why would an independent Scotland be any different?

The excellent drama *Happy Valley* was seen so widely across the US that actor James Norton recently said, 'random Americans come up to me on the street and talk to me about Hebden Bridge. They watch it with subtitles on, but they love it.'

Indeed, I've sat with friends in Norway lapping up *Downton Abbey* on the Norwegian state broadcaster NRK. But they can watch this vivid, British portrayal of class inequality – we have to stew in it.

I for one would cheerfully swap the BBC's endless fixation with all things Tudor, inter-war and upper class for lavish SBC productions of Scottish classics like Robert Louis Stevenson's *Kidnapped*. This was last adapted for British TV in 1978 by a co-production between Harlech TV in Wales and Germany's Tele München – not the BBC. Meanwhile, the best model for iScotland is the Danish Broadcasting Corporation (DR), funded from income tax and responsible for hit series *The Killing*, *Borgen* and *The Bridge*. In 2014, there were two or three Danish TV series in production at any one time. In 2019, there were 20, plus 25 films being shot on location in Denmark, prompting the country's drama school to double its student numbers. In short, the world wants more Danish TV than Denmark can handle, thanks to the streaming boom. Ditto the other Nordic countries. An SBC won't get there overnight, but *Outlander* – viewed in 40 countries – demonstrates the world's fascination with Scotland. What a day it will be when a Danish-style SBC feeds that interest – not better funded, more confident foreign broadcasters.

New England and Auld Europe

Is it disloyal to abandon England? Well, most folk south of the border would actually be waving us off. A 2021 poll of English voters for the *Telegraph* found only a fifth strongly oppose Scottish independence and most young English folk aged 18–34 believe Scotland would thrive as an independent country. England is ready for change and Scotland won't be disappearing – but reappearing. Other English folk believe Scottish independence is the constitutional cataclysm needed to weaken establishment control south of the border and revive the English liberal/Remain-voting left. Singer and campaigner Billy Bragg argues that Scotland's departure from the union would encourage a new constitutional settlement, with PR elections and a reformed upper house to represent English regions; 'I'd certainly vote for a new England.'

In 2021, two European academics based in Oxford (Andrea Pisauro and Janina Jetter) went a step further, creating Europe for Scotland (EfS). They drafted a letter asking the EU Commission to confirm that Scotland can easily rejoin the EU and it's been signed by 15,000 British and European citizens, including English musician and Bowie collaborator Brian Eno:

> Those of us who think the project of a united Europe is critically important want to see it grow, not shrink, so I applaud Scottish desire to be reunited with Europe.

And novelist/screenwriter Ian McEwan:

It falls to Scotland to take responsibility for its
own future. Should it decide on independence, it
will thrive within the EU as other small nations do.
Leading figures in Brussels have promised 'the door
will remain open.' Now is the time for them to hang
out the welcome sign.

And British historian/Kings College professor, David Edgerton:

Scotland should have the right to choose between the
English Union and the European Union – between
dictat and democracy.

And Italian professor Alberto Alemanno:

The EU must stand by the Scots who, like any other
people of Europe, should be entitled to choose their
future in the European Union. If it's no longer an
option to be part of both the UK and the EU, it is not
Scotland's fault.

And German professor Ulrike Guerot:

Scotland historically and culturally belongs to Europe,
independently of the state formation it currently
belongs to. This is why I signed this European
solidarity appeal for Scotland.

These leading members of European civic society get it.

They realise Scotland is not a natural part of isolationist
Britain, but essentially European.

Amazing. It's not just that prominent European figures harbour
a secret sympathy for Scotland. It's that they've put their heids
o'er the parapet, risked pelters or non-comprehension by their
ain folk – and taken a stand for us. Not directly on the question
of independence but on Scotland's right to EU membership.

Now, none of these esteemed signatories is daft.

Clearly there's no way for Scots to rejoin the EU except as an independent country. But folk from other countries won't tell us what to do.

They've helped clear a path – if we choose to take it – by urging EU officials to provide an accession assurance to Scotland before indyref2 so there's none of the confusion, mixed messages and blatant lies that surrounded the vote in 2014. These folk see a plucky, single-minded, gallus little nation when we too often see bickering, division, stuck polls and uncertainty.

So c'mon. Other countries have off days, disappointments and moments of disorientation. That doesn't define them any more than guddles define us. Scotland is evolving into the social democracy England will struggle to become and it's clear independence is an option that will not wither and die. Notably, political parties in Scotland didn't ditch Yes – the losing argument in 2014 – as British parties dumped Remain in 2016. That Yes constancy is a beacon for the left in England. And there's a far better future for all our countries working together as voluntary independent members in a beefed up Council of the Isles than in the present, unequal, involuntary union of the UK. Jings, in time we could have as much respectful cooperation and joint working as the Nordic Council.

Finally, there's the hardy perennial – we already voted on independence in 2014.

Yip, that's true. But the underlying issues have not been resolved in the intervening decade. There were downright lies about EU membership in 2016, there's a continuing slump for Scotland's economy because of England's Brexit, the SNP has won eight straight elections on an indyref2 mandate and the agreement for a Northern Ireland border poll allows a rerun every seven years. We are in a different political space today and cannot move on without a second referendum to reset our politics and let Scots move on, one way or t'other.

Alex Salmond did describe the 2014 vote as 'once in a

generation'. That was political rhetoric not a personal promise, which he was in no more of a position to make than Gordon Brown's unfulfilled pledge of 'something close to federalism'. Sovereignty in Scotland rests with the people, not any political leader. Besides, if Salmond is taken at his word about the 'one-off' indyref, Boris Johnson should have been found 'dead in a ditch' in October 2019 when Brexit failed to materialise. Strange that one extravagant claim was dismissed as 'just Boris' whilst Salmond's was promptly etched on a tablet of stone. In any case, the Tories don't deny the right of Scots to have another referendum. They simply argue now is not the time. Be real. Now will never be the time because the next independence vote will likely be won.

Enough already. The classic worries have answers which are just as satisfactory or wobbly as those supporting the status quo. Why is that never enough?

Perhaps a majority of Scots will never take the plunge. Perhaps though, these hard-to-dispel worries serve as a proxy for something else. Something less tangible. Something softer. Something given little house-room in political debate. Something rarely discussed outside music, poetry and the arts. Something vital.

How we feel about ourselves. How fully we trust one another. Whether we consider ourselves capable of heavy lifting – on our own account, at our own direction, at our own speed and in our own name. That's different to venting impotent rage at Tory governments. Since most of us didn't vote for them, it often feels the damage they do isn't really our fault.

A vote for independence is different. Riskier. More uncomfortable. It represents the end of innocence, diversion, excuses, dodged responsibility and any remaining vestiges of victimhood. It means aiming higher, owning aspirations, getting out of the back seat and steering the car. It invites expectation, judgement, responsibility and the absolute certainty of making mistakes along the way. All of that weighs heavily on those Not to the Manor Born.

But there's something even harder for 'no-nonsense' Scots to acknowledge – the feeling of rip-roaring excitement that reverberated around Scotland in early September 2014, when a new country was almost born.

For a few weeks with Yes in front, a different future beckoned – a new start, generating creativity and optimism, attracting like-minded folk from across Britain, Europe and the world and reactivating our own reserves of ingenuity. All triggered by the fabulous possibility we might spend the next 50 years creating a new child-centred, green economy, instead of mitigating the woeful, hurtful, immobilising, hope-denying crap that pours out of Westminster.

Aye it was optimism.

Aye it was David and Goliath.

Aye, the powerful emotions on display in 2014 might appear naïve and even embarrassing in hindsight. After all, only the brave or slightly unhinged are openly upbeat in a country that's mastered the dark arts of studied detachment and gallows humour. So, since 2014, many Scots have hunkered down, curbed our enthusiasm, called in the accountants (no offence) and watched this precious, exciting idea of a new country get bogged down in problems, details and 'what iffery'.

Yet memory and hope endure, and those powerful yet rarely expressed feelings explain why half the nation still backs independence.

So, why should Scotland quit the straitjacket of the UK?

Because like love, children or the biggest promotion possible, it would demand our all. A capacity greater than anything we currently understand or expect from ourselves. Because an independent Scotland would thrive, not just tick over. Because age-old social ideas about fairness, community and solidarity would finally be applied to the business of government. Because we could win the Eurovision Song Contest.

Be daft. Be serious. Act as if we own the place. Fail, learn, trust and succeed. And that's it really. No land of milk and honey, no righting old wrongs and no taking all night.

Folk need inspiration to progress but it can feel foolish, even childish to dwell on such precious motivating life forces, in the face of the corruption, duplicity, sharp practice and 'tough love'.

Consider. At the time of writing, women in England are being fined by NHS England for claiming free prescriptions during pregnancy. Yes, they were entitled. But only if a midwife did the paperwork correctly. Since many overworked midwives failed to tick the right box, hundreds of pounds must now be repaid or young mums will be taken to court. No exceptions.

Scotland abolished prescription charges for everyone 12 years ago and the world didn't end. With independence we can build on that better direction – without looking constantly over our collective shoulder. That demands optimism. And contagious stories of inspiration. Out loud. In the open. Repeatedly. So, folk can engage emotionally and dare to dream.

Yip. The D-word.

Dreaming is tough to do in public – not because Scotland is an inspiration-free zone, but because hopes, stories and anecdotes aren't much favoured by politicians or a soundbite-seeking media. 'Floaty' emotional responses are regarded with deep suspicion in our brisk, modern Scottish world. We aren't asked to be upbeat, positive or hopeful in public very often. Indeed, we are home to a world first – the only double positive that's actually a negative. Aye right.

So, expressing optimism in Scotland is hard. And when it's done half-heartedly, you'd rather hear nails dragged down a blackboard. Far easier to avoid the whole unsettling experience and watch Humza Yousaf pick his way through First Minister's Questions instead.

Better still, stifle hope completely (that awkward wee bugger) by insisting an independent country will inevitably mirror the current strengths and weaknesses – actually let's just make that weaknesses – of the Scottish Government. Now, if Holyrood was making a total mess of things compared to Westminster this might be a useful exercise. But – whatever the eye-catching errors, negative headlines and fair criticism – it generally isn't.

Scotland has lower levels of child poverty, shorter NHS waiting times, more affordable homes, fewer rough sleepers, better supported carers, less student debt and public procurement that operates without VIP fast lanes or crony contracts. Scotland has cut climate emissions further, boosted renewables, electrified rail lines, rolled out free childcare, led the world with minimum unit pricing for alcohol and free period products and free school meals for all children in primary years one to five, while England's offer, 'explained' in a 21-page booklet, is so complex that an Eligibility Checking System (ECS) has been launched to help. Which probably costs the same as just giving all primary kids free lunches.

All of this is why, a February 2023 report by the tough-talking Institute of Fiscal Studies concluded Scotland's tax and benefits system is more progressive than anywhere else in the UK. And it's probably why three in five Scots said Nicola Sturgeon made Scotland a better place, in a poll conducted two days after her resignation.

It's also why two-thirds of Scots sampled in the Social Attitudes Survey said they could trust Scottish ministers to work in their best interests in November 2022, amidst a ferries' fiasco and controversy over Gender Recognition Reform. Only a third of that figure said the same about Westminster. 63 per cent said Holyrood gives ordinary people a say in how Scotland is run. 57 per cent said the UK Government can't be trusted to make fair decisions.

So even dragging their collective feet or presiding over missed targets, public service failure and personal controversy, Holyrood Ministers aren't held in the low regard Scots reserve for Westminster. Voters seem quite capable of distinguishing between turbulent weather and a foul political climate. But there's more. Performance within a constrained devolution settlement is no predictor of outcomes in a truly independent country. Then we must stop resting on our laurels about out-performing an unreconstructed rUK and tackle our under-performance compared to like-sized, progressive, resource-rich, small northern neighbours.

Independence will give Scotland the chance to turn away from failing British defaults and adopt or adapt systems developed over centuries by better functioning Nordic and Low Country neighbours. They're ready to help if we're not too proud to ask. That's a far more promising policy future than constantly letting out the seams on jaickets that fit someone else.

But there's an even bigger point to make. It's not just leaders and governments that mark democratic milestones. More important – though far less commented upon – is the growing political consensus within Scotland itself.

Scotland's settled will

Ardrishaig-raised Labour leader John Smith – quoted by Humza Yousaf in his acceptance speech – first used the idea of a 'settled will' 30 years ago to describe the steam gathering behind devolution. But once achieved, that settled will didn't disappear or stagnate. It matured, deepened and stands revealed today in Scotland's collective belief in the power of fairness, society and democracy. Actually, that belief is probably more powerful than backing for any constitutional outcome. The question is – which arrangement best protects, enhances and enables it.

The answer's been made easier by successive sell-yer-granny-style Conservative governments at Westminster. In contrast and by comparison, Scots can see their kind of country very clearly. They vote for it at every election and are infuriated when Scottish outcomes are 'only' equal to the UK average. The outline of the new Scottish state flickers into life with each collective flinch at a postponed CalMac ferry or burst of anti-migrant rhetoric from Suella Braverman.

It's important, though controversial, to note that this precious settled will even includes Scottish Tories. Of course, it's entertaining to highlight tensions between Douglas Ross and his frothing 'die-in-a-ditch' English counterparts. But the

Scottish Conservatives' alignment with the rest of the Scottish Parliament on issues like EU membership, Scottish Child Payments, proportional voting and Personal Care, is proof positive that the Scottish political spectrum is not the palette you'll find down south. Back in 2001, the *Herald* reported:

> Henry McLeish continued to play cat and mouse
> with opposition MSPs yesterday as the SNP and Tories
> suspected a U-turn on his multi-million-pound plans
> for free care for the elderly.

No, you didn't misread that.

Twenty years ago, Scottish Tories were trying to make sure Scotland leapt beyond miserly British norms by demanding that Scottish Labour stick to its free personal care reforms. Labour Ministers south of the border so opposed Scottish Labour's initiative that the DSS, headed by Alistair Darling, tried to scupper it by withholding £23m. Jings, with friends like these... Presumably the Scottish Tories hoped free personal care would tear Labour apart. It didn't, but the initiative alerted voters to the bigger progress that could be made without the dead hand of Westminster interference. Even now, despite huffing and puffing, Scottish Tories are more like Nordic welfare-state-supporting Conservatives than the hard-right, state-dissolving maniacs at Westminster.

And that's because they keep better company – progressive Scots not Braverman, Patel and Jacob Rees-Mogg, a man so patriotic he pays almost no tax, moved his business to Ireland, holds an Irish passport and is registered for tax in the Cayman Islands.

But Scottish Labour today won't go the extra mile on any radical policy, lest it shows up Keir 'Middle England' Starmer, validates Scotland as another country and whets the Scots' appetite for more. Scottish Labour should be outflanking the SNP right now, pushing for Home Rule – complete control over tax-raising, public spending, borrowing, energy and immigration. But the

Scottish party has delegated custodianship of the constitution to Gordon Brown – a former premier who's now more interested in building English regionalism than the federal Britain he promised in the heat of battle. The era of respected, senior Scottish Labour MPs able to push the London party for constitutional change ended with David Cameron's election, a decade of austerity and the rise of the SNP. Labour now has just one solitary Scottish MP. Why would Keir Starmer upset the whole UK apple cart to appease the Scots with a federal structure for the UK – an idea that proved so unpopular in 2004, that even the highly-distinctive Geordies rejected the idea of a North-East assembly?

Nope. Scotland doesn't much matter to UK Labour and contrary to assertions there have been only four elections since 1918 where Scottish votes changed the UK outcome. If Labour wants to win at Westminster it needs to win in England.

So, John Smith's settled will hasn't gone into deep freeze, but his party will not support its continuing growth. A bit like disowning a puppy when it becomes a semi-mature hound or abandoning a child when it becomes a teenager, Scottish Labour only supports baby steps for Scotland, and that's not good enough. There are smart people of good conscience in the party. But they can't explain why progressive Scotland must wait (endlessly) for conservative Britain to catch up and cotton on.

The last ten years have demonstrated something to one and all. Scotland is a social democracy stuck in a conservative country. *And stuck, it cannae thrive.*

Agreed, thriving was once o'er hopeful – above our station and beyond expectations. But ten years on from the indyref, simply ticking over just isn't good enough. Not for our children, who will leave a Scotland that stays tethered to a backward-facing, under-performing, archaic, unequal and isolated Britain. And whisper it, belonging to the worst-performing economy in northern Europe isn't good enough for us either. Our eyes have been opened.

Every crony millionaire contract, starved public service, and broken promise about EU membership confirms Scots have been conned by the old Etonians who run the British Establishment. They might have screwed up so royally they'll spend the next five years out of power, regrouping. But they'll be back. They're always back.

Scots know that with 100 per cent certainty. What vestige of self-respect remains if we don't act on that knowledge?

We have resources other countries would give their eye teeth to possess. We know that our settled will – if taken seriously – could build a country quite different to England. And with the highest levels of trust in the UK, high levels of solidarity between citizens and strong compliance with rules, a Holyrood government can implement the progressive policies other parts of the UK can only dream of.

We know what we want and what we need. Now we have to do the scary thing and go get it.

And there, some folk falter.

Does indy mean SNP rule forever?

Actually, that's far more likely in the present halfway house of devolution. Despite its current travails, the SNP will continue to attract the lion's share of votes from Yessers and unless Labour, Tories and the Lib Dems create a Holyrood coalition, there's no way one unionist party can seriously loosen the SNP's grip on power.

But what about the 'Rainbow Parliament' of 2003 when Solidarity, Scottish Socialists, a Hospital candidate, a Senior Citizens' MSP plus independents like Margo MacDonald and Dennis Canavan all made their mark? The constitutional divide has steam-rollered independents and small parties right out of the system. But there's no use girning, no way around our current democratic reality and no way back. The most effective direction for those who want to 'lose' the SNP is actually indyref2. If it's a Yes vote, the SNP is unlikely to wither on the vine overnight, especially if Labour opposes self-determination right to the bitter end. Successful independence parties in other countries have generally been 'rewarded' by their electorates – just as Scottish Labour was rewarded for delivering devolution. For a while.

But once the new landscape becomes familiar and the constitutional divide is over, Scots will finally vote as they want. Not for the least worst party, not holding their noses (as many Scottish Labour, Tory and Lib Dem voters currently do every General Election) and above all, not 'wheeshting' for indy or for Keir Starmer in Number Ten. Very rapidly our proportional voting system will deliver a parliament that resembles other small European independent neighbouring states with no automatic majority for any one party and no expectation of anything other than coalition government. In short, if you'd rather have the SNP in power indefinitely, keep backing the status quo.

Still, unaccountable fears remain. What happens if the Westminster Scottish Secretary cannot swing in with steadying/undemocratic Section 35 vetoes, on legislation they don't like? What happens when there's no other stifling/steadying hand on Scotland's tiller? What happens when history starts again, on our watch? What will it be like to drop the bravado and permanently abandon the temptation to follow our ancestors elsewhere?

What will it be like, at long last, to dig where we stand and fix our own country – to adjust to life as modest winners and not the world's best-loved losers? I'd give anything, truly anything to find out.

So, what do you feel? If Scotland becomes an independent country, what will happen? What is your instinct about Scotland's capacity to manage itself? Does the idea scare you rigid? Is it too hard to believe a small country can be a success – or just THIS small country? Do you fear retaliation from a wounded England? Does belief seem too much like hard work? Do differences with rUK seem too trifling and the prospects for improvement, too remote? Above all, does Scotland look like a pup – too barren, difficult and empty a country to be successful?

All these fears, presumptions and anxieties lie between Scotland and a rational consideration of the case for independence – together they produce a hesitation more profound and hobbling than the old trope about Scots being too poor, too wee and too stupid for independence.

That suggestion is easily refuted. But others lurk beneath, unspoken and infinitely more powerful. That Scots are too angry, too disputatious and too Celtic. Too disorganised, too chippy and too hesitant. Too much like the insubstantial side salad beside England's meaty steak. Too unaccustomed to leading. Too lacking in drive. Too keen to consult, too indecisive. Too accepting of raw deals. Too comfortable, risk averse and unwilling to endure the early hardships of independence. In other words – too complacent and too feart.

Is that who we are?

I remember a conversation about independence with my late mum who very probably voted No in 2014. She left school at 14 without qualifications but was, like many of her formally under-educated generation, sharp as a tack. When I asked what she was thinking about the big vote she pondered awhile and said, 'Yes Scotland has come a long way, but...'

There was no need to finish the sentence. I was my mother's daughter. I was brought up to see the world through her eyes as well as my own. I could sense her reservations.

It sat in the stuff we didn't talk about. The baggage collected over centuries at the tail end of the British Empire – the unaccountable but deep-seated belief that things which can work in other countries will not work here. The instinct not to get above your station, lest that invites mockery and disaster – writ large across a whole country.

But here's the thing.

Independent or devolved, we've got to get over it. Scotland has made remarkable strides thanks to rising levels of self-government, self-knowledge and self-confidence – they do all go thegither – much of it arising from community control of land, energy and other assets.

But we haven't shifted the deep-seated, subliminal belief amongst many people that anything driven by Scots will end up flawed, parochial, kitschy or in some other way, unviable.

The fear that Scotland is the ultimate Slow Horse.

This mindset is (maybe unwittingly) fuelled by a profound lack of trust in the capacity of 'ordinary' people amongst the great and good – by every profession and every political party including the SNP. It arises from centuries of British elitism and top-down control plus a media preoccupation with large countries that's stopped us knowing more about the small Nordic states which are also the world's happiest, wealthiest and most equal.

So, to cut a long story short, this book focuses not on the controversial cart of currency, but on the sturdy wee pony of confidence. For one reason.

Scotland is already another country. We just need to launch the lifeboat and sail away. But weed currently fouls the propellers. So it's time for a deep dive.

PART ONE

The Deep Dive

I HAVE A salesman pal who reckons he can sell a car to anyone. He figures out who's buying and builds a positive default by running through all its advantages.

It's grey – a great colour for not showing the dirt. Yes.

It's a five door – great for luggage and adaptable. Yes.

It's got a hybrid engine – that'll save money on petrol and get you into Low Emission Zones. Yes.

It's brand-new but registered with one owner which takes £1,500 off the selling price – a great bargain. Yes.

So, would you like a test drive?

No? Really?

If you're even halfway ready to buy, and after all that trilling, it's hard not to say Yes again. That's how selling works. An unstoppable ramping up of positivity.

So let me try to sell you Scotland.

It is the Saudi Arabia of renewable energy – yes.

It was an independent state until 300 years ago and has retained its own distinctive systems of education, law, religion and belief and public ownership – yes.

Its government is at least as efficient and generally more successful than Westminster – I know there's been an argument about this one, but comparing all the data actually – yes.

It has a distinctive culture and more progressive voting history than the rest of Britain – yes.

Governance standards at Westminster have collapsed – yes.

Brexit's been a disaster and the only way back into the EU is as a new country – yes.

So, do you back Scottish independence?

Er... Why do so many folk still hesitate? And it's not because anyone thinks Westminster would procure Hebridean ferries any more efficiently than Holyrood.

If the selling proposition is right, then what's the problem?

Maybe hesitation comes from a deeper place.

Change is hard

I was confused.

Sitting in my primary school classroom in 'troubled' Belfast, windows criss-crossed with wide Sellotape to encourage large injury-minimising chunks of glass after any explosion, I was neatly correcting a British history book strewn with factual errors. Yip, I'd have hated to teach me too.

'England' and 'Britain' had been used sloppily and interchangeably throughout the text and I fondly imagined the school would prefer someone to put that right. Two detentions later I understood differently. But I was still amazed no adults seemed to care. I wasn't a young Republican. Au contraire – I lived in one of Belfast's leafiest suburbs beside a Scottish Presbyterian Church. But even by the age of 9, I had been about. Born in Wolverhampton, wheeched across the Irish Sea aged 3, then wheeched up the A9 to grandparents' council houses in Wick and Banffshire ever year for lengthy summer holidays – and back again. So happily, I knew the difference between England, Scotland, Ireland, Northern Ireland and Britain early doors.

Time passed.

One day, aged 13, I walked across the garden to the spot where my dad used to dump cut grass and dead headed roses. I used to rescue the best blossoms and drop them into jam jars to make rosewater – which never worked. But the fascination with those perfect petals remained, until the day we left our house, street, school friends, haunts and wee childish plans for the future behind and moved from Belfast to Glasgow in 1973. Lock, stock, barrel and goldfish.

I had no idea why we had to go.

Yes, there were bombs – you could hear the booms at night, ricocheting round the hills that encircle the city. But they were distant.

Yes, the school at the end of our road had been burned to the ground. But that could have been an accident.

Yes, the garden gate was padlocked shut every night – like many others.

Yes, a bicycle trip to the newsagents had been interrupted by a paramilitary parade, the city centre was a barely visited place guarded by soldiers with rifles and dad once came home with a bullet hole in the car bonnet. He didn't seem as excited as us.

None of this was problematic because it was normal.

It was all we children had ever known.

And that scared my parents to the core.

My dad had been a pilot in Bomber Command and my mother was one of five children growing up in a Wick single end. They both knew hardship. But they also knew freedom. The idea of surviving one war to bring up children in another didn't appeal. So, with just three months' notice, and after 13 happy (we thought) years, they took the big decision to move to Scotland, leaving the rose-pile, a chunk of my identity and the early portion of our young lives behind.

I saw nothing wrong with our life in Belfast.

Even now, the childish refusal to really leave survives in my own mixed accent. My brother can imagine us walking through each room of our old house and can describe the carpets and wallpaper. Each of us actually visits when we go 'home', even though the house was demolished long ago.

We didn't want to leave.

Yet my parents were absolutely right.

As children, we had grown 100 per cent accustomed to limitation, suspicion, segregation and the constant, albeit usually distant threat of violence. Our very ease with it scared mum and dad rigid. Segregation was systematic, well organised and thorough – so much that I grew up believing my massive primary school contained every conceivable strain of humanity. But there were no Catholics. Thanks to the sectarian partition of neighbourhoods, there couldn't have been. And though our lives were happy and comfortable, the 'situation' was beyond weird. It took parents steeped in another culture

– Scotland – to see that clearly, believe in better, act decisively and leave.

Now to be crystal clear, I draw no parallel between a malfunctioning 'United Kingdom' and an actual war on the island of Ireland. None whatsoever. There is no comparison – and that's my point.

Even when children were dodging the bullets, even with bombs, hi-jacking, murders and checkpoints as motivating factors – most loving, protective parents opted not to leave.

Change is never easy.

And new is hard.

So, caution about leaving the massively familiar UK is understandable. But caution shouldn't be confused with happiness about the status quo. And frustration with folk who won't immediately go the extra mile is not just counter-productive – it's unfair. Advocates of independence would do well to reflect on their own reluctance to embrace important change until non-negotiable deadlines come along.

I should have an electric car. I should've converted my heating from gas. I should do Pilates every day. I should join a choir. There are so many good things in pastures new. And they take... well what do they take that stops us instantly progressing from one thing to the next? Emotional energy. Time. Headspace. Those vital things that become disposable luxuries in pressurised lives.

Let's face it, the vast majority of people don't change banks when they're being fleeced. In fact, the whole British economy operates on the basis that consumers will thole bad deals rather than change – because disruption is so time-consuming and we suspect 'they're all at it'.

People are primed to make the most of what already exists – the weather, sporting disappointment, even collapsing systems of governance. There's an instinct to complain but accept the hand we've been dealt. There's not enough time to read up, make an informed choice, conjure up a different future and create a route map to reach it. It's normal to plough on.

And this caution acts like a form of political gravity – demanding vast reserves of energy and organisation from those blasting off in different directions.

So, let's go easy.

Independence may seem like a no-brainer to Yessers, but that may reflect temperament as much as rational argument.

I think back to the Civic Assembly formed in 1997 to advance devolution, at which a perceptive Kiwi visitor, Robert Reid described the Alliance party he had just set up in New Zealand, composed of Maoris, farmers and women – an unusual combination, I observed.

In fact, according to Robert, the party was really divided into personality types – stone-throwers, alternative builders and institutional plodders. They needed each other but despised one other too.

Not a week has gone by over the intervening quarter century, without that astute insight springing to mind. I observed exactly the same tensions in Channel Four's People's Parliament programme where I was Speaker for five years in the 1990s. Once again friendships bridged political differences and were largely based on temperament.

I'd say most Yessers tend to be enthusiasts and practical people who generally learn through doing, want to get the show on the road and are confident big problems can be sorted en route. I certainly fit that profile.

But sometimes, optimists are captured by their own enthusiasm, certain there will be a practical solution if only situations are confronted and transformed. Often that may be true but taking the bull by the horns scares the bejeezus out of everyone else and enthusiasts sometimes fail to do the necessary paperwork, inclusion and planning.

That's why all temperamental types are needed in a successful society. They each carry grains of a larger truth.

Yessers spend their lives breathing enthusiasm into every project they encounter and particularly into the possibilities of a Scottish state. The No camp and Westminster Government have historically done the opposite – undermining the value of everything distinctive about Scotland – from its cultures and languages to its natural resources.

And so a symbiotic relationship has formed.

The more negative the opposition, the more relentlessly upbeat and self-starting the indy movement.

No access to the BBC – simple.

Indy Live set up their own citizen broadcasting outfit, which is crowd-funded and works on a shoestring. They don't just cover indy-related gigs but dozens of wider events exploring Scottish culture and identity that have been passed over by the big broadcasters.

Don't get me wrong. This is admirable, loveable, and fabulous.

But there's a pattern.

The BBC and official Scotland carry on as if the indyref never happened and 50 per cent support for fundamental change isn't alive in Scotland right now. The mainstream is untouched, unmoved, and more concerned about maintaining control than dropping its guard to let new voices in.

We have an enthusiasm imbalance every bit as profound as the democratic deficit.

And nowhere is that mismatch more profound than at the heart of the independence movement, where the SNP – Scotland's political establishment – has acquired the unenthusiastic demeanour of the British state to counterbalance what it perceives as the crazy, relentless energy of Yessers.

Yessers shouldn't curb our enthusiasm.

Not at all.

It is the currency of the Yes movement.

But we should understand other temperaments, otherwise we can't easily tackle caution, hesitation and pessimism about Scotland's future. Happily, some of these fears are just baggage. But unhappily, some of that baggage has clung on for centuries like a massive barnacle, and won't be prised off without a good dunt. So here goes, with a series of utterly negative propositions about Scotland some folk secretly believe, but feel too embarrassed to voice.

Is Scotland a pup?

Do we know the fantastic deal we've got, as we head towards independence in this country? Do we really know what we've got?

Or do we secretly think Scotland is a bit of a pup?

You know, a bit lacking in the important assets department.

A bit barren.

A bit underpopulated.

A bit damp and dreich.

A bit remote and northern.

A bit off the beaten track.

And therefore a bit insufficient as we set off into the wide blue yonder as a new state, solo, on our tod with just... you know, Scotland.

Where it always rains.

Always.

In 2007, BBC News reported Land Rover was promoting a new colour called Stornoway Grey. A Western Isles councillor claimed the name was 'offensive, inaccurate and inherently degrading'. Land Rover said Stornoway Grey was one of its strongest colours and helped to 'keep' the Western Isles on the map.

The same year a BBC weather presenter apologised after calling the Western Isles 'nowheresville'. Local MP Angus Brendan MacNeil offered weather presenters a visit to his constituency. The Met Office forecaster said he 'deeply regretted' his choice of words.

Aye right.

Fifteen years ago, these two stories, prompted me to try and put 'nowheresville' on the map with a radio series cycling up the Western Isles and a book – *Riddoch on the Outer Hebrides*. On that glorious, memorable two-week cycle, it rained just once along the lovely single-track road by Scarista beach, heading for Luskentyre, Harris.

And yet, despite telling everyone there is no bad weather only inappropriate clothing, I had a few inappropriate problems of my own.

Half-mast plastic over-trousers were dripping rainwater into trendy cutaway trainer socks I must have 'borrowed' from a step-daughter. Served me right.

My recently washed cycling jacket had clearly lost its waterproofness and the unaccountably girly decision to wear lip-gloss in a fairly substantial headwind left me cycling with two wands of hair permanently plaited across my face.

And then... amidst the rain, in the rolling waves of the beach at Nisabost, I spotted company. A group of people swimming in the surf – some fully clothed. One woman wearing a swimsuit was caked with white sand despite an air temperature of just 10 degrees. Curious, I shimmied down to the beach and almost got dragged in. I asked if they are locals. They laughed.

'No. We're from Scotland.'

That kinda said it all.

'Locals think we're crazy going out to swim in the rain. And friends think we're crazy –we take just £20 each cos there's nowhere to spend money. We just swim when we want, and go walking wherever. It's great.'

Hell's teeth, I thought. These guys are right.

Feel the rain and do it anyway.

And the weather promptly cleared up. Now, there's no denying it does rain cats and dogs out west, but 15 years ago Hebridean islands (including St Kilda) had to import water and in 2022, Scotland's east coast experienced its driest January since 1940.

Climate is changing, but the narrative about Scotland's land, weather and resources remains defiantly gloom-laden. Why not – it's been centuries in the making.

For the record let it be stated that the main motive of the Sutherlands... was to improve the wretched

conditions of the people on their estates. A way of
life was thereby destroyed, but it could probably
not have survived in any case. All enlightened
opinion agreed at the time the numbers living on
the congested lands in the north had to fall if any
economic progress was to be achieved.

This *Scotsman* editorial was written not in the 1880s, during
brutal clearances on the Duke of Sutherland's estates – but in
the 'enlightened' 1970s.

Astonishing.

Somehow the great and good still believe our land, people
and climate are to blame for the emptiness of Scotland – not
our landowners. No wonder a fifth of the country is managed
as a driven grouse moor. The received wisdom is that our
straths and glens are so utterly barren, Scots should be glad
that absentee toffs are willing to take them off our hands,
keeping a few low-paid locals in substandard tied housing
to help rich foreigners shoot small birds. Scotland really is
such an unproductive pup of a country – so barren as to be
fundamentally worthless.

This of course is nonsense. Propaganda. Easily rebutted
by looking at the relatively large populations sustained on
tree and lochan-covered Arctic tundra in the Nordic nations
still further north. Or, 'the mountain ledges the sheep cannot
reach with their wealth of alpine herbs'.[1] Or trees growing
tall in the central reservation of the A9 – beyond the deer and
sheep that have been allowed to reduce the surrounding land
to a yellowed desert.

*Ok, most of the Scottish landmass has neither Mediterranean
sun, nor Surrey-style rolling fields. But Scots are living in
a possible paradise – if we change our patterns of landownership, land-use and above all, our mindsets.*

The great and good have been raining on Scotland's parade
for centuries and – whether deliberately or unconsciously

---

1 Smout TC, *Nature Contested*, EUP, 2000, p131

– they've stifled expectations and deflated optimism. They'll convince you that what we've got – or in the case of quasi feudal Scotland what they've got – just isn't all that special. Nothing to see. No point squabbling. No need to change use or ownership. Just move on.

We must find the energy and optimism to tackle all of this.

Because from a different perspective – the upbeat perspective that accompanies the move towards independence – Scotland is actually peachy.

Take the rain. There's no point denying the west coast in particular gets a lot of it. Enough to qualify as a globally rare coastal temperate rainforest.

Sure, we have also midges. Wee blighters. But the rain and snow also mean we also have water – one of the most precious resources on Earth. Of course, the abundance of H_2O means Scots don't really rate it – but just across the border, the 19 privatised water and sewage companies of England certainly do. With an unprecedented 500-year summer drought in 2022, which caused the Thames to shrink by five miles, there are predictions southern England will run out of fresh water in less than 30 years. Sir James Bevan, chief executive of the English Environment Agency, suggests Scotland could be the answer to his country's water woes with England staring into the 'jaws of death', as an ever-growing population outstrips water supplies. Peter Murphy, director of consultancy firm UK Water observes:

Loch Ness has more water than all of England and Wales combined. And that's just one loch – Scotland has more than 31,000 freshwater lochs, and most are unused. Scotland has a small population and about 100 times more water than it uses. The country's hydrological cycle is only going to improve – climate change means Scotland is going to get warmer, and therefore wetter. Scotland's population will probably increase too, but we should all be thinking about investment and opportunity. Scotland lends itself to

water collection – rerouting water to England would
cost less than HS2.[2]

Right, ignore the gloom attached to the idea of Scotland
getting even wetter. Focus first on Mr Murphy's contention that
more rain constitutes an 'improvement' in a hydrological cycle,
which means the best kind of new independent country these
days, is a wet one. Focus second on his alarming talk about
Scottish Water being siphoned off to southern England. Now
I'll grant you that sounds more like a Boris Johnson gimmick
than a real proposal and it was indeed kick started by Mr
Wheeze himself in 2014 when the London Mayor argued water
could be exported south via a £14 billion series of canals on a
natural 'contour' down the spine of England from the Scottish
borders to the sacred south east. Alex Salmond expressed
interest in selling some of Scotland's publicly owned water
supplies, but the current Scottish government isn't so keen and
says neither bulk shipping nor pipelines are financially viable.
Obviously they also worry the UK Government could make
a 'Natural' water Grid perform like the National electricity
Grid where Scots are surcharged for the privilege of consuming
our own assets.

In short, give folk like Boris a teacup and he'll take a 1,000
litre container.

Mind you, it is legally Scotland's water. But with chronic
shortages in England and a track record of welching on deals
and imposing new rules on Scotland via the Internal Market
Act – can we be certain it will stay that way?

Already privately-owned Thames Water has approval for
a £13 billion investment in pipes, restored canals and new
waterways to transfer water from the north via the Severn
to its increasingly barren patch. Maybe it's alarmist to think
Scotland's water might also head south. And maybe it's a mean
thought anyway. If we have that much water, why not share

2 https://www.heraldscotland.com/news/18890231.pipe-dream-
ministers-block-boris-johnson-inspired-bid-export-scots-water-england/

some with our nearest neighbours?

Well, generosity might be fine if everything else in the privatised English garden was rosy. But it's not. Thames Water paid no corporation tax between 2011 and 2015, lost 677.2 million litres of water through leaky pipes EVERY DAY, distributed £392 million in profits to shareholders and paid its director £851,000 in salary, bonuses and other perks.[3]

In other words, 'free' or cheap Scottish water won't make these private companies clean up their act. It'll just boost shareholder profits and allow the southern water crisis to continue. And there's a wee kicker. In 2017 over 50 per cent of Thames Water belonged to pension and sovereign wealth funds owned by foreign governments. So English Water IS owned by the public sector - of other countries. It's called taking back control.

Which tells us a few things.

It's great that Scots live in a rainy country with loads of water.

It's great that Scotland's Water remains in public hands – though wastewater plants aren't – and with only 4 per cent of river overflows monitored in Scotland, compared to 90 per cent in England, there must be some doubt about the official claim that 87 per cent of Scotland's waters are in 'good ecological condition'.

But there's no doubt sharp-elbowed charlatans manage the whole water and sewage system down south and English ecologists would give their eye teeth to have a publicly accountable system like ours.

And it's reasonable to ask what apart from independence will guarantee that our water isn't commandeered as a cheaper solution than fixing leaks as southern droughts get worse.

So don't knock it. Rain, is one of Scotland's greatest natural assets, gives us hydro energy at the flick of a switch, the lush, green beauty of the west coast plus the lochs and river systems that make Scotland Scotland. Instead of pining for a climate

---

3 https://www.ft.com/content/cb794b64-3454-4328-986e-d93a397ce96f

we will never have, how about cheerfully settling for the one we've got?

Accepting our homeland just as it is also means accepting ourselves.

Taking responsibility for our shared home – the whole physical and marine terrain – is part and parcel of growing up and being Scottish. Or at least, it should be.

Look north, to see how national self-acceptance has been integral to the success of small independent countries.

Take Iceland – essentially a giant cauldron sitting astride two juddering tectonic plates. The sub-Arctic island, home to one third of all lava flows on earth, has 30 volcanoes and 12 small earthquakes every day. But, the islanders don't thole their volcanoes, they love them.

The redoubtable Katrin Oddsdottir, secretary of the country's pioneering crowd-sourced constitution, told me her parents appeared at her primary school, many years ago and wanted to see her immediately. 'My sister must be dead,' Katrin thought. 'Why else would both of them be here?'

She was taken to a sideroom, parents ushered in and the teacher tactfully withdrew. As Katrin steeled herself for the worst, her mother leaned over and said: 'There's the most amazing volcanic eruption on the other side of the island. We're all going to watch – will you come too?'

You've got to love these guys. Icelanders thrive not despite their volcanoes but because of them.

One day, dreaded and long overdue eruptions from Katla and the Laki fissure will once again decimate the country. In 1783, clouds of poisonous hydrofluoric acid and sulphur dioxide contaminated the soil, killing half of Iceland's livestock, destroying crops and causing a famine that killed a quarter of the human population. The destruction extended across the globe for a year, obscuring the sun and spreading a poisonous fog that caused food shortages which may have triggered the French Revolution.

Yet still the Icelanders love their volcanoes. This unusual, remote, dangerous, striking, geothermally heated country is home. And home has made Icelanders who they are. Daring.

It's why they grabbed the opportunity to declare independence while Denmark was occupied during WW2 – even though economists believed their sole national asset was a collection of sulphur mines. Sixty years later, they ditched an application to join the EU after near bankruptcy in 2008. As soon as their own currency stabilised, the old instinct for independence and self-sufficiency kicked in again.

Icelanders have a strong belief in their own capabilities thanks to accepting, valuing, loving, surviving and actually owning the land (and sea) that is home. Not turning away in horror or disbelief at the lava-strewn boulder fields but using familiarity and engineering skill to turn that harsh land and the constant threat of eruption into a source of cheap, constant geothermal energy.

There's a Nordic saying – there is no bad weather, only inappropriate clothing.

Maybe that can be adapted for countries.

There are no barren lands, only outsider perspectives.

And maybe, there is no frozen north, just slightly spooked southern visitors.

That may seem a bit unfair, but over the centuries, some prominent writers have been fiercely negative about 'north Britain'.

Take that acerbic Londoner Dr Samuel Johnson, who visited Scotland in 1773 and spoke of a land almost totally covered with useless, dark and stunted heath and matter incapable of form, concluding that

> an age accustomed to flowery pastures and waving
> harvests is astonished and repelled by this wide
> extent of hopeless sterility.[4]

Nice.

Naturally, Johnson's verdict was recorded for posterity

---

4 Smout p12.

– not so the verdict of local people.

Fortunately for us, modern Scottish historians have evened things up. Professor TC Smout makes this profound observation in *Nature Contested*:

> I can trace no fear of the natural world in native born commentators. It was the visitors for whom it was famously alarming.[5]

He quotes an anonymous account of Strathnaver in Sutherland, written in the 17th century, which describes

> a country full of red deer and roes, pleasant for hunting in the summer season... stored with all kinds of wild fowl... with diverse lochs, full of fishes.

Professor Smout remarks,

> our author is neither repelled nor intimidated by his environment. On the contrary, for him Strathnaver is a delightful place, Virgilian in its pastoral peace, rich in natural resources with excellent hunting grounds for pleasure and the perfect spot for a second home in summer.[6]

Admittedly, a century and many miles sat between Dr Johnson and Smout's anonymous writer. But how could they have had such radically different views of roughly the same terrain? Perhaps, the local saw what was present with all its possibilities, whilst the visitor saw only what was absent – the 'flowery pastures and waving harvests' of his own southern home. Different perspectives are fine. But in Highland Scotland, the visitor's view is the one that has stuck.

The same thing happened in the Nordic countries, whose

---

5 Ibid.
6 Ibid p13.

mountainous fjords and Arctic territories were depicted by visitors as places of terror and bleakness. Ironically, this may have aided Norwegians in Arctic Finnmark, fleeing Nazi occupation during the Second World War. Few occupiers believed anyone could survive in such a godforsaken wilderness. Except, as Jan Baalsrud demonstrated in his incredible escape to Sweden (powerfully retold in the film *The 12th Man*) the land was not empty. Locals hid, transported and shielded the injured resistance fighter all the way to freedom, despite ferocious winter conditions. Locals who knew and cherished every inch of their frozen land.

Back in Iceland, the painter Johannes Kjarval (1885–1972) was one of the first to paint his country as he saw it – as it actually is – without contrived traces of the visual comfort that might appeal to Danish patrons and their sensibilities. Kjarval – described as the Nordic Van Gogh by our own Richard Demarco – depicted the vivid Icelandic sward with mosses and lichens that turn red, yellow and green in changing seasons amidst sharp, uneroded, unforgiving contours of a country strewn with the newest rocks on earth and red, sulphurous rivers which contrast starkly against white, snow covered conical mountains – an island wrestling with its own never-ending vulcanicity.

Kjarval is loved in Iceland, partly because he was a genuine Bohemian who owned nothing but a tiny hut, staying with friends and strangers, to paint Iceland outside in the 'plein air'. He handed over most of his works in lieu of rent before moving on. As a result, almost every extended family has a Kjarval – a slice of their own cultural identity. But mostly the man is loved because he gave Icelanders the real Iceland – depicted lovingly and with great, grounded detail.

This is the opinion of a visitor to Kjarvalsstadir – the Reykjavik museum dedicated to his work:

Elsewhere, landscapes are full of trees and flowers – in Iceland they are necessarily focused on the rocks and the underlying geography. Kjarval paints the

rocks in detail, and that is something I have rarely
seen before. Each bump, each tiny crystal, each
fragment of lichen is there. But, at the same time, he
conveys the dynamism of Iceland's landscape – where
the rock boils and flows and shifts and reshapes
itself. He also captures something of the uncanny
aspect of the landscape, the feeling something could
be watching you, that the rocks could somehow
be alive, that something is going on that you might
occasionally catch in the corner of your eye.

Indeed, Icelanders have an ancient belief that elves or *huldufolk*
(literally hidden people) inhabit rocks, causing new roads to
divert around oddly shaped boulders in the lava fields – in
case they are elf churches.

In recognising all of this and refusing to apologise for the
country's landscape and superstition, Kjarval captured its
intense, unusual beauty and gave confidence and self-respect
to its people.

And the point of this northern excursion?

Compared to Iceland (and indeed all the Nordic nations)
Scotland is a green, verdant, lush, fertile and productive country.
But thanks to estrangement from our own land, lochs, rivers,
coasts, mountains, bogs and foreshores – owned by absentees
and lairds for generations – such loving self-acceptance hasn't
happened. Yet. And that vastly limits appreciation of Scotland's
abundant resources – ourselves included.

I know this preoccupation with land and the distant past
may strike a dud note for urban Scots – who are the vast
majority. But forgive me for regarding this as a bit of political
reflexology. In the same way pressing the ball of the foot can
release pressure in the kidneys, pressing home the damage
done by Scotland's weird land inequality may release a great
deal of tension in the whole body politic.

Scotland is still basically out of bounds for the average
citizen in a way no other country in the developed world

would tolerate. Our land – our home – is either the private, guarded domain of the landed gentry or a physically demanding landscape accessible by only the very tough or fairly wealthy.

As the American writer Katherine Haldane Grenier put it:

> Victorian men participated in a range of... 'manly pastimes' in the Highlands: hunting, fishing, hiking, camping, climbing mountains. Renditions of parts of the Highlands, such as the Cuillin, as 'desolate', 'sterile' and 'inaccessible' implicitly elevated the achievements of those who went there.[7]

If our land isn't for the ordinary Joe or Josephine, then what is 'progressive' Scotland really about?

Anyway, labelling the Highlands as desolate and wild helped legitimise an 'improvement' mentality that almost destroyed the humble Scottish bog – now acknowledged as a carbon store on a par with the forests of the Amazon.

Back in the 17th century, Sir Robert Gordon opined that a bog was

> a bounty of merciful providence [which provided] inexhaustible mosses wherein are digged the best of peat.[8]

But within 200 years, 'improvers' like Andrew Steele were claiming that Scotland's bogs were

> immense deserts... a blot upon the beauty and a derision to the agriculture of the British Isles.

Indeed, bogs so challenged the 'improving' sensibilities of

---

7 Haldane Grenier, K, *Tourism and Identity in Scotland 1770–1914*, Oxford: Routledge, 2005, p110.
8 Ibid p20.

Victorian landowners they spent vast sums getting poor locals to 'reclaim' them. William Aiton, for example, drained the 'great moss' at Blair Drummond, boasting that in the process,

> several hundreds of ignorant and indolent
> Highlanders were converted into active, industrious
> and virtuous cultivators and many hundreds of acres
> of the least possible value rendered equal to the best
> land in Scotland.[9]

Aye, whatever.

But landowners also sought to 'improve' the awe-inspiring wilderness of Scotland's mountainous terrain by removing locals, since nothing as tatty as ordinary human life could tarnish the mystical experience of the sublime – 'a fear which fills the mind with great ideas and stirs the soul, as in a storm.'

Indeed, once Victorian society had decided the terrible desolation of Scottish glens was actually terribly beautiful, local Scots were rapidly cleared so as not to spoil the view. While the Englishman Edwin Landseer painted The Monarch of the Glen in 1851, thousands of real local people were cleared from surrounding glens to make way for aesthetically pleasing emptiness, deer and 'sportsmen'. In the 1830s, English reform campaigner William Cobbett was outraged that Edinburgh – which he regarded as the world's finest city – was not surrounded by thriving agricultural villages because aristocrats preferred their estates empty, rural and 'unspoiled'. He also raged against the Clearances:

> All that we have been told about [Scotland's] sterility
> has been either sheer falsehood or monstrous
> exaggeration.[10]

Cobbett got it in one.

---

9 Ibid p20.
10 Green, D (ed.), *Cobbett's Tour in Scotland,* Aberdeen: Aberdeen University Press, 1984.

Scotland's sterility – sheer falsehood

The 'falsehood and monstrous exaggeration' of Scotland's sterility has continued unabated, ever since. And because Scots today have less connection than our forebears, a wedge has been driven between us and our land. Between us and the spectacular country that's shaped us – one of many schisms that support the stultifying myth of the Scots' split personality.

But sticking with land for a minute, there has been epic projection of southern uneasiness onto our own rich and epic landscapes: massive and casual manipulation of the land and its people; and relentless rejection of Scotland – just as she actually is.

If women have been bent out of shape by the impossible demands of the male gaze – and we have – poor old Scotland has undergone the same cruel fate, viewed alternately with outright disapproval and weird, exalted excitement by powerful outsiders. Forced to pout, pose, disguise, discard and deny her very self, Scotland has been feared, rejected, drained, 'improved' and admired by 'owners' who rarely stayed longer than a summer shooting season.

And even by a Scottish Government which has chronically undervalued her offshore wind resource in the ScotWind sale.

It's time to take responsibility for putting this right, because Scottish landscape is not just beautiful, it's also a beautiful construct.

In *Making Scotland's Landscape* on BBC Scotland, Professor Iain Stewart observes that almost all of Scotland's 'natural' landscape is essentially man-made:

> The only thing that happens naturally is rain. As soon as it hits the ground, it is ours and we do with it what we will. Today there are scarcely any rivers or natural large bodies of water left untouched by human activity. Scotland's waters have become some of the most managed on earth.

That may be shocking to hear. But it's also hopeful. Our glens are not naturally empty. Our lochs are not naturally devoid of fish. Scotland is currently managed and we can manage it better to support people not grouse, improve biodiversity and help communities decarbonise. We must. That's our mission and our duty.

Democratically owned, one fifth of Scotland would not be an empty, poisoned grouse moor. It would be a peopled, mixed woodland, with bogs and precious wetlands. Are we ready to help that transition/reversion actually happen? Because if we aren't, this glorious country will continue to do less for the world's ecology than it should and still less for our national self-esteem. We cannot view Scotland as a dodgy inheritance or a downright stranger, when it is simply and marvellously our irreplaceable home.

Still, some will question whether estrangement from the land really has such a negative impact on our modern, largely urban sensibilities. I'd humbly suggest a lot of hard work has been put in over the ages to ensure that it does. Why else do so many Scots agree with Samuel Johnson, that:

> the noblest prospect which a Scotchman ever sees, is the high road that leads him to England.

Ach, you'll say, that was then.

Just one choice quote, designed to rile. Ignore it. Well, one or two, actually.

> What enemy would invade Scotland, when there is nothing to be got?

asked Johnson, warning an Irish friend against union with England:

> Do not make a union with us, Sir. We should unite with you only to rob you; we should have robbed the Scots if they had anything of which we could rob them.

Of course, when oil was discovered, Scotland's robbability quotient rapidly changed.

And even though 18th century Scotland, unlike England, provided a basic primary education for most children in parish schools, Johnson remained unimpressed:

> Knowledge is divided up among Scots like bread in a besieged town, to every man a mouthful, to no man a bellyful.[11]

James Boswell, irked by Johnson's refusal to concede the existence of highly educated Scots, cited Lord Mansfield, Chief Justice of the Court of King's Bench. But Johnson denied that Scotland could derive:

> any credit from Mansfield, for he was educated in England. Much may be made of a Scotchman if he be caught young.

Ok – Samuel Johnson had some toe-curling views on many things and a fairly big problem with Scotland. If alive today, he might be a shock jock on GB News beside Neil Oliver and David Starkey. But his views are just ancient history, right?

Sadly, each harsh, outsider's view of Scotland simply laid groundwork for the next.

And Johnson's groundwork was pretty substantial. He literally shaped the evolution of modern English with his *Dictionary of the English Language* in 1755. He was – according to the *Oxford Dictionary of National Biography* – 'the most distinguished man of letters in English history'.

A powerful opponent, channelling all the negativity in the English psyche about the alien northerners who'd recently backed a French prince and nearly taken over his green and pleasant land.

Post-Culloden England held Scotland in fear, some loathing

---

11 https://www.samueljohnson.com/scotland.html

and a lot of naked contempt. Scots then proceeded to drink the Kool-Aid.

And this downbeat view of all things northern, this learned aversion to our own domain endures. As a result, we are haunted by a fear of being Northern; of being left behind because we are so damned remote.

Remote.

When Scotland sits slap bang in the middle of the North Atlantic and further south than the most productive, successful, Triple A credit-rated countries in the world? Honestly.

The situation is far simpler. We – who are custodians of Scotland – have allowed our land to become a foreign-owned, tradeable commodity and our country to be portrayed as peripheral. We have taken that warped portrait to our hearts. And we must remove it.

Being in denial about our Northernness means failing to embrace our own physical and cultural riches. It means behaving as if we're louche southern types used to piazzas, outside eating and a Mediterranean diet, who've been unaccountably dumped near the North Pole.

It means tittering at the mere mention of Norway – such an indy cliché/unattainable goal/utter irrelevance where a pint costs £700 – whilst drinking in comparisons with countries so much larger as to be quite irrelevant – like America, population 320m.

We are northern people who inhabit an energy rich, geopolitically important, North Atlantic island. We live here – not anywhere else. Sure, it's good to see oorsels as ithers see us. But only up to a point. Let's spend time making Scotland the centre of our universe, because when we love our own country, geography, climate and latitude, we can recognise and harness its never-ending opportunities.

Like wind. Another resource traditionally viewed in a fairly negative way. Ferries cancelled. Bridges closed. Travel disrupted. In the old days, wind drowned fishermen, whistled through homes and made life cold and miserable Even today, thanks to wind, the best coiffed styles of men and women gang aft agley.

Yet wet and windy is the ideal climate for a modern country seeking independence, since wind and hydro are the cheapest and most reliable sources of renewable energy to be found anywhere in the world. Happily, Scotland has some of the highest wind speeds and most consistent air-flows in the northern hemisphere.

But wind is intermittent, cry the critics.

Jings, so is breathing.

And an independent Scotland could join ambitious plans for a North Atlantic grid so the occasional calm day in Scotland could easily be offset by renewable energy from another part of the continent, or indeed our own fully developed hydro and tidal energy resources.

So will we continue to undervalue the potential of our wind, rain, seas, mountains, rivers, peat-covered islands, blanket bogs and glens or – like our independent neighbours – abandon the Northern cringe and sing from the rooftops about the splendour of our home?

Judging countries by their anthems

Read the lyrics to the national anthems of the Nordic countries. Compare with our own battle and monarchy-obsessed polemics. Read and weep.

Norwegian national anthem
Yes, we love with fond devotion
This our land that looms
Rugged, storm-scarred o'er the ocean
With her thousand homes.
Love her, in our love recalling
Those who gave us birth.
And old tales which night, in falling,
Brings as dreams to earth.

Norsemen what so ever thy station,
Thank thy God whose power
willed and wrought the land's salvation
In her darkest hour.
All our mothers sought with weeping
And our sires in fight,
God has fashioned in His keeping
Till we gained our right.

Swedish national anthem
Thou ancient, thou freeborn, thou mountainous North,
In beauty and peace our hearts beguiling,
I greet thee, thou loveliest land on the earth,
Thy sun, thy skies, thy verdant meadows smiling.
Thy sun, thy skies, thy verdant meadows smiling.
Thy throne rests on mem'ries from great days of yore,
When worldwide renown was valour's guardian.
I know to thy name thou art true as before.
Oh, I would live and I would die in Sweden,
Oh, I would live and I would die in Sweden.

Finnish national anthem
Our land, our land, our fatherland,
Sound loud, O name of worth!
No mount that meets the heaven's band,
No hidden vale, no wave-washed strand,
Is loved, as is our native North,
Our own forefathers' earth.
Thy blossom, in the bud laid low,
Yet ripened shall upspring.
See! From our love once more shall grow
Thy light, thy joy, thy hope, thy glow!
And clearer yet one day shall ring
The song our land shall sing.

Icelandic national anthem
Oh, God of our country! Oh, our country's God!
We worship Thy name in its wonder sublime.
The suns of the heavens are set in Thy crown
By Thy legions, the ages of time!
With Thee is each day as a thousand years,
Each thousand of years, but a day,
Eternity's flower, with its homage of tears,
That reverently passes away.
Iceland's thousand years.
Iceland's thousand years.
Eternity's flower, with its homage of tears,
That reverently passes away.

Danish national anthem
I know a lovely land
With spreading, shady beeches
Near Baltic's salty strand;
Near Baltic's salty strand;
Its hills and valleys gently fall,
Its ancient name is Denmark,
And it is Freya's hall
And it is Freya's hall

Praise King and Country with might
Bless every Dane at heart
For serving with no fear
For serving with no fear
The Viking kingdom for Danes is true
With fields and waving beeches
By a sea so blue
By a sea so blue

British national anthem
God save our gracious King!
Long live our noble King!

God save the King!
Send him victorious,
Happy and glorious,
Long to reign over us,
God save the King.
Thy choicest gifts in store
On him be pleased to pour,
Long may he reign.
May he defend our laws,
And give us ever cause,
To sing with heart and voice,
God save the King.

Even 'Flower of Scotland' lacks the upbeat, easy connection with nature found in these Nordic anthems.

O Flower of Scotland,
When will we see
Your likes again,
That fought and died for,
Your wee bit Hill and Glen,
And stood against them,
Proud Edward's Army,
And sent them homeward,
Tae think again.
The Hills are bare now,
And Autumn leaves
lie thick and still,
O'er land that is lost now,
Which those so dearly held,
That stood against them,
Proud Edward's Army,
And sent them homeward,
Tae think again.

Not much beats the landscapes of Scotland. And yet our

official national anthem is a dirge about Kings and Queens and our unofficial Scottish anthem alternates between defiance and mournfulness. There's nothing loving or admiring about the physical landscape of Scotland in either 'national song'. That's understandable in God Save the Monarch, but in a song designed to stir Scottish hearts? Is vaguely pledging to whack the English in battle again REALLY more uplifting than falling in love with our own gobsmackingly beautiful country?

Perhaps our hesitation has a simple explanation. In contrast to the Nordic nations, the Scots haven't got Scotland. One big reason for overlooking its beauty, is that by and large, it isn't and never has been ours.

That limits connection, pride, security and confidence about the land and our place upon it. That creates a tendency to downplay its productivity, beauty, natural splendour and capacity.

And that places a subliminal brake on the demand for complete control.

You realise what's missing when you visit countries like Finland and Estonia, whose people are head over heels in love with the physicality of their own countries. They see beauty in bogs. They see their national character reflected in hundreds of miles of indistinguishable conifers. They see glory in the depths of forest. They rejoice in knowing that during the Second World War, 'Forest Brothers' dug into snow tunnels for months on end, able to survive and push back Red Army invaders. One thing helped this self-love develop in Finland and Estonia.

Land reform – the first change made by each post-independence government in 1918. According to Estonian independence leader, Marju Lauristin, the main reason her people hung on during 50 years of Russian occupation after ww2 was that early, momentous re-distribution of land which gave ordinary Estonians skin in the game. They strategised, sang, organised and resisted their way through half an awful century because they knew the country belonged to them. Theirs would indeed become a land fit for heroes. They could make it so.

Today these Baltic states are still conducting a slightly breathless love affair with their own land – and thus with themselves. You can see folk worship landscapes that are essentially massive, tree-strewn bogs. You can hear the soaring ecstasy of Finlandia – Jean Sibelius' tribute to the relatively barren country he urged towards independence.

Yet there's nothing like this widespread, universal, unapologetic, familiar, no-holds barred, unconditional love for our own landscape in modern, post-feudal Scotland.

Ochone.

By contrast, we see jeopardy all around because we still look at our land with the critical, disappointed, frightened and occasionally sublime-obsessed eye of the outsider.

But the good news is – that can change. A 'loving' gaze existed before the tragic internal exile of the Clearances – and it can exist again.

Duncan Ban MacIntyre to the rescue

In 1768 'Moladh Beinn Dòbhrain' or 'Praise of Ben Dorain' was published by Donnchadh Bàn Mac an t-Saoir or Duncan Ban MacIntyre – transcribed from the poet's own recitation, since he couldn't read or write and had committed all his verse to memory, aided by the rhythm of a pibroch pipe tune. Iain Crichton Smith said of 'Ben Dorain':

> Nowhere else in Scottish poetry do we have a poem of such sunniness and grace and exactitude maintained for such a length, with such a wealth of varied music and teaming richness and language. The devoted obsession, the richly concentrated gaze, the loving scrutiny, undiverted by philosophical analysis, has created a particular world, joyously exhausting area after area as the Celtic monks exhausted page after page in the Book of Kells.[12]

12 Smith, IC *Towards the Human*, (1986), Saltire Society, Edinburgh. pp133–35.

For the uninitiated, Beinn Dorain is one of the most instantly recognisable Munros in the southern Highlands – a huge conical peak louring over the A82 north of Tyndrum:

> Her riches are endless: fresh springs of water,
> New bursts of bushes, green glittering leaves,
> Luxurious greens, of all shades and tones
> In the spring of the breeze,
> In sunshine and under
> The cloudless blue sky.
> I have loved her so long –
> This passion so – comprehensive and strong …
> Sustains its renewal each day in the song –
> Diamond light
> On the trees and high slopes
> Rising, the conical top all swirls round,
> Like music, to dance in,
> Elegant forms, mutual, joined,
> Connected in movements
> With separate purpose…
> There is order
> In their assembly,
> A small group of deer
> On the steep edge, ascending –
> Their step on the cliff-edge
> Certain and bright
> Overlooking the bare field,
> The unvisited corrie –
> With access to nourishment free,
> All around them, nothing
> To pay.[13]

It is wonderful, rousing, upbeat and uplifting stuff – even if

---

13 Duncan Ban MacIntyre with Alan Riach (Translator) *Praise of Ben Dorain*, Kettillonia, Angus, 2013.

most Scots don't recognise Ban MacIntyre's name. But I'd guess they long to share his intimacy with the land around him and jettison the dead-weight of our own exclusion.

It could reasonably be argued that Scotland doesn't need independence to achieve that. Many of the levers needed to end the feudal pattern of landownership are already in the hands of a Scottish Government that opts not to use them. But as veteran land reform campaigner Andy Wightman has observed, the change in outlook needed to elect a government that truly dismantles feudalism and redistributes land is of the same magnitude as the change in outlook needed for independence. Or put another way, the energy released by independence might also dismantle one of Scotland's oldest inequalities. Conversely, with the timorous status quo, how much further will we ever get?

Meantime, let's learn to love this country – water, bog, rain, cloud and all. Scotland has a coastline which would cover a third of the planet, if stretched across its diameter. In a future Scotland with democratised land ownership, we could have community sawmills, sustainable timber for building and home heating, fishing opportunities galore, watersports almost everywhere and integrated renewable energy systems that also extract heat from the water around us, using Scottish technology that's powered industrial cities like Drammen in Norway for the last 15 years but has only recently and tentatively been adopted here – its country of origin.

All of this really matters because Scots must decide if the country we'll inhabit after independence is a going proposition or a hopeless pup. Our estimates of its worth have been influenced by a perception of Scotland as inhospitable, barren and essentially useless. A perception we have unwittingly embraced.

From a different perspective, the whole of Scotland is lush. The second most northerly county in Scotland is called Sutherland – named by Vikings, who considered it so southern as to be positively Mediterranean compared to their own fjord homelands. Now, this is not to say we should take all our bearings from the perspective of Viking raiders. Clearly large parts of Scotland are unsuitable for conventional farming – but they sit beside seas with huge possibilities for tidal energy and aquaculture, beside ideal sites for wind energy which could power glass houses, vertical farming and hydroponic agriculture, supporting larger, more stable human populations. This is why Norway has always been so well populated, despite having a third of its territory in the Arctic. Hydro energy was developed on rivers, so early industry travelled there, creating a dispersed, rural settlement pattern the country chose to maintain after independence. In stark contrast, Scotland's discovery of coal, and the steam engine, made industry portable, so it quickly concentrated around the central belt, leading to the dangerous assumption that everything beyond is unable to stand on its own two unsubsidised feet. In fact, the resources of rural Scotland – Highland and Lowland – are staggering, yet vastly underestimated by most Scots.

So, let's reassess and prepare to fall head over heels in love.

So, what are we like?

Having done some mental rearrangement regarding dear old Scotia – how about ourselves? What are we like?

Well, there's the good stuff, which we naturally shrug off. And the bad stuff, which we hug close and store deep down.

Like the fear we are contrary bams.

Violent.

Warring.

Chippy.

Sullen.

Always settling old scores.

If it's not the grumpy, aggressive Groundskeeper Willie from *The Simpsons*, it's the fabulously morose, pessimistic Sergeant played by John Laurie in *Dad's Army*.

Indeed, you can forget Sean Connery, Ewan McGregor,

Annie Lennox, Rod Stewart and Scottie from Star Trek – 2015 research found Groundskeeper Willie was the character most Americans associate with Scotland, a place they considered to be 'a rural, undynamic environment"

Of course, that was before *Outlander* exploded onto American screens and Donald Trump's time as President rather lessened America's world clout as arbiters of worth. Or taste.

If Scots wanted a serious argument about national stereotypes, we could throw in David Hume, Adam Smith, John Muir, Elsie Inglis, Mary Slessor, Andrew Carnegie and inventors like Baird, Bell and Watt. And if wanted to win, we could just hand over a copy of Elspeth Wills' *Scottish Firsts* or Arthur Herman's *Scots' Invention of the Modern World.*

But both books only accentuate our fall from grace – how many famous firsts is Scotland racking up today? Of course, no-one is counted famous until they're deid. But still it's the negative images of Scotland that have stuck – particularly, the simmering threat of violence.

Not difficult when the classic Hard Man was so powerfully portrayed in William McIlvanney's 1990, novel *The Big Man*, later made into a film about a Glasgow prize fighter, starring Liam Neeson and Billy Connolly.

The royal motto of Scotland is 'Nemo me impune lacessit', Latin for 'No-one attacks me with impunity', or in Scots, 'Wha daur mess wi me?'

Confrontation and aggression.

Is that what Scots are about today?

Is that what we were ever about – in the main?

It's not just history that gets written by the victor.

It's the assignation of national temperament, outlook and personality.

Mud sticks. And mud slows progress. It's meant to.

Let's face it, in a history written by the victors, Scots were never going to be painted as the cheery folk. We blotted our collective copybook too many times – resisting control, skirmishing at the border, fighting for independence, backing

England's main enemy, openly rebelling against the Hanoverian monarchy and nearly winning.

Just like the Irish.

And it's true – Scots have been fighters.

During the European wars of the 16th and 17th centuries 40,000 Scots fought as mercenaries in the service of Russia, Prussia, Austria, Sweden, Italy, Turkey, Spain, Portugal and France. Scots were also hired to fight in Ireland – nick-named Redshanks because they dressed in plaids and waded bare-legged through rivers in the coldest weather.

The clan system of medieval Scotland did absolutely produce fighting men.

But it also created ties of family loyalty that made life viable in tough conditions. Until heads were turned by alien ideas about hierarchy and status, clan chiefs were owed loyalty by their *clann* – the Gaelic word for children – not rent because chiefs were stewards or custodians of the land, not outright owners. Yes, there were feuds – but there were also systems for resolving disputes. The Morrison chiefs were brieves or hereditary judges of disputes on the island of Lewis for centuries, just as the MacCrimmon family provided pipers to several generations of Clan MacLeod chiefs and Clann MacMhuirich – anglicised as Clan Currie – were employed by the Lords of the Isles as bards, lawyers, doctors, musicians and clergymen.

There were acts of thuggery.

There was also a democratic tradition and a powerful, shared culture.

But one has been given far more attention than the other.

I remember a trip to Cladh Hallan on South Uist, 15 years ago for a Radio Scotland series I made about the Outer Isles.

Our bumpy journey in a transit van, behind the small car of local crofter Neil McMillan, took us through sand and machair to the outline of Bronze Age terraced houses occupied between 1400 and 400 BC. Two mummified adults were found there with three children, ranging in age from newborn to adolescent. Both skeletons had been buried in a crouched posture, with arms wrapped around knees drawn up against the chest.

Strange.

Describing the rest of the find, Neil stood close to us, shielding the frisky wind from the microphone with his wiry frame. The softly spoken crofter didn't seem to feel the chill – but then, Neil was standing on sacred ground.

> You know the first porridge was made on this site
> and we've been eating it ever since... the recipe
> spread all over the world, right from where we are
> standing.

Neil spoke as though he still couldn't quite believe it. A single summer's excavation work by Sheffield University unearthed a heritage so rich and productive, locals scarcely recognised it as their own.

To everyone's surprise, no weapons were found – though the excavation team did find fragments of moulds for swords and spears, as well as dress-pins and razors. Some beautiful Bronze Age swords had been unearthed years earlier in a nearby peat bog – evidence of skilled craftsmen and traders at work, since the ores needed for bronze production could only have been imported from much further south.

According to island-based archaeologist Kate MacDonald,

> the swords would have been status symbols, a bit like
> having a Porsche today. You can't drive a Porsche at
> the speed it was designed for, but owning it says a lot
> about how much wealth or power you have.

In short, Neil's ancient ancestors were peaceful, resourceful and smart. Not constantly warring or untouched by progress, as he and many islanders had been led to believe.

Further up the coast, at Howmore, in the ruins of an old

chapel, Kate said we were standing at a monastery which was the Early Medieval equivalent of St Andrews University. Modern monasteries are removed and marginal. But two thousand years ago, they housed the thinkers who created modern Europe. Back then, the Outer Hebrides was not an isolated island chain. In a world of international, sea-based trade, excellent boat builders reigned supreme, and where boats, traders and islanders gathered, the intellectual skills of civilisation flourished. At Howmore, without signposts, fanfare or acknowledgement, we were standing at one birthplace of the modern world.

Who knew?

The point is that Scots were as peaceful as anyone else – resourceful folk in a powerful geopolitical location. That hasn't changed. But embedded ideas about aggression and marginality make that positive inheritance hard to accept.

I had another mind-blowing, perception-altering exchange with the late Professor of Scottish Architecture Charles McKean who often blew a gasket trying to convey his frustration at 'castles' being used as evidence of Scotland's feuding and uncivilised past.

Charles wrote in the arts and politics quarterly *The Drouth* in 2014:

> The ubiquitous heritage presentation of Scottish
> renaissance country seats as military objects...
> fundamentally perverts Scottish history, preventing
> a real understanding of how they worked... at the
> centre of their estates, functioning as the centre of
> power, culture, hospitality and the regional economy.
> Their classification as castles, not only isolates them
> from the contemporary poetic, musical, artistic and
> literary cultures of the country... but also from
> the rest of Europe. When one [compares] their
> allegedly defensive panoply of turrets, gun loops
> ... and crenellations with contemporary European

fortifications, it is perfectly clear these castle-like houses were militarily risible. Nothing more than a martial decoration superimposed upon a modernised habitation – like so many on the Loire. [But] Scottish renaissance architecture became invariably interpreted in military terms. For a country forced to identify itself with the military values of the Empire, the authentic architecture of the Scottish past, often proved far too peaceable.

Yip, there's much more to Scotland's early existence than 'our martial story'. Yet the image of angry, brooding, violent, feuding Scots is always the one that endures.

No wonder. It took several centuries to create.

The framing of Scots as cannibalistic, violent murderous thugs began when natives of Ireland and Scotland took up arms against England.

Anti-Scottish tracts had been published by the English Church in the early Middle Ages when Scotland backed France during the Hundred Years' War. Camden's *Britannia* published in 1586 observed that Scots (especially Highlanders)

Drank the bloud out of wounds of the slain: they establish themselves, by drinking one anothers bloud and suppose the great number of slaughters they commit, the more honour they winne.

This idea that Scots were cannibals apparently arose from a mistranslation of an early text by St Jerome. But thanks to *Britannia*, Scotland's mythical cannibalism was written into history as fact and subsequently embellished by various English writers – including historian Edward Gibbon who declared himself astonished that a 'race of cannibals' might be living near David Hume while the Great Man was producing world-shaping ideas about philosophy and economy. Thus, the cannibalistic hare was kept on its non-existent feet helping to invent Sawney Bean – the head of an incestuous, lawless and cannibalistic family whose 48 members lived in caves on the Galloway coast. Although completely fictitious, the family was said to have murdered and eaten over a thousand victims.

That total makey-uppey was published in the *Newgate Calendar* in 1720 – the most popular book in London after the Bible and *Pilgrim's Progress* – and helped lay the ground for other representations of Scots as vicious, animalistic and profoundly uncivilised.[14]

According to Glasgow University history professor, Murray Pittock, Highland Scots especially were portrayed as brutish thugs, figures of ridicule and no match for Lowland Scots and supporters of the Protestant Hanovarians. Highlanders were feminised in a parody of the female disguise used by Bonnie Prince Charlie or savage warriors who needed the guiding hand of industrious Lowland Scots to function. Either way, not to be trusted.

Scots-baiting culminated in that offensive verse of God Save the King, which was dropped (officially) when the song became the British national anthem in the 1780s.

Lord, grant that Marshal Wade,
May by thy mighty aid,
Victory bring.
May he sedition hush,
And like a torrent rush,
Rebellious Scots to crush,
God save the King.

Of course, crushing looked fully justified in the late 18th century since Scottish forces had risen twice against British Hanoverian monarchs. But after Culloden a cunning British state found a less confrontational way to deal with its erstwhile enemies – it co-opted them. As Calum Maclean recounts:

---

14 https://www.exclassics.com/newgate/ng9.htm

Every Gaelic-speaking Highlander, irrespective of creed or denomination, was a potential nationalist, a Jacobite and rebel. Towards the end of the century there was formulated the brilliant policy of enlisting the 'secret enemy' to destroy him as cannon fodder. Highlanders were again dressed up in kilts and, by the ingenious use of names such as Cameron, Seaforth and Gordon old loyalties were diverted into new channels.[15]

So, after Culloden and the abolition of the clans, the only way to play pipes, wear tartan or speak Gaelic – essentially the only way to maintain your identity – was to join the British Army that very possibly killed your father. Since land had been confiscated from Jacobite families, kinsmen and supporters, emigrating or joining the British army was also the only way to earn a living. So vanquished Scots became part of the British fighting machine and died in large numbers. In 1759, General Wolfe sent Highlanders into the Battle of Quebec declaring,

they are hardy, intrepid, accustomed to a rough country, and no great mischief if they fall.

Brave, disposable fighters.

The die was cast.

Poverty, clearance and dispossession meant the British army became the only game in town, boosting the idea of Scots as 'natural' fighters. The resulting cultural confusion is still paraded every year – to international acclaim – in the massed pipes and drums of the Edinburgh Military Tattoo.

But mercifully, military tradition is just one side of Scottish culture.

There's another side, embedded in folk traditions that have been recovered and restored by decades of patient work by the Royal National MOD, the Traditional Music and Song

15 MacLean, CI, *The Highlands*, London: Batsford, 2006, p63.

Association of Scotland, the Feisean movement, Dougie Pincock's National Centre for Excellence in Traditional Music at Plockton, the Scottish traditional music course at the Royal Conservatoire of Scotland, and a dazzling array of top notch music festivals from Ceolas on South Uist, to Glasgow's Celtic Connections – Europe's premier folk, roots and world music festival, which has just celebrated its 30th birthday.

If you want to revel in the incredible way non-military piping defines modern Scotland, watch the amazing Danny MacAskill weave his bike down the Cuillin of Skye, to Blackbird, one of the pulsating tracks on Grit, the final album composed by the genre-bending piper and composer, Martyn Bennett.

There's more to our musical culture than military traditions – and that's not to knock our world-beating pipe bands.

But our default attachment to the 'war pipes', has left us inclined to dismiss other traditions – like the uilleann or 'elbow' pipes – as Irish. Ditto step-dancing. Now fair play to Michael Flatley – who has a Riverdance patent on the whole damn thing. But of course, Scots stepdanced too. If our forebears had danced the Highland Fling in low croft houses, we'd have taken one another's eyes out.

The point is that preoccupation with the sublimated violence of military tradition denies Scotland's other, earlier, enduring, peaceful, creative and world-beating musical heritage. And it drives the narrative that violence is an inherent part of the Scottish personality. Wars, we just couldn't stay away from them. And once opportunities for organised combat dried up, Scots divvied up cities and fought one another.

Now, let's be honest, there's no escaping the modern armies that have patrolled the schemes of Glasgow and the west of Scotland. The gangs, hard men, swords and shocking everyday levels of violence made world headlines in 1968, when Frankie Vaughan arrived in Easterhouse with a weapons amnesty and hundreds of chibs, swords and blades handed in, including kitchen knives 'borrowed' by dozens of kids keen to meet the famous crooner. Still, since then, there's been big change. In 2005, when

Strathclyde Police created the Violence Reduction Unit (VRU), Glasgow was the 'murder capital of Europe' with 137 homicides. All sorts of crackdowns had failed, so Strathclyde tried a pioneering new approach treating violence as a public health issue. The VRU's empathetic outlook – working with deprived communities, talking to gang members and dumping old punitive, judgmental attitudes – produced results. By 2018, Scotland's homicide rate had more than halved and police authorities from London to the Horn of Africa were copying the VRU approach.

As London burned in 2011, Glasgow and Edinburgh did not. As 'copycat riots' broke out in Birmingham, Bristol, Coventry, Derby, Leicester, Liverpool, Manchester, Nottingham, West Bromwich and Wolverhampton, the streets of Scottish cities stayed quiet. And eventually, the 'British riots' were correctly renamed the English riots.

That's not to be complacent about Scotland – the plague of domestic violence, the ruthlessness of drug syndicates or the epidemic of self-harm. Real progress needs a reduction in poverty and inequality – hard to do when Westminster calls the shots on taxation, benefits and the economy. But Glasgow is no longer the murder capital of Europe.

And that is some kind of progress.

Has it sunk in?

We've been sold the idea that Scots fight at the drop of a hat for so long, it's got under our skin and into our collective subconscious.

There was always another story – the inventiveness, the early literacy, the legions of doctors and engineers, poets and philosophers and the generosity and hospitality of ordinary people who owned next to nothing.

But the prevailing message was even more powerful. Be afraid of your ain folk. Be afraid of your warring Celtic natures. Be afraid of your selves. Be very afraid.

Actually, an echo of this exists in the SNP's own nervousness about the popular movements that sprang up in the aftermath of the 2014 referendum. They had to be managed and distanced, not backed or embraced in case… what?

Of course, managing rather than empowering punters is the instinct of every British political party. And since some feared rammies at public events, Nicola Sturgeon's prolonged absence at All Under One Banner marches may have seemed reasonable. A case of the top people keeping their powder dry and distant from association with the words of one random, extreme-sounding bam. There's doubtless something to that. But the desire to appear acceptable in the eyes of polite society almost always means keeping the immediacy and urgency of working-class culture, popular movements and street demonstrations at arms-length, as if Scots are like some half-lit fireworks – always liable to explode uncontrollably, right in your face.

And we're not.

We're liable to question. Liable to feel a duty to get off our backsides to create a different future for our country. Liable to march in the rain and sing like linties. Yes.

But liable to become violent or aggressive – no more than anyone else.

Forgive me if I repeat this because it cannot be restated enough.

Over the long years of the indyref there were only a couple of eggs thrown at Jim Murphy. Scots are almost tediously democratic.

Not violent people

So why the SNP's wariness of the burgeoning non-party Yes movement?

Well, a political party always wants control.

Scotland after the indyref was louping and self-organising as energised activists sensed a different society just around the corner, after long decades being taken for granted by Labour. But that energy, seemed like a threat to the SNP. The same way youthful energy looks like trouble on a stick to yer maw. No offence mums – you are usually right.

But not in 2014.

Jonathon Shafi, main organiser of the Radical Independence Campaign recalls the ever-rising tide of excitement in November 2014, when he took a deep breath to hire the Radisson Blu, with an 800 capacity, for the first RIC conference. Tickets sold like hot cakes and he had to upgrade to the SECC a day later:

> I remember going to the Clyde Auditorium, known for hosting concerts rather than left-wing meetings, with a slight air of disbelief. We booked it, with 3000 seats. Alongside that, we hired the adjacent Crown Plaza, the Science Centre, and the nearby Garden Hilton. These would service break-out spaces and creche facilities. In less than two weeks, all those venues were sold out.

The SNP, however, seems to have seen this as a potential threat.

> After we announced our new venue, the SNP booked the Hydro, on the doorstep of our conference on the same day. This event, replete with foam fingers and the trappings of a presidential-style rally, would serve to anoint the new leader of the SNP, the independence movement, and Scotland. It was denied at the time, but the message was clear. Nothing should rival the SNP in its claims to represent the totality of the independence cause.

Now, we'll never know their actual motivations, but the SNP leadership has since studiously avoided involvement with the wider Yes movement, inadvertently confirming its characterisation as a rowdy, critical and unruly mob, in the eyes of the media and 'law-abiding' supporters. Even though these massive marches were universally peaceful, well organised and impressively self-policed, with the 'Silent Clansman' – aka

Elgin bus driver, Paul Jamieson – back turned to the small but inevitable unionist counter-demonstration at every march, earphones on and arms folded with his message conveyed wordlessly to every passing marcher like a kilted latter-day Jimmy Reid. Don't get riled, don't get angry, it's what they want, ignore them. In fact, as marchers encountered the megaphone-wielding unionists, most waved while others sang.

There was no violence and no arrests.

My own memory of those extraordinary gatherings is dominated by the little things. Marchers stopping to help a wheelchair user stuck at a curb; trying hard not to trip over a clutch of wee dogs for two long hours and that tremendous banner of the Old Firm for Indy carried by Celtic and Rangers fans, burying the hatchet for an afternoon in support of a bigger shared goal.

Why was that so important?

Because each other cheek turned, each act of restraint, each refusal to rise to the bait defeated that tired old national stereotype.

The massive marches involving hundreds of thousands of people were a triumph of popular self-organisation – yet they were roundly ignored by SNP leaders, though John Swinney did appear at Perth, in 2019.

Why the bodyswerve? Was it fear of 'the mob'? Did broadcasters take their cue from the missing FM and decide 100,000 'leaderless' people on the streets constituted no more than a pointless gathering or rabble?

If so, that's shameful.

Demonstrations are the preserve of those without institutional clout and the streets are essentially a working-class domain. Middle class society has other, more discreet ways to influence events – networks, contacts, societies, powerful neighbours and golfing companions. So, it's not surprising middle-class professionals find the resort to public demonstration a bit unsettling. Mind you, if marches don't have a confrontational moment, they're too boring to merit a column inch or a broadcast second. See fairness, see mince. Witness the furore over one sign and one confrontational challenge to a BBC reporter outside the Perth Tory hustings in the summer of 2022.

Couple all of that with the pervasive belief that 'proper' democracy happens in buildings, featuring well-spoken folk in suits, and it's no surprise broadcasters gave independence marches a miss.

Fling in the banal difficulty that staffing is low at weekends because TV news bulletins are much shorter than usual and you have a perfect stack of excuses.

But interestingly it's always been the absence of cameras that's riled the peacefully marching crowds – not missing SNP leaders . One frustrated Yesser after a massive Glasgow march in 2016 tweeted:

It's almost like a point of principle for BBC now. If the whole population of Scotland marched at the same time on the same day in every town & city in the country, they would still not report it.

Another observed:

No violence, no thuggery, no mess, just happy, hopeful people looking to the future. [We] need to stop expecting the BBC to care.

But as pro indy marches got bigger, so did the problem of 'balance' in the eyes of a nervy BBC. Even though Better Together didn't rely on street action for impact, the Beeb still needed an 'equal and opposite' show of strength on the streets before a single marching Yesser could be broadcast. Yes, that was always crazy. The strength of the No campaign was never its command of the streets but its control of the establishment, the great and good, institutions like banks, newspapers and the royals. The Yes movement had little institutional underpinning and relied on song, slogan, culture, social media, street protest and excitement to express itself.

The Yes and No campaigns were always very different beasts and there would never be 'balance' in their activities. Yet BBC Scotland ignored massive Yes demonstrations because tens of thousands of 'No Thanks' campaigners had not also hired buses to cross Scotland on their day off (in all weathers) to demonstrate enduring belief in the strength of the Union. If No didn't exactly replicate the energy and street presence of Yes, there could be no balance and therefore no coverage.

See the logic of BBC balance – see mince.

Aunty has belatedly conceded this was a mistake – sort of.

But it's never acknowledged the same failure during the post indyref period when the political DNA of Scotland changed completely. Does this all matter? Yes it all does.

The American sociologist and *Tipping Point* author Malcolm Gladwell has theorised that after 10,000 hours of any activity participants become expert, relaxed, accomplished and comfortable with their own talent.

His examples include Bill Gates, who was ahead of everyone else in computers because he attended a progressive Seattle high school where pupils had been coding since they were teenagers – and the Beatles, who played eight-hour gigs in German clubs long before they invaded America and topped the UK charts. Their opportunity to practice early and often – along with their own raw talent – allowed Gates and the Beatles to invent software and modern rock and roll respectively.

So, here's the thing. More than 10,000 hours have passed since the first independence campaign began and far more than 10,000 people have been involved. That long hard slog has produced a sizeable body of very capable people – able to set up websites, hire halls, livestream demonstrations, digest hideously complex information about borders, currencies and EFTA v EU membership arguments and therefore well able to question the wisdom of SNP policy and the authority of its leadership. Maybe that capacity explains Nicola Sturgeon's wariness of the grassroots Yes movement. But it's a wariness her successor Humza Yousaf must abandon. Able, activist, confident, outspoken Yessers aren't going away. Indeed, as the years pass, more and more are getting their wings and joining the 10,000 hours club.

My guess (after 30 years working in BBC News and Current Affairs) is that all those marches, rallies and public events would have been covered if the First Minister had been there. And such involvement would have produced a different SNP. Maybe 'realists' think it would have been an election-losing SNP. Or a Scottish version of the Catalans, whose peaceful leaders were jailed, exiled and otherwise hung out to dry by the international community after a Declaration of Independence in 2017.

Since Catalonia is frequently trotted out as a cautionary tale for indy-supporting Scots, it's worth saying that the parallel drawn is quite unfair.

The terrible carnage of the Spanish Civil War and the violence perpetrated until the 1970s by the dictator Franco mean Spanish politics is still volatile. Bodies of Franco's victims are being exhumed and a national DNA bank has been established to help locate and identify remains of people in unmarked graves. Indeed, Spain still has one of the highest number of forced disappearances in the world, second only to Cambodia.

That could hardly be more different to the history of peaceful protest and dissent in Scotland. And yet the myth of the powder-keg Scots lives on and seems to have persuaded the main party of independence – albeit subconsciously – to maintain a lofty detachment. And though it wasn't openly talked about, that detachment wasn't missed by Yessers. And it hurt.

Gerry Hassan observes:

The SNP has morphed into being like Labour before them – 'a Court Party' controlling patronage. This, of course is how politics was also done pre-1707, when

Scotland was independent and the monarch's court
was the locus for all power.

An SNP loyalist could easily point out that the party
itself was long dismissed as a trashy flash-mob before their
victory in 2007; that trying to dismantle the British state
in the face of establishment hostility was no mean feat and
that the stereotypical characterisation of Scots as basically
ungovernable placed pressure on SNP leaders to prove the
opposite and avoid any association with the tiniest outbreak
of indiscipline.

But it meant they also avoided connection and the chance
to experience that fabulous, motivating, uplifting feeling of
common cause. Ultimately, a leadership that chooses not to
mix weakens and alienates the rank and file. And a leadership
that fails to tackle damaging stereotypes about its ain folk,
unwittingly perpetuates them.

So, the Yes movement has become a bit like the SNP's mad
aunt in the attic – something the party must accommodate
but would rather not acknowledge.

Meanwhile, it's also fair to say Yessers are impatient for
change. Not like girny 'are we there yet' bairns, but like folk
terrified that a rare opportunity is disappearing fast. Like the
inhabitants of all unequal nations, Scots have deep-seated doubts
about entitlement to life's bounty. So, we grab at whatever's
passing. Even though, as the Bard succinctly put it, 'you seize
the floo'er, its bloom is shed'. Indeed, 'Tam o Shanter' has been
recited so often, Scots can't say we haven't been warned about
the downsides of grabbiness. It's true that political moments
come and go, but just as often real breakthroughs only happen
after the weary traverse of a few false summits.

Courage. Patience.

There's no sign the indy-supporting half of Scotland has
given up – and that's fairly amazing given the bruising contest
to replace Nicola Sturgeon as leader; the shock resignation
and subsequent arrest and release of Peter Murrell as Chief

Executive and a very bumpy honeymoon for Humza Yousaf.

Anxiety is understandable – but though SNP support has fallen, support for independence has remained quite constant. That's no cause for complacency. If Yes gets stuck at 48–50 per cent, Scotland gets stuck in Groundhog Day. And if the SNP's political domination falters, smaller pro-independence parties will struggle to take up the slack.

But it's important to keep things in perspective.

Even with 'just' 72 thousand members, the SNP is a larger party than all other Scottish parties put together and the UK Lib Dems. It has had serious internal divisions before and survived. And the departure of the old guard gives the chance for a real reset. Besides, whatever happens to the SNP, it's a vehicle – independence is the cause.

And so long as Westminster remains hopelessly dysfunctional, that cause will get hundreds of thousands of Scots out of bed, on their feet, chapping doors, in polling booths and on the streets demanding the opportunity to choose a different future.

Yessers aren't going away.

And Scots are not the same folk we were in 2014.

The speed with which many No voters changed their minds after the Brexit vote suggests support for the Union was already dwindling. Many No voters have been on a journey since their side 'won' in 2014 even if it's been more individual, personal and private than the very public, collective journey embarked upon by many Yes voters.

So naturally there are feelings of disappointment and disorientation as the 'old guard' of the SNP steps down. Between them they've helped take independence from a barking, minority pursuit to a credible idea supported by half of Scots, with such clear capacity to go further that no British government dares do the decent democratic thing and transfer powers for another referendum.

But the SNP's achievement is shared with the un-resourced campaigners of civic Scotland who've helped create a bulwark against collapse – a new progressive centre ground beyond the Labour Party and its old trade union base. The activists who pop up in every community project. The doers, thinkers, writers, Yes groups with street stalls, speakers circulating round a seemingly endless circuit of well attended meetings; the journalists who run the *National*, jeopardising their own careers by open political attachment in an industry whose staff never wear their hearts on their sleeves; think tanks like Common Weal, enabling funders like the Scottish Independence Foundation, online magazines like *Bella Caledonia*, bloggers too numerous to mention, and of course Business for Scotland and its information-disseminating wing, Believe in Scotland.

All these folk have demonstrated curiosity, intelligence, tenacity, patience and the ability to self-organise in under-acknowledged bucket-loads. Take the self-taught streamers Independence Live, who still pitch up faithfully in all weathers to make sure the big events in this new, civic Scotland, reach the self-educating Yes-leaning public, who also contribute 90 per cent of the group's funding. What would happen if these largely voluntary efforts had even been given state backing? Now, I suspect the bold lads and lasses of Indy Live might not totally welcome the restrictions that would inevitably bring. But is that why it hasn't happened?

In 2016, a man very familiar with ambitious start-ups and myself approached Bauer Media with a view to buying their Medium Wave frequencies and creating a new, more rigorous and independence-friendly, national radio speech and music network. Bauer at that time were hardly using MW – just rebroadcasting the musical offerings of Radio Forth, Clyde etc on FM. We approached the Scottish Government for a start-up loan, mostly to assure other investors we had government support, but got nowhere. Because broadcasting is a reserved issue.

We were well aware of that, yet still ready to bet our shirts (and mortgage our homes) to test the water. We met Bauer anyway, and were told the family-based company had a policy of never, ever selling company assets.

Maybe that was just some opening hardball, but without support it was hard to find the energy to go on, risking our personal livelihoods for a project that looked set to be disowned by important players on our own side.

Ochone.

Still, as Buddha observed, this is not an easy world and others have far greater troubles.

So, most folk in the Yes movement have simply shrugged off the hurt of being slightly disowned and got on with it. After all, deep down, disempowered people expect to be ignored by the great and good and may even think it's what they deserve. It's definitely what everyone's comfortable with. A pecking order where the Queen Bee sits at a safe distance from the workers in the hive.

But Scotland must get beyond all this, to raise confidence about the capacity of Scots and to make those who invoke the 'bloodthirsty Scot' sound as laughable and totally out of touch as they really are.

It's one reason the late great Jimmy Reid made such efforts to deter strikers in the successful UCS '70s sit-in from behaviour that might reawaken the tired, old stereotype. The fact his 'nae bevvying' rule has remained in common parlance for so long, is testimony to his canny instinct – that the crude caricature of a brawling, drunk, intolerant Scot hovers constantly in reserve, awaiting deployment.

It hasn't changed much over the centuries.

But it just isn't true.

New Scots, solidarity and Van Man

One great example of the new Scotland happened on 13 May 2021, when chef Sumit Sehdev and mechanic Lakhvir Singh were threatened with Home Office deportation at Kenmure Street in Glasgow and rescued by hundreds of neighbours including one nicknamed 'Van Man' who risked injury by diving straight under the Border Force van, giving anti-deportation networks time to surround and peacefully blockade it. An eight-hour stand-off ensued between the police officers who were called to the scene and members of the public who formed a human shield around the van.

Watching film of that siege still brings tears to my eyes.

It is completely beautiful and hugely significant in the development of Scotland's progressive 'settled will'.

The characteristics of a nation are only partly reflected in its written rules. More telling are the things we do, think or say spontaneously. But though they may happen in the flash of an eye – they're often the product of years, even decades of practice, discipline and organisation. The Kenmure Street siege was a prime example of that – the glorious outcome of local, neighbourhood, voluntary and official support systems built up over two decades since Syrian refugees were first dispersed to Glasgow.

Resistance to deportation began in 2005 when dawn raids by the Home Office prompted the award-winning Glasgow Girls campaign and the creation of grassroots support networks. At first led by sympathetic Scots, they are now mostly run by former asylum seekers, including Pinar Aksu from the Maryhill Integration Network, who read the 'Kenmure Street agreement' which allowed the two detainees to be released.

But what happened that day was not down to chance. The quick blockading action owed something to straightforward neighbourliness, something more to the memory of refugees like Soloman Rashid, deported from Dungavel to Iraq and later killed there, and a great deal to the No Evictions Network, the Unity Centre, Positive Action for Refugees, Refuweegee, Glasgow Destitute Asylum Network and countless other networks organising quietly across Glasgow for years. Reluctant to seek publicity lest that jeopardise their effectiveness, these groups have proven adept at delivering food, shelter and legal support. So, whilst the identity of 'Van Man' was known throughout Pollokshields, locals carefully kept his name off social media.

These networks also include dozens, maybe hundreds of research students and academics with relevant degrees, arising from the Scottish Government's decision in 2014 to do something different with its new devolved control over refugee management. It devised a 'New Scots' policy where asylum seekers would not be sitting apart for years while the Home Office processed their claims but

> supported to integrate into communities from day one of arrival, and not just when leave to remain is [finally] granted.

This strategy brought together councils, statutory bodies, charities, faith groups, the Scottish Refugee Council and academics, like UNESCO Professor of Refugee Integration at Glasgow University Alison Phipps and Professors Alison Strang and Alastair Ager from Queen Margaret University.

According to Alison Phipps, they agreed social bonds should be placed at the heart of the New Scots Policy:

> Social bonds create neighbours who meet, greet and eat with one another. That's what keeps people safe, especially when state structures creak or fail.

And essentially social bonds went swinging into action when the Kenmure Street Two were lifted... and released. But social bonds go further. In many parts of Scotland asylum seekers are thriving instead of just marking time.

In Glasgow, migrants and refugees have set up the African Calabash restaurant on Union Street (with 24 staff), the Soul Food Sisters Collective and a laundrette business, 'Fluff & Fold'. Argyll and Bute Council has housed 21 refugee families on Bute since 2015 and some have moved successfully into enterprise. The Rayan in Rothesay is a Halal take-away restaurant run by a Syrian project manager and his wife who won rave reviews for food they contributed to a local market stall. Nearby Syrian-run

Helmi's award winning patisserie has welcomed Billy Connolly as a customer and in Stornoway, Syrian refugee Mohammed Edris turned 30 years' experience of running an upholstery firm in Homs into a Hebridean business that reupholsters old furniture using Harris Tweed.

Meanwhile the Scottish Islands' Federation has offered free online business training with modules in English, Spanish, Farsi and Arabic.

According to Professor Phipps, it's taken decades of collaboration and behind-the-scenes work to turn Scotland into a world leader in refugee integration. In stark contrast to the hostile environment and managed decline of safe asylum routes introduced by successive Westminster governments, managed integration schemes in Scotland are working pretty well.

We should celebrate that difference.

Although the Kenmure Street protesters didn't have devolved powers on their side – immigration is reserved to Westminster – they were exercising the ancient, basic power of hospitality – asserting common decency in the treatment of refugees and asylum seekers, many of whom had just been able to vote for the first-time ever, in Scottish Parliamentary elections.

Of course, there is racism and sometimes anger about asylum seekers appearing to upturn the pecking order in local housing lists. Journalist Gary Younge, the first black columnist in Britain, has criticised Scotland for thinking racism is 'nothing to do with us'. But he also paid tribute to the Kenmure Street siege:

> There's a moment that exists now, when lots of
> Scottish people, not all of them, are imagining what
> an independent Scotland looks like – which takes
> race seriously and sees the potential to be different,
> more progressive. I do see potential there in a way I
> rarely see in England.[16]

16 https://www.heraldscotland.com/politics/23396522.men-bats-shouted-n-word-gary-younge-racism-scotland/

And that's what makes Kenmure Street so special.

We know the ugly side of life.

Those activists showed a beautiful side, where folk spent long, resolute hours by that white Home Office van, fuelled by sandwiches and cups of tea from neighbours until they halted the deportations. And almost exactly a year later, the same thing happened in Edinburgh when Home Office officials tried to remove staff from a restaurant in Nicolson Square and were forced to leave without detaining anyone.

But why are we surprised by this instinct for solidarity? Peaceful, non-violent direct action is so embedded in the history of Scotland, it's almost in our genes.

Think of the trade union and Labour movements which began in the west of Scotland. Think of the suffragettes and 1915 Rent Strikes by the women of Govan.

Think of the Holy Loch protests against Polaris nuclear submarines by 'the Eskimos' 50 years ago.

Think of the Scottish factory workers who blocked the supply of Rolls Royce engines to the Pinochet regime in the 1970s – a story powerfully retold in the film *Nae Pasaran*.

Think of poll tax protests against warrant sales in the '90s, the women's peace camp protesters at Faslane, protests at Dungavel detention centre in 2016 which won a promise of closure callously rescinded by the Tories a year later, and the petition signed by a third of the Shetland population in 2006 that stopped the deportation of Thai national Sakchai Makao.

Think about the sit-in that stopped the demolition of Govanhill Baths (yards from Kenmure Street) when a dozen locals chained themselves to the cubicles and occupied the building for 140 days – the longest occupation of a public building in British history. It's since become the venue for countless community campaigns and aims to re-open as a local wellness centre.

Think about the seven pupils at Drumchapel High School whose successful campaign stopped the detention of their friend Agnesa Mursela in 2005, produced a Glasgow Girls musical, a film, a temporary halt to dawn raids and almost a new chapter in Scottish political history, when Roza Salih – who arrived as a 12-year-old Kurd without a word of English – narrowly missed becoming an MSP in 2021.

In short, Scots have a long history of acting to prevent injustice and to protect threatened minorities. Such solidarity is a sign of vitality... and one official measure of a nation's happiness.

In 2022, while all eyes were on the GERS figures and Scotland's balance of payments, another index got less attention – the UN's World Happiness rankings. Finland came top for the fifth year in a row, Denmark stayed in second place and Iceland bypassed Switzerland to take third place. Britain came 17th.

The report assesses how people in more than 150 countries evaluate their own lives using six criteria of which only one is 'hard cash'. According to American wellbeing academic Jeffrey Sachs:

> The lesson of the World Happiness Report is that
> social support, generosity to one another, and
> honesty in government are crucial for well-being.

Well, well.

At a glance we can see that Scotland's determination to mitigate benefit sanctions, extend generosity, protect asylum seekers and get through Covid without a 'partygate' government – all mean that an independent Scotland would start higher in the Happiness stakes than 'mothership' UK.

Because the Index doesn't just measure state generosity – it also measures how spontaneously generous we are towards one another. On the solidarity front, Scots score in lots of unexpected ways. Take the Tartan Army whose members regularly fundraise for kids' charities in the cities they visit. Or the thoughtful behaviour of Dundee United fans in the Netherlands which prompted a local paper in August 2022 to report:

Supporters of the Scottish club Dundee United...
made an impression on the Nieuwmarkt yesterday.
Thousands of fans threw a party and then left the
square spotless. Employees of the surrounding cafes
are happy with it: 'It's always fun with those Scots.'

The fabulous reputation of Scotland's fans abroad is another
measure of the country's increasing confidence. Years ago, a
poll found the happiest people in Britain were the folk who had
lost both referendums – Remain-voting Scots. Why? Because
we still have the hope of a better life and a better country –
and we've got one another.

Liz Truss once talked about a family of nations.

Aye, whatever.

Relations don't trash the pensions of other family members
just to make a point.

Indeed, if the UK was an actual family, social services would
surely have had a quiet word by now with Scotland's heavy-
handed, don't speak unless you're spoken to constitutional
'parents'.

But there's another measure indirectly measured by the
World Happiness Index – how generous folk are towards
political opponents.

Once again – despite all propaganda to the contrary –
Scotland actually scores well.

Whisper it.

Scots are generally peaceful, keen systems builders and
stubbornly democratic.

But will independence open Pandora's Box?

Will old scores get settled, pitched battles begin and Celtic
Twilights become the order of the day? Will Jeremy Clarkson
be banned.

Unionist commentators certainly think so.

There are a few things to say.

First, unlocking the pressure cooker of Britishness will unquestionably release pent-up hopes and emotions. Britain was built on the exploitation of its own folk, Irish people, the Windrush generation, colonial subjects and the physical resources of Scotland. Competition, unfairness and class conflict has been built in with the British bricks for centuries, creating one of the most inherently unequal states in Europe.

So the dispossessed expect social and political change – not just the great and good of Edinburgh taking over where Westminster left off. That'll demand focus, restraint, skill and courage from everyone, especially political leaders, who must deliver fast to keep everyone onboard. Independence isn't the end of Scotland's story, but just the start of restoring fairness to a country and power to a working class that's known precious little of either.

So yes, independence will release energy. And if you find the prospect of an energetic country different or even challenging – that will seem scary. Old traditions will have to be married with new ways of doing democracy, amidst swirling expectations of payback and compensation. Prominent unionists will expect plum jobs, ambassador roles and preference to keep them sweet and a new independent country on the road. Yessers may hope for a return on years of campaigning and being sidelined in their careers. Tens of thousands of folk will sell shoeboxes in London to buy islands, castles and posh flats here. But these are not problems – they are by-products of success, release and their choice.

Happily, in our new mongrel nation, there will be a lot of choice about. Yet for those more familiar with Hobson's Choice, even that may seem stressful. Will the 'right' decisions be made; will forceful elements be over-represented; will things keep moving if every part of the status quo is revised simultaneously?

The answer of course is to take change slowly and democratically via citizens assemblies where possible, in the knowledge new systems can be changed if they don't work out. Small mistakes are not a crime - they are inevitable in any new project.

Yet a terrible fear of failure, judgement and criticism stalks those habitually excluded from power. And in Scotland that's been almost everyone. So irrational fear of the unknown can turn the luxury of choice into the certainty of a poisoned chalice.

It's crazy.

But it's human.

Survey the following choices and notice if you feel mounting panic or excitement. Or a bit of both.

When Scotland becomes independent, will there be a Declaration of Independence in Scots, Gaelic, English or Urdu? And if Scots – which Scots?

Will there be readings from Rabbie Burns, Duncan Ban MacIntyre, JK Rowling, Jackie Kay, Liz Lochhead, or the lot – and who decides?

Will the new Parliament be given legal form by some foosty auld judge or that thorn in the flesh of all legal authority, Aamer Anwar?

Will music be provided by the SSO or the Grit Orchestra?

Will the gig be held in Glasgow, Edinburgh or Scone?

Do we need to involve the Stone of Destiny – or is that all wrong?

Will Scotland become a Republic or does that need another vote? Will we vote on EU membership too – will we get sick of voting?

Can Orkney and Shetland opt out? Would they?

Would we establish a second revising chamber – like the regionally representative one Westminster parties never actually create?

If so, would the Gaelic Western Isles, the Nordic Northern Isles, the shinty-playing Highlands and the Rugby-mad Lowlands find common cause to demand a massive Norwegian-style funding shift to rural Scotland that reverses the present culture of managed decline?

Who'd be our first Poverty Tsar – a Professor, a group of randomly chosen claimants or Darren McGarvey?

I don't know about you, but I'm feeling no panic.

An even wider range of options is likely, challenging and

interesting - all at the same time. And that's fine.

There's enough variety in this 'multiform Scotland' to create a fabulous new country and put our capacity for inclusion and negotiation immediately to the test.

That's either scary or energising depending on your life experience and point of view.

All bets will be off, so handling heightened expectations won't be easy. But better that than bending ourselves even further out of shape to keep an old Victorian pecking order intact.

Besides, where is the evidence that Scots would self-destruct let off the British leash and given half the chance? It's not the experience of devolution over the last quarter of a century. It's not the countries and constitutions exiled Scots have created abroad. And it's absolutely not the jaw-dropping evidence of people power across Scotland as communities without formal power, experience or cash have taken over islands, bridges, parks, moors, forests, lochs, old churches, schools and other assets neglected by a top-down state and small army of absentee lairds. (More on that fabulous legacy of community heavy lifting in a minute.)

No, this fear of mayhem comes from elsewhere – in the constructed fear of our own warring natures. Time for another deep dive.

Take *Jekyll and Hyde*, by Scottish author Robert Louis Stevenson – regularly cited as a prime example of the Caledonian Antisyzygy, which according to the *Concise Scots Dictionary*, means

> the presence of duelling polarities within one entity, considered characteristic of the Scottish temperament.

The idea was promoted by Gregory Smith in a 1919 book, responding to figures like TS Eliot who contended there was no value in Scottish provincial literature, just an absence of coherence or an anchor in any single language. Smith responded that such diversity and the union of opposites formed the basis of Scottish literature. Which sounds fair enough.

As William McIlvanney said of his troubled cop Laidlaw, 'He knew nothing to do but inhabit the paradoxes', and according to the *Guardian*, McIlvanney made that sound like Glaswegian common sense.

But according to the late Ted Cowan and Douglas Gifford, who explored Gregory Smith's legacy in *The Polar Twins*, the Scots' perceived penchant for internal discord went far beyond the literary world:

> Smith did not restrict his observations to creative
> writing, but implied that these antithetical
> characteristics informed all of Scottish culture and
> were to be discerned throughout Scottish history
> [and] everyday life.

It was just a swift canter from there to the notion that Scots are fundamentally torn. Forever in two minds. Thrawn and contrary – swinging endlessly between the civilised and the monstrous. Folk whose passionate hearts constantly fight their rational heads. And if you think that has nothing to do with the cause of independence, how often was the heid/hert dichotomy raised during the first referendum? It's as if Scots (uniquely) cannot hope to have both vital body parts moving in the same general political direction, which is a wee shame for independence and kinda useful for unionism, since emotional constipation, social stagnation and political deadlock help dampen spirits and keep things constitutionally static. Which is handy. Scots have literally 'been in two minds' for the last 300 years, trying to negotiate two competing identities – British (in public) and Scots/Gaelic (in private).

You think I exaggerate? Take Edinburgh, whose New Town is the very embodiment of Britain.

After Culloden, the need to expand beyond the overcrowded Old Town combined with a desire to appeal to triumphant Hanoverians. So, in 1767 James Craig devised a New Town plan reflecting their love of classical antiquity – and street names reflecting their naked power.

George Street – the largest and most prestigious thoroughfare – was named after King George III. Queen Street was named after his wife. Princes Street, originally planned as 'St Giles Street', was named after his sons, Hanover Street after his family and Frederick Street after his dad. St Andrew's Square and St George's Square (later Charlotte Square) were named after the patron saints of the two recently unified nations, (cue the rictus grin) while Thistle Street and Rose Street represented their national emblems.

Welcome to Edinburgh – the most British city in these islands with the most Brit-averse Parliament.

But the duality of Scottish life reaches far beyond the capital and further back in time.

When Victorian Scotland was transformed from a rural, agrarian Gaelic-speaking country into a modern urban, industrial nation, it was transformed

> from being one of the most feared and detested parts of the kingdom, a constant source of unrest and instability, [into] Caledonia, Britannia's devoted sister, a model of propriety and bastion of moral virtues... a pillar of the Empire, her name a trademark of world repute and her voice respected in international affairs.[17]

Small snag – apart from the dreadful poverty – this rise to glory coincided with the disappearance of Scotland's own sense of national identity.

Cairns Craig has argued that Scotland's history became increasingly regarded as redundant, irrelevant and surplus to the needs of the times. Historical writing shied away from exploring the nation's own history and this 'historical failure of nerve' resulted in the 'strange death of Scottish history',

17 Findlay, W, *Victorian Paradoxes,* Tours 2005, Presses universitaires François-Rabelais pp43–57.

condemning the nation to evolve in a sort of limbo.[18] Or as TC Smout lamented, in its rise to Victorian greatness, Scotland 'gained a century and lost its history'.

Meanwhile post-Culloden there were (at least) two contradictory versions of almost everything. Mapmakers visited distant parts of Scotland and, without Gaelic, invariably changed what they saw. The misnaming and loss of local placenames mirrored the experience in Ireland, later critiqued by playwright Brian Friel in his play Translations. In Scotland, many of the enduringly popular 'Highland Dances' like the Gay Gordons and Dashing White Sergeant sprang from the English military barracks, not indigenous tradition. So for any aspect of Highland culture – dress, piping, dance or speech – at least two competing versions emerged. But British cultural values became the safest to espouse and highbrow English traditions the most profitable to learn.

Perhaps this explains why Scots have traditionally been 'in two minds.' Not because of some irresolvable confusion or mental weakness but because we've been ducking and weaving (skilfully) between two competing identities for centuries. Mind you, skilful isn't the adjective most scholars apply to the watchful, wary Scots:

> Scottish culture is characterised as split, divided, deformed. This is a not unfamiliar view of Scottish culture, epitomised by Walter Scott, in which Scotland is divided between the 'heart' (representing the past, romance, 'civil society') and the 'head' (the present and future, reason, and by dint of that, the British state)[19]
> Now this is getting to the crux of matters.
> Britain has not a hope in hell of appealing to the heart.

It is a state with a tax-base not a nation with a culture. If Britain did have a culture, it would be based on compliance,

---

18 Craig, C, *Out of History*. Edinburgh, Polygon, 1996, p43.
19 McCrone D, *Understanding Scotland*, Routledge, (2001).

hierarchy and a weird, feigned nostalgia for the 'good old days' when men were men, serfs were serfs, MPs were elected by a handful of folk and the little people knew their place.

It's the constituent nations of Britain (England, Scotland, Wales and Northern Ireland) which touch citizens with distinctive cultures, histories, politics, languages, dialects, voting patterns, folk memory and civic structures like law, education and religion.

So, the distance between the British state and the Scottish nation – between head and heart – is the chasm Scots must forever loup, if we remain within the union.

So long as we remain convinced duality is inescapable, many Scots will struggle to accept one state, one nation, one government and one country, believing we need the constant working of two antithetical forces – Westminster and Holyrood – head and heart – to stop us overdoing either the Celtic or Anglo-Saxon parts of our complex, collective make-up.

Tastily tragic – but just plain wrong.

Why are the Scots alone cursed with this heart/head divide? Are we different to every other nation on earth and how can the deeply damaging split in loyalties and cultures end, except by full, self-government?

As it is, there's no escaping the dualism encouraged by the British state. It winks at us – in the town centres of a generally Republican country, where Queen, Victoria and Albert Streets take puzzling pride of place. In the BBC's insatiable preoccupation with early English monarchs, whose cruelty, achievements and cross-border attacks on Scotland must be lapped up as if they are our own. It sits in that other obsession with WW2 as a more meaningful reality than the present – when head and heart combined to fight Nazi occupation and Britain had 'its finest hour'. Even though that hour is past and the rest of Europe has pivoted to face modern not bygone realities. It sits in the assumption that might is right and anarchy will descend if the great and good are challenged in any way. In the belief that adversarial systems of law, governance and industrial relations provide better outcomes than limp-wristed collaboration and compromise. Above all, it lives on in the blinkered belief that British systems are automatically better than 'foreign' ones – even as this archaic, unequal, unreformable state sinks further down every international league table.

That's the British side of the great divide – on the other sits Scottishness. Hesitant but happier with compromise, more pragmatic, less bothered about status and the precedents set by ancient history and bolstered by a legal system that gives more weight to modern legislation than the dead hand of precedent. More on what we're like later.

Both identities possess Scots – in very different ways.

Scotland commands emotional loyalty because it's a nation. Britain commands tax returns because it's a state. Imagine how our confidence and collective headspace would improve if those identities were aligned?

Because as things stand, Britain is not a nation state (head and heart combined) but a union of four stateless nations (total guddle).

And that's a vitally important distinction.

Britain's four nations stopped being states at different times in history – but they never stopped being nations exerting cultural clout. Indeed, as David McCrone observes,

> following the Union of 1707, Scotland was left with
> a deficit of politics and a surfeit of culture.[20]
> A British political head and a Scottish cultural heart.

But that long period with a 'surfeit of culture' – but without a bespoke, national parliament – was still crucial for Scotland.

Alan Riach – poet and professor of Scottish Literature at Glasgow University – suggests the exploration of national identity has a long lineage in the work of Scotland's major writers, radical and conservative, citing Walter Scott, who wrote about Scotland from the Borders to the archipelagos of Orkney and

---

20 Ibid.

Shetland; Lewis Grassic Gibbon's *Scots Quair*, which addresses the whole of Scotland, from the farming community of *Sunset Song*, to the small town of *Cloud Howe*, and the industrial city of *Grey Granite*; while his contemporary Neil Gunn, whose work mostly describes the Highlands, also set novels in Edinburgh and Glasgow helping to create 'an all-in view of national identity and potential'. And of course, James Robertson's award-winning, and epic 21st century novel, also fits the bill – *And the Land Lay Still*.

Alan Riach argues:

> The epic scale of these works of fiction was self-consciously intended to address the matter of the nation. And the nation, in Scotland, means difference. To know who and what we are, we have to find out about others. These works encourage that healthy curiosity.[21]

Nice one.

Maybe looked at differently, the old idea of disputatious Scots, can be viewed quite positively.

Which healthy nation is not in a state of constant flux, attempting to marry old traditions with new realities and adapt old understandings of social and democratic balance to include previously ignored minorities?

Indeed, centuries of ducking and weaving – through choice or compulsion – may have left Scots better prepared for a modern world full of difference and thus, massively dependent on negotiation, compromise, friendliness and mutual recognition. Better perhaps than countries whose leaders vow to 'die in a ditch' if they cannot assert their own will over all-comers. (Looking at you Boris.)

Cairns Craig mentions that:

> The fragmentation and division which made Scotland

---

21 Riach, A, 'Scotland, mongrel nation: healthy curiosity and zombie priorities', *The National*, 7.10.16.
http://eprints.gla.ac.uk/152799/1/157299.pdf

seem abnormal to an earlier part of the 20th century
has come to be the norm for much of the world's
population. Bilingualism, biculturalism and the
inheritance of a diversity of fragmented traditions
[became] the source of creativity rather than its
inhibition in the second half of the 20th, century and
Scotland ceased to have to measure itself against the
false 'norm'... of the unified national tradition.[22]

So, perhaps with long experience of exploring our own
rich and varied cultures, Scots can abandon the simplistic
preferences of the social and political monoglot – we've
learned there is so much to admire, pick over and choose
between in life. Professor Riach puts it this way:

William McIlvanney once famously called Scotland a
'mongrel nation' and was happily praised for doing so.
Edwin Morgan's exemplary lead in finding out what
'others' are all about is key to all the arts: in study and
discovery, you exercise that most valuable thing, the
intrinsic optimism of curiosity.

He goes on to say that kinship across differences is the foundational
story or founding myth of Scotland, with a legacy stretching from
Columbus to Malcolm Canmore, and he describes kinship as:

the understanding that a nation is made up of
different groups, languages, geographical areas,
terrains, economies and cultural preferences.

So, the best leader for Scots is one who can uphold kinship
across 'the variousness of this nation's people' and encourage
'the intrinsic optimism of their curiosity'.
Sure, from the perspective of Type A cultures (no offence

22 Craig, C, *History of Scottish Literature*, Aberdeen University
Press, 1990.

to headstrong folk), Scotland's cooperative, consensual model may look flabby and weak, the same way rowans bending in the wind look less majestic than unbending mighty oaks – until lack of flexibility causes their branches to snap and break.

Scots have a different conception of leadership – not meekly following just anyone but not racing blindly ahead with the unimpeachable confidence of the uber-entitled either. I'd guess Scots would be quite happy with the kind of non-starry, collective leadership that characterises the Nordic nations. Until the Danish TV hit series *Borgen* mirrored the rise of Denmark's first female Prime Minister – few outside the country had even heard of Helle Thorning-Schmidt. That's how proportional, consensual systems normally operate – with steady progress, and relatively low-key leaders.

Admittedly, Scotland has looked decidedly high-key, after eight years of the far-from-retiring Alex Salmond and another eight with the internationally recognised Nicola Sturgeon. Scotland's got used to governance by a single, very well-known, controversial and almost God-like figure. It's given the country an appearance of clout and international status, precisely because so few countries with proportional voting systems are led by such powerful individuals. But it's also manacled Scotland to this idea of top-down, patrician, British-style leadership.

Scotland's limited proportionality and constitutional stuckness have together produced massive and very unusual majorities for one party – the SNP. But despite the fondness of frightened people for one single and highly visible figurehead – a lynchpin who can knock heids together and 'get things done' – that's not generally a recipe for success. Unless it's First Minister Andy Murray. Wee jape.

The truth is that teams work, cooperation works, participation works, and 'my way or the highway' eventually goes the way of the old oaks.

So, yes, Scots will probably always argue, precisely because we know that it's the blend of views, the mixture of outlooks and life experiences, 'the variousness of this nation's people' that produces kinship. Our foundational story. Not being telt. By anyone.

Scotland's democracy will hopefully proceed carefully, knowing many cultures exist in every corner shop and each sentence and it is therefore unwise to assert one way, one route or one single, overarching, governing idea.

That's how we hing and it's how we need to make our public domain hing too.

Will Scots be sniffy, dictatorial and exclusive come the day? I think not. Even though Scottish literature has been woefully missing from the British syllabus, body politic (and thus our own curriculum) for long decades, it's unlikely that petty exclusion will happen in reverse when Scotland's own story is finally front and centre. We know very well – all too well – there's more than one tradition in our nation.

The same feeling of mutual acceptance will never occur for Scots within the UK. A nation of five million cannot hope to achieve cultural parity with 55 million neighbours, except on their terms. It's a size thing, and truly nothing personal. And neither will be the gradual easing out of empty British tropes when Scotland becomes a nation-state, embarks on the long process of reuniting head and heart and throws all the old stuff about sullenness and contrariness to the four feckin winds. So that's four gloomy, deep-seated fears about Scotland aired and hopefully dispatched. There are a few more to go.

Have the best left?

My mother was a vigorous, smart but formally uneducated woman with some profoundly gloomy, inherited Caithnessian defaults. One of the most maddening and oft repeated, was that 'the best left'. By which she meant that in centuries past, with starvation, eviction and clearance gathering pace in the Highlands, the folk with their heads screwed on did the smart thing and got the hell out.

With the clear corollary that those who stayed were essentially slow, stupid and hesitant. The dross.

Like herself, myself and our entire family.

This vicious self-criticism was annoying. Likewise, my grandmother's proud yet baffling claim that 'We're a family of leavers,' meaning, I think, that she'd succeeded in getting as many of her offspring as far from their hopeless place of birth as humanly possible.

Perversely though, both women absolutely loved Wick and there was no chance of any other holiday destination for our 16 childhood summers than the long trip north from Belfast, to get 'home'.

You know, the home they were all busily trying to leave.

Families. Go figure.

But as with ever other bit of weed fouling Scotland's propeller, there's a fragment of truth in all that stuff and a crateful of savagely unfair, self-destructive criticism.

So here we go again. Better out than in.

Caithness writer, Neil Gunn eloquently described the shame of the Highlanders unable to protect their cultural heritage in this section of *Butcher's Broom* where his character Davie considers the Clearances.

There was a shame in it however he looked at it. And this shame got linked up with all their land, with the bitter shame of the clearances, with a recognition of some inner futility and weakness in their character, a fatal central dividing within them, paralysing all power of decisive action.

Yip, there's that dread duality at work again, along with something even worse – a terrible guilt and merciless masochism, of the kind scrawled into the window of Croick Church by evicted Sutherland families awaiting deportation in 1845: 'We are the wicked generation'.

This gloom might affect only Highlanders. And since

that cohort more than halved in number between 1831 and 1911, you might conclude that this self-harming, flagellation is nonetheless a minority pursuit.

But right across Scotland in the last century, there were families of leavers. So much so, that leaving seems to be in our blood.

Two million Scots travelled overseas between 1830 and 1914 – one and a half times more than the emigrant cohort from England and Wales and more even than Ireland if migration to England is also counted.[23] According to Tom Devine, Scotland took second place in a European league table of outward migration per head of population in the 19th century and rapidly 'emerged as the emigration capital of Europe'.[24]

What a sad title. And what a bitter reflection – not on our land, people or capabilities – but on an economic and social system that created a pool of landless labour whose members had to accept poverty wages from landowners and city industrialists or leave Scotland altogether.

How could this silent exodus do anything but damage morale and national self-confidence for generations? After all, if Scotland was so great, how come its young, skilled folk were and still are leaving?

It's a good question that needs some answers.

First, staying was stacked against Highlanders.

In the late 1700s, before the Napoleonic Wars blocked trade with the continent, many crofters had been moved to the coast to collect kelp, because it produced an alkali for glass and soap manufacture. It was such unpleasant work that the government passed the Ships' Passengers Act in 1802 to keep people available for landowners by making emigration prohibitively expensive. Nice. But demand for kelp plummeted during the wars and by 1815, it had been completely replaced in the manufacturing process. So, before the formal clearances had even begun, large

23 *Scottish Historical Review*, 1994, Vol 73, No 195–6, p92.
24 Devine, TM, *The Scottish Nation*, London: Penguin, 1999, p468.

numbers of Scots were living on precarious, infertile, coastal plots of land, deliberately made too small to sustain a family. Then in 1846 the potato blight sweeping Ireland and Europe finally hit the Scottish Highlands prompting outbreaks of typhus and cholera. By 1846, a whopping three quarters of the entire crofting population of the Northwest Highlands and Hebrides were completely without food. Take that in. Yet, according to *The Economist*, this famine demonstrated not that the ownership of land was cruel and unfair but that

> the departure of the redundant part of the population
> is an indispensable preliminary to every kind of
> improvement.

With politicians, lairds and 'thought leaders' in agreement about the need for emigration, it was hard for the people to resist.

But it's important for Scots to know that against all the odds, many of our forebears did just that.

Land raids erupted across the Scottish Highlands in the 1900s, encouraged by the revolutionary mood in Ireland and Russia and the creation of a Crofters' Party which won seats across the Highlands in 1885, helping to force through the Crofting Acts. Twenty years later the Highland Land League affiliated with the fledgling Labour Party – also created in Scotland – leading to the Land Settlement (Scotland) Act 1919 which created 4,584 new holdings. But bureaucracy, landowner intransigence and lack of finance meant this scheme met only a tiny fraction of the demand for land. From 1912 to 1943, the Department of Agriculture received 33,196 land applications, but settled only a quarter.

> Thousands of men [12,916 to be precise] withdrew
> their applications for land and applied instead for
> passage on the emigrant ships. Almost all the 300
> people from Lewis who boarded the *Metagama* (in
> 1923) were young men with an average age of 22,

off to Ontario where they had each been offered
40 hectares of land. Another country held out the
opportunity Scotland had promised but failed to
provide.[25]

Wee quibble. It was Britain that promised returning soldiers
a Land Fit for Heroes and it was the British Government that
failed to deliver. Scotland had no parliament, no voice and
no say in the matter.

Meanwhile in the Scottish Lowlands, tenants fought their
own battles against a law of hypothec, which gave landlords
security over their property driving up rents.[26] They formed the
Scottish Farmers' Alliance and defeated landlord candidates in
the 1865 and 1868 elections. The 1883 Agricultural Holdings
Act (Scotland) finally gave tenants the right to compensation
for improving land – 150 years after Norway.[27]

In short – the folk who stayed in Scotland were not some
kind of compliant dross – they were doughty fighters. They
didn't give up. They organised, got political and got results
but not enough to stem the exodus, for another reason that
would surprise my mum – so many Scots were skilled workers
and thus able to command higher wages elsewhere. Our system
of parish schools had long produced a literate population with
six universities and colleges in a country of less than a million
people. Many skilled workers, left for England, the Baltic
States, North America and later Africa as doctors, engineers,
missionaries, explorers and traders.

So, some of 'the best' did leave; some came back; some
stayed, organised and fought back; others stayed and simply
managed to survive. Impressive.

But that's not how we see the past or the impossible choices
our ancestors faced.

25 McIntosh Gray, A and Moffat, W, *A History of Scotland: Modern
Times,* Oxford: Oxford University Press, 1999, p28.
26 Devine, TM, *The Scottish Nation,* London: Penguin, 1999, p453.
27 Ibid.

Back to my Caithness family who are slightly hostile to Gaelic and backed a local campaign for place-names to display Norse placenames instead of the Gaelic road-signs springing up around the Highlands 20 years ago. Even though my mum's birthplace of Wick/Vik is clearly Norse for bay – Gaelic was the predominant language of Caithness, according to the first national census in 1801, though 90 years later the number of Gaelic speakers had crashed to just 4,068 and by 1951 only a handful was left.

Why? Families forced by clearance and poverty to work for merchants in the heaving herring yards of Wick – Europe's busiest herring port in the 19th century – had to choose between a future, an occupation, a livelihood and a language. It was Gaelic, exclusion and poverty or English/Scots and the chance of a better future. People didn't consciously or easily turn their backs on old lives, languages, customs and beliefs. They had no choice.

> Agricultural improvement' in the early 19th century
> sealed the association of English with progress
> and civilisation. The Gaelic element of Caithness'
> heritage was something to be cast off and discarded,
> even denied. So total was this process that it seemed
> impossible Gaelic was ever spoken [in Wick].[28]

Academic William Findlay extends that process to the whole country:

> In the name of modernity and progress and with the
> blessing of Scotland's own intellectual elite, the historic
> balance of Scottish society was destroyed forever.

As Fiona Paterson comments:

> The Gaelic identity [Neil] Gunn constructs is
> wrought with pride in where one has come from,

---

28 Domhnall Uilleam Stiùbhart, *Caithness of the Gael and the Lowlander*, Bratach, 2008.

coupled with shame of failing to do that heritage
justice… his characters struggle to maintain
traditional values in the face of change.'[29]

That in a nutshell is what Scots have been struggling with for
centuries – maintaining traditional values in the face of change.
    And we struggle still.
    Emigration has had a long-lasting impact on our economy,
culture and collective confidence. Quite unjustly.
    Our ancestors were stiffed, fleeced and given no real
alternative but to knuckle down or leave. Still, many stayed,
fought and created the political parties and movements that
gave British families stability and dignity, until that hard-won,
post-war settlement was dismantled by Margaret Thatcher.
    It's time to forgive our ancestors for leaving and forgive
ourselves for doubting them. We aren't the dross. Neither were
they.
    It's our political and economic systems that are the pits.
    And we can change both.

The mighty muscle of community buyouts

For years, I've been watching audiences as they view the 2019
film about the Faroe Islands, made by myself and Al McMaster
from Phantom Power and it kinda breaks my heart.
    One Faroese interviewee is asked about Scottish
independence. Let's remember where he's coming from – a
country of 18 utterly barren islands, connected by tunnels,
reliant on fishing and located in the stormy North Atlantic
between Shetland and Iceland with a population of just
55,000. Essentially Livingston on the rocks.
    So Tór Verland Johansen starts his answer: 'We look at
you and think, what's the problem?'

---

29 Paterson, Fiona E (2020) 'The Gael Will Come Again':
*Reconstruction of a Gaelic world in the work of Neil M Gunn and
Hugh MacDiarmid* MPhil(R) thesis.

People in the watching audience smile and lean forward.

He goes on to list all the assets possessed by Scotland. Oil and gas are not mentioned.

'Renewable energy, whisky, tourism, great universities, beautiful country and above all...' and at this point folk are sitting on the edge of their collective seat, 'you are a friendly people.'

The disappointment is palpable – every time.

No-one quite says it but as people sink back in their seats, their disappointed, irritated thought bubbles are almost visible. Is that all? Friendly? What use is friendly in a dog-eat-dog world?

Ah Scotland.

Friendliness is a godsend. A beautiful thing. And given the relentless commercialisation of modern life – an amazing thing. Friendliness speaks of an open nature, freed from knee-jerk suspicion and defensiveness. It's the basis for trade, cooperation and discovery and the opposite of hierarchy, status, suspicion and fear. And if you want to know how unimportant friendliness is, live in a society without it. Without the exchanges and acknowledgement that make mutual understanding possible.

It's like bones without cartilage.

Sore.

And whilst we actually know that, we also doubt that being 'a friendly people' is anywhere near good enough if we aim to navigate the choppy waters of independence.

It makes us sound simple and naive. Like Jack from the Beanstalk fairy tale – the friendly lad conned into trading the family cow for a handful of magic beans. Aye, fair enough, he did eventually retrieve goods stolen by the giant, including a bag of gold, an enchanted goose and a magic golden harp.

But still. He was gullible. Keen to believe the best of people. Friendly. Vulnerable.

It's better to be tougher. Harder. More focused. Less anxious to please.

And thus, less like ourselves.

Which is a crippling outlook that fuels another contrived but deep-seated worry.

Are 'ordinary Scots' up to the task?

It's heart-breaking that we harbour such serious doubts, when Scotland has quietly become the community-buyout capital of Europe. Right now, thousands of Scottish citizens in hundreds of buyouts are running everything from islands and schools to hydro-electric dams and petrol pumps, affordable housing, restaurants and creches. They're doing it without experience, formal structures, overseers, outsiders or clipboards. They've transformed the shape of land ownership, so that 70 per cent of folk on the Western Isles now live on community-owned land. And these super-capable people are running assets that councils, churches, lairds and charities could not – profitably and sustainably. And we still think Scots are incapable of running their country? C'mon. Scan the list of asset-owning development trusts and see if a single part of Scotland is missing.

A Greener Hawick
A Heart for Duns
Acharacle Community Company
Action Porty
Aird Community Trust
Alva Development Trust
Alyth Development Trust
Annexe Communities
Antermony Development Trust
Appin Community Development Trust
Applecross Community Company
Arbirlot Community Trust
Ardentinny Community Trust Ltd
Ardgour Area Fund
Ardoch Development Trust
Ardrishaig Community Trust

Ardrossan Community Development Trust
Arisaig Community Trust
Arran Development Trust
Arrochar & Tarbet Community Development Trust
Assynt Development Trust
Auchinleck Community Development Initiative
Aviemore and Glenmore Community Trust
Baldernock Community Development Trust
Balerno Village Trust
Ballater (RD) Ltd
Balquhidder, Lochearnhead and Strathyre Community Trust
Banchory & District Initiative Ltd
Barmulloch Community Development Company
Barr Community SCIO
Barra & Vatersay Community Ltd
Barrhill Development Trust
Beith Community Development Trust
Belhelvie Community Trust
Bellsmyre Development Trust
Birse Community Trust
Bishopton Community Development Trust
Blackhall Community Trust
Blairgowrie and Rattray Development Trust
Bothwell Futures
Braehead, Broomridge & District Community Development
Trust
Braemar Community Limited
Breadalbane Development Trust
Bridgend Farmhouse
Broadford and Strath Community Company
Brora Development Trust
Brunswick Youth Centre
Burnfoot Community Futures
Burntisland Community Development Trust
Callander Community Development Trust
Cambusbarron Community Development Trust

Camuscross & Duisdale Initiative
Carbost Pier Ltd.
Carloway Estate Trust (Urras Oighreachd Chà rlabhaigh)
Carluke Development Trust Ltd
Carradale Community Trust
Carrick Castle Community Trust Limited
Cassiltoun Housing Association
Castle Douglas Community Centre Development Trust
Castle Douglas Development Forum
Catrine Community Trust
Clackmannan Development Trust
CLEAR Buckhaven & Methil
Coigach Community Development Company
Coldstream Community Trust
Colinsburgh Community Trust Limited
Colintraive and Glendaruel Development Trust
Colonsay Community Development Company
Comann Eachdraidh Sgire a Bhac
Community Action for Erskine
Community Alliance Trust
Community Central Hall
Community Development Company of Nesting
Comrie Development Trust
Connect Community Trust
Craignish Community Company
Crail Community Partnership
Cranhill Development Trust
Creetown Initiative Ltd
Crieff Community Trust
Cromarty Community Development Trust
Crossroads Community Hub
Culbokie Community Trust
Cumbrae Community Development Company
Cupar Development Trust
Dalavich Improvement Group (DIG)
Dalbeattie Community Initiative

Dalgety Community Trust
Dalmellington Parish Development Trust
DART (Darvel Area Regeneration Team)
Development Coll
Dingwall Community Development Company
Dollar Community Development Trust
Dufftown and Mortlach Development Trust
Dumfries High Street Ltd (T/A Midsteeple Quarter)
Dunadd Community Enterprise
Dunblane Development Trust
Dunlop & District Community Company
East Loch Lomond Community Trust
East Nairnshire Community Organisation (SCIO) known as
ENCOMM
Eday Partnership
Edinburgh Old Town Development Trust
Eilean Eisdeal Trust
Ekopia Social Investments Ltd
Ettrick and Yarrow Community Development Company
Evanton Community Trust
Eyemouth & District Community Trust
Falkland Community Development Trust
Fauldhouse & Breich Valley Community Development Trust
Ferguslie Park Housing Association
Fetterangus Community Association
Finderne Development Trust
Fintry Development Trust
Fittie Community Development Trust
Fochabers Village Association
Forgan Arts Centre
Forres Area Community Trust
Fort Augustus & Glenmoriston Community Company
Fountainbridge Canalside Community Trust
Fraserburgh Development Trust Ltd
Fuse Youth Cafe
Future Hawick

Gairloch and Loch Ewe Action Forum (GALE)
Galston Community Development Trust
Garbh Allt Community Initiative GACI
Gargunnock Community Trust
Getting Better Together Ltd
Glasgow Eco Trust
Glen Urquhart Rural Community Association
Glenbarr Community Development Association
Glenboig Development Trust
Glenelg & Arnisdale Development Trust
Glenfarg Community Hall Group
Glengarry Community Woodlands
Glenkens Community & Arts Trust
Go Golspie
Gorebridge Community Development Trust
Govanhill Baths Community Trust
Govanhill Community Development Trust
Grantshouse Development Company Ltd
Great Bernera Community Development Trust
Greener Kirkcaldy
Grow 73
Growing21
Hartwood Community Development Group
Healthy n Happy Community Development Trust
Helmsdale & District Development Trust
Here We Are (Cairndow) Ltd
Huntly Development Trust
Inchinnan Development Trust
Innerleithen Community Trust
Inspire Inveraray
Inverclyde Community Development Trust
Invergordon Development Trust
Iomairt Chille Chomain
Iona Renewables
Island of Hoy Development Trust
Island of Kerrera Development Trust

Islay Development Initiative
Isle of Canna Community Development Trust
Isle of Cumbrae Initiative Community Company
Isle of Eigg Heritage Trust
Isle of Gigha Heritage Trust
Isle of Luing Community Trust
Isle of Rum Community Trust
John O'Groats Development Trust
Johnstonebridge Community Centre Trust
Killin and Ardeonaig Community Development Trust
Kilmadock Development Trust
Kincardine Community Association
Kinghorn Community Land Association
Kinloch Historical Society
Kinlochleven Community Trust
Kirkcolm Community Trust
Kirkconnel & Kelloholm Development Trust
Kirkcowan Community Development Trust
Kirkcudbright Development Trust
Kirknewton Community Development Trust Ltd
KPT (Keir, Penpont, Tynron) Development Trust
Kyle and Lochalsh Community Trust
Kyle of Sutherland Development Trust
Laggan Forest Trust
Lairg & District Community Initiatives
Lambhill Stables
Lanark Community Development Trust
Largo Communities Together
Latheron, Lybster & Clyth Community Development Company
Lenzie Community Development Trust
Lesmahagow Development Trust
Leverhulme Community Hub
Linlithgow Community Development Trust
Linwood Community Development Trust
Lismore Community Trust
Local Initiatives in New Galloway

Lochcarron Community Development Company
Lochgoil Community Trust Ltd
Lochwinnoch Community Development Trust
Lockerbie Old School Community Hub
Lossiemouth Community Development Trust
Luss & Arden Community Development Trust
Machrihanish Airbase Community Company
Maryhill Burgh Halls Trust
Mayfield & Easthouses Development Trust
Meigle and Ardler Community Development Trust
Milngavie Community Development Trust
Minginish Community Hall Association
Moffat Town Hall Trust
Moniaive Initiative
Morar Community Trust
Morvern Community Development Company
Mount Blair Community Development Trust
Muir of Ord Development Trust
Mull & Iona Community Trust
Muthill Village Trust
Nairn Improvement Community Enterprise
Neilston Development Trust
New Cumnock Development Trust
Newburgh Community Trust
Newcastleton & District Community Trust
Newlands Community Development Trust
Newmains Community Trust Ltd
Newton Stewart Initiative
Newtongrange Development Trust
North Uist Development Company Limited
North West Mull Community Woodland Company Limited
North Yell Development Council
Northmavine Community Development Company (NCDC)
Oban Communities Trust
Old Luce Development Trust
Old School Thornhill

One Dalkeith
Ore Valley Housing Association
Out of the Blue Arts and Education Trust
Papay Development Trust
Peebles Community Trust
Penicuik Community Development Trust
Pentlands Community Space
Pinwherry and Pinmore Community Development SCIO
Point & Sandwick Trust
Polbeth Community Hub SCIO
Portgordon Community Trust
Portpatrick Community Development Trust
Portree & Braes Community Trust
Portsoy Community Enterprise
Possilpark People's Trust
Preston and Abbey Community Trust
Princess Royal Sports & Community Trust
Raasay Development Trust
Rannoch Community Trust
Renfrew Development Trust
Renton Community Development Trust
Rogart Development Trust
Rosemount Development Trust
Rosewell Development Trust
Rousay, Egilsay and Wyre Development Trust Ltd
Sanday Development Trust
Scalpay Community Association
Scourie Community Development Company
Shapinsay Development Trust
Sinclair's Bay Trust
Skerray Limited
Sleat Community Trust
South Islay Development
South Kintyre Development Trust
South Loch Awe-side Community Company
South Seeds

South West Mull and Iona Development
SPOTT Community Association (2019)
St Andrews Environmental Network Limited
Staffin Community Trust
Stanley Development Trust
Stepps Community Development Trust
Stonehaven Town Partnership
Stoneyburn and Bents Future Vision Group SCIO SC046760
Storas Uibhist
Stow Community Trust
Stranraer Development Trust
Strathard Community Trust
Strathblane Community Development Trust
Strathdearn Community Developments
Strathdon Community Development Trust
Stratherrick and Foyers Community Trust
Strathfillan Community Development Trust
Strathglass and Affric Community Co Ltd
Strathmore & the Glens Rural Partnership
Strathnairn Development Company
Stromness Community Development Trust
Stronsay Development Trust
Sunart Community Company
Sustaining Dunbar
Swamp Creative Media Centre
Tain & District Development Trust
Tarbert and Skipness Community Trust
Tarland Development Group
Tarves Development Trust
Tayport Community Trust
The Ardchattan Centre Ltd
The Ballantrae Trust
The Boyndie Trust
The Cabrach Trust
The Dornoch Area Community Interest Company
The Ecology Centre

The Environment Trust (West Dunbartonshire)
The Eskdale Foundation
The Findhorn Village Conservation Company
The Garve & District Development Company
The Girvan Town Team
The Glendale Trust
The Isle of Jura Development Trust
The Knoydart Foundation
The Langholm Alliance
The Langholm Initiative
The Leanchoil Trust
The Pairc Trust
The Pavillion (Greater Easterhouse)
The Stornoway Trust
The Three Kings Cullen Association
Thenue Housing Association Ltd
Thornhill Community Trust
Thurso Community Development Trust
Tighnabruaich District Development Trust
Tiree Community Development Trust
Tomintoul & Glenlivet Development Trust
Torry Development Trust
Trossachs Community Trust
Tullibody Community Development Trust
Twechar Community Action
Tweedsmuir Community Company
Udny Community Trust Company Ltd
Uig Community Trust Company (UCT)
Uig Development Trust
Ullapool Community Trust
Uplawmoor Development Trust
Upper Eskdale Development Group
Urras Oighreachd Ghabhsainn
Vale of Leven Trust
Valley Renewables Group
WAT IF

West Ardnamurchan Community Development Company
West Calder & Harburn Community Development Trust
West Granton Community Trust
West Harris Trust
West Kilbride Community Initiative Ltd
Wester Loch Ewe Trust
Westray Development Trust
WHALE Arts Agency
Whitburn & District Community Development Trust
Wick Development Trust
Winchburgh Community Development Trust
Woodlands Community Development Trust

Impressive.

And a powerful riposte to the niggling worry that Scots won't manage the transition to independence fairly and professionally.

Well, why not – when it's been done almost a thousand times over in every part of Scotland.

The rules mean buyouts and asset transfers must be costed, consulted upon and agreed by the whole community. If any other country had completed so many well-constructed, legally binding, life-enhancing examples of people power we'd regard it as an extraordinary place. Instead we call it Scotland – where the ability to negotiate change is so undervalued by politicians and the media that it makes no headlines. There are few dramas, conflicts or failures to speak of – and that doesn't sell papers. It doesn't feed any of the narratives of hopelessness that drive political discourse and so the revolutionary change in Scottish confidence at community level has made no news at all. And it should – it must.

Strontian – the school builders

Lead was mined above the remote village of Strontian on the Ardnamurchan peninsula from 1722 till the late Victorian era – along with lead, silver, zinc and a rare, new carbonate mineral called strontianite. There used to be a hat factory in the village making helmets for the lead mines in one of the larger houses. Women and children plaited two hats of different sizes out of straw and filled the gap between them with clay that baked in the sun.

Why am I telling you this?

Because that self-help tradition came back into play in 2018 when Strontian became the first community in Scotland to build and own its primary school – not a private school but part of the Highland Council network. How did they do it?

Gradually.

In 2007, the Sunart Community Company was set up to buy a couple of bits of land in Strontian for a village green and footpath. The management committee soon realised there was a much bigger possibility – a £800k community hydro scheme which could pump-prime community development for decades to come. What had that got to do with schools? Haud on. With a huge volunteer effort, locals raised the cash in community shares just before Westminster cut tariffs and effectively halted community hydro. Boosted by that success, the community then created a 50-page, lottery-funded 30-year development plan. Rather than use expensive charrettes (the formal and expensive way of mediating public opinion favoured by central and local government) the document was displayed at the local agricultural show and locals put beans beside their favourite options. That encouraged the tiny Strontian community to embark on its next enormous project – building its own new primary school. Their problem wasn't the usual one of declining roles – quite the opposite. Thanks to population growth, the 'old' Strontian primary was at bursting point and didn't meet standards for classroom and play space. The obvious solution was to merge primary pupils with the local secondary school but that was impossible for ten years because the secondary had been built using PFI and couldn't be altered in any way. The council's proposed solution was to spend £1m on portacabins. But the community's idea was far better. They would buy the land, create a building that could serve as a temporary primary school, lease it to the council till the PFI was paid off – and then, if the schools merger finally went ahead, the Strontian community would own a building capable of conversion into four affordable homes.

Huzzah.

Happily, Highland Council agreed to the community's idea, so Strontian Community School Building Ltd was set up. Eager volunteers got £155k worth of community shares sold, which unlocked other funds so they could commission the construction of four connected houses that are now being used as a primary school. This success mattered hugely – for other remote areas fighting off depopulation, for cash-strapped councils spending megabucks on inappropriate, centrally conceived services and for Highland Scotland's conceit of itself. Despite the low expectations of most politicians, Scots generally excel at heavy lifting in their own communities, given half the chance. And as the Strontian folk have gone on to demonstrate, community effort is habit-forming.

The Sunart Community Company also acquired the seabed licence from Marine Scotland so the community now owns land and leases on the jetty and slipway.

In 2017, VisitScotland closed the local visitor information centre in Strontian village so the community company bought the building and now has a community-owned visitor centre staffed by a rota of ten local artists selling local craft products, rather than the tartan tat selection often found elsewhere. That's quite an achievement. And finally, Sunart Community Hydro – the project that got the whole community going – donated another £15k to local good causes recently, bringing the total pot of cash unlocked by these grants to a whopping £1.1 million in under three years. Not bad for some ex-lead-miners and crofters.

Eigg – the pioneers

Another Highland community has taken a quarter of a century to turn itself around.

In 1995, Keith Schellenberg, the problematic, absentee owner of the Hebridean island of Eigg for 20 years, finally agreed to sell. But not to the community. That would happen, he said, 'over his dead body.' Despite petitions, modest fundraising, public support and a determination by 65 islanders to somehow raise the necessary millions, Schellenberg quietly sold the island to another absentee owner, the mysterious 'fire artist Professor' Maruma.

The brazen disrespect was breathtaking.

The impact on hopeful campaigners hard to bear.

The powerlessness almost impossible to thole.

Clearly it didn't matter how the people of Eigg felt about their island being traded on the open market like a prize bull. It didn't matter what alternative possibilities they had painstakingly created over the previous five years. Might was right. Ownership was 9/10 of the law. Their own ideas were banjaxed.

For a few months.

During which time, lengthy discussions ensued about the best way forward, including working with the new owner. But that quickly fell away as the true nature of 'Professor' Maruma emerged. Without rehearsing the whole extraordinary story, Maruma was exposed as a man who bought his title from an American university, found the cash to buy Eigg not from a unique painting style as he claimed but via loans from two creditors, one of which foreclosed in 1996.

Suddenly another opportunity emerged – and another setback. The Eiggachs sought cash support from the National Heritage Memorial Fund, but its offer of a £1 million grant came with strings attached. Namely that islanders would own just 49 per cent of the island with nature charities and the council owning the rest. The islanders walked away. By May 1997, the NHMF let-down didn't matter. Members of the public had come to the rescue to meet the £1.56m asking price – it included a six-figure contribution from one anonymous donor. The islanders finally bought Eigg on 12 June that year – it was a helluva party – and 25 years later, their custodianship is counted a massive success in every conceivable way.

And this matters because it was ordinary ingenuity and people power of every possible kind that created the opportunity for islanders to thrive. Before the 1997 buyout, the absence of mains electricity meant homes on the island were powered by dirty diesel generators. A decade of planning and fundraising later, Eigg Electric was born, combining wind, water and solar with underground cables to provide 24-hour renewable power to every home on the island.

Now each house on the grid is allocated 5kw of energy and triggers a trip switch if it consumes more. That hardly ever happens thanks to smart meters on every kitchen table and a highly developed sense of energy use. Across the island electric cars, cycles, customised golf buggies and even electric wheelbarrows are doing all the heavy lifting. The ambitious aim is to be carbon net zero by 2030.

Biodiversity has been boosted by a quietly epic effort by father and daughter Wes and Tasha Fyffe who've been restoring native woodland on bracken covered slopes. Aided by skilled application writer Rebecca Long, the pair won a grant from Forestry and Land Scotland to replace the old, unmaintained spruce plantation (planted for the grant income by Keith Schellenberg) with saplings grown from locally collected seeds of hawthorn, alder, rowan, hazel and elm, plus oak from acorns gathered near Arisaig. The small team cleared land in the 'old' plantation to grow 20,000 seedlings in poly tunnels and plant them out during the pandemic years, humping the tiny trees uphill by quad bike where possible – but mostly carrying them by hand. It's now one of a handful of tree nurseries that operate on Scotland's islands.

Most of the felled trees were taken to a mainland sawmill (prompting plans for a shared, portable Small Isles sawmill), but some's been kept for island firewood and local building projects – lowering the cost and carbon footprint of imported material. Long ago, the islanders set up Eigg Construction – a subsidiary of the Trust – after the buyout to refurbish the many dilapidated croft houses. Later, a new generation of local self-builders was created when the Trust offered plots of land for free (to be repaid if the resulting home is ever sold). So, building projects are fairly constant and there's a loose cap of two homes a year so locals stay involved in construction and the award-winning Eigg Electric isn't overloaded. The latest big building project – with locals working for off-island contractors – was expansion of the pier building that houses the tearoom, craft shop, grocery shop, island trust office and bike hire. It reopened in 2022 as a new island hub powered by a biomass boiler and PV panels from the tearoom roof – with a new shower and toilet block, drying room and washing machines. The rest of the green hub is business units to support new start-ups and a new coastguard room with excellent broadband courtesy of Hebnet (Hebridean Network), a community interest company set up by Eigg builder and yachtsman Simon Helliwell and Ian Bolas from neighbouring Rum. They've taken island internet from dial-up to high-speed broadband and the duo have taught other remote west coast communities how to do the same thing, enabling islanders to work on mainland projects without constant travel. Another eco boon.

Stu McCarthy of The Isle of Eigg Brewery raised almost £200,000 in a crowdfunded share offer and since a carbon-zero brewery was the investors' top priority, the new brewery is using PV solar panels for power, with a Tesla Powerwall for storage and plans to use an electric delivery vehicle for mainland delivery.

Meanwhile, below the basalt ridge of An Squrr sits the deserted township of Grulin, whose people were cleared on a whim by an incoming sheep farmer in 1858. He stayed just four years. The old black houses have collapsed and fallen into the ferns. Efforts to rebuild them by original Eigg Trustee Tom Forsyth in the ' 90s were blocked by the authorities. Without animals to keep down the bracken, Grulin looked set to become a museum piece.

But now the land is being worked again by young farmer Sarah Boden, who left as a child and returned in 2010 to build a home and start a family with Pictish Trail musician Johnny Lynch. He runs the record label Lost Map Records from Eigg – one of a clutch of island bands and professional musicians who together put on a brilliant Celtic Connections 21st anniversary concert in 2018. Sarah runs 350 sheep and 20 cows and belongs to a new ecological hill farming movement, while Frances Carr and her husband Stephen Nelson have created an oyster farm.

What kept them all going in the face of obstruction, dead-ends and high-handed intransigence?

They talked a lot. Being on a small island with one shop, they met a lot. But they also organised a lot. Trust board members divvied the island into beats and went go out to visit those who didn't attend meetings, so no-one could complain about being left out. As human ecologist and Isle of Eigg Trust founder Alastair McIntosh put it, 'the people of Eigg made the island "unlairdable"'. That didn't mean direct action – unless you include using the farm tractor to deliver drums of diesel to freezing elderly tenants against instructions. It did mean running Eigg as if the people were in charge – because actually, they always had been.

You may see where I'm going with this.

Eiggachs have always been ready to harness their own resources, natural and human, and have never waited for off island expertise.

Over 25 community-controlled years they've produced a circular local economy with a burgeoning of storytelling, music making, application writing, project management, lacemaking, fencing, website construction, wind turbine maintenance, quarrying, boiler servicing and a steady supply of new, affordable, island-built, energy-efficient homes and organic willow weaving.

This sustainable, joined-up action was coordinated by

no-one from high command. Eco-ingenuity seems to have arisen spontaneously on Eigg, the minute remote control ended.

It's a taster of the kind of energy ready to be released with independence. And it's no coincidence that the vast majority of these can-do islanders are also instinctive Yessers.

This kind of leap from dependency to self-sufficiency is happening all over Scotland. But since there is no single big bang – the kind of story the media understands best – no-one knows. Well, you do now.

And yet still, I imagine there will be a niggling voice.

Aye but those are remote areas where people are used to working together. What about the cities, the schemes, those areas of mass deprivation? There won't be any of these go-ahead ventures there – right?

Wrong.

Lochgelly – the mining town reborn

It was the thing towns dread –in 2004, Fife ex-mining town of Lochgelly was voted the 'Worst Place to Live in Britain'.

Helen Ross, now Treasurer of the Lochgelly Community Development Forum remembers it well.

> Journalists sat at street corners, waiting till mangey dogs walked past to take pictures. Everyone's heart sank because behind the scenes, we were doing so much and working so hard to change things. But pits had closed, and the town was full of three storey flats no-one wanted – there were even maisonettes on top of those flats. Improvement plans had been hatched but demolition had to take place before renewal could begin – it was going to be a very long-term process.

Six years later there was another blow when the town received a Plook on the Plinth nomination as the most dismal town in Scotland. It read:

Lochgelly imparts a funereal air and the Lochgelly
Centre, the heart of the community, lies boarded up
waiting redevelopment.

Of course, it hadn't always been like this – and that's what's
hurt townspeople most. The Fife town – now in the poorest
ten per cent of communities on the Scottish Index of Multiple
Deprivation – was once a weaving and agricultural village and
after the discovery of ironstone and coal, it became one of
the main centres of mining in Fife. Lochgelly miners – a self-
regulating and self-sufficient, community minded bunch – paid
a penny from their wages to build their own Miners' Institute.
Soon after, subscriptions paid for a Cooperative Society and
around Fife, libraries and schools were built. But as the mines
closed, that self-sufficiency crumbled.

By 1998 local women Christine McGrath and Eileen
McKenna decided they'd had enough. Lochgelly had become a
forgotten town and the two women were determined to turn it
around. They formed a local regeneration group and recruited
Helen Ross. She recalls: 'We had different personalities,
different skills and a lot of life experience.'

That was an understatement.

Helen has worked as a window dresser, telephonist, driving
instructor and market trader as well as travelling round the
world. She'd worked for insurance companies, credit firms,
and local councils. Together with Christine (an expert form-
filler) and Eileen (a talented planner) they formed a strong,
determined team.

Their timing was good. Fife Council and Ore Valley
Housing Association (OVHA) had just started work with the
community on the Lochgelly Masterplan. This ultimately led
to five housing developments and an award-winning Business
Centre beside the refurbished Miners Institute. The Lochgelly
Centre finally got its refit and was extended to include a 415
seat theatre, library, local office, e-commerce suite, sports hall,
creative classrooms and a café.

Satisfied that 'hardware' issues were now being tackled, the Regeneration Group reformed as the Development Forum (LCDF) decided to tackle the big 'software' problem – how locals felt about their own town.

Relaunching the annual gala and parade in 2006, the process of social change began, followed by a community Christmas light switch-on event, which involved fundraising for the lights, closing the road, organising a torchlight parade and a Christmas Craft fayre where Mr and Mrs Claus gave children free selection boxes donated by local businesses. These simple things were transformational.

Helen remembers: 'When we saw about a thousand people coming down the road carrying lights – we all burst into tears. It was such a beautiful sight.'

The next advance resulted from what seemed like another setback.

In 2010, world-renowned planning expert Andres Duany led what newspapers described as 'a ground-breaking charrette' (planning forum) but what locals less charitably described as 'a shovette' – a culture crash in which imported professionals seemed to run roughshod over locals. But the culture-clash ultimately did some good, unlocking funding to transform the much-loved, B-listed Town House into rented flats. New flats have also been built on other vacant and derelict sites in the town bringing 31 new affordable homes to the town centre.

Another important legacy of the Lochgelly charrette was a change in Scottish government practice, recognising that local people know their towns better than professionals who should listen, help shape community aspirations but always encourage local people to do the leading.

A final happy outcome was that Fife Council recruited Hazel Cross to work in the town.

Helen Ross recalls:

Believe me she had a hard time when she came in because of the feeling generated by the charrette but

Hazel won everyone around, she really listened to us, could see all the work that had gone on, valued us, rolled up her sleeves and made us a promise she would help. We call her Miss Lochgelly, even though she comes from Methil, cos she's always there at the back of us – she's excellent.

One of Hazel's early achievements was 'intercepting' the Indoor Climbing and Bouldering Centre originally looking for space in Glenrothes or Kirkcaldy. Hazel pointed out that Lochgelly was just off the A92, with its own train station, and the advantage of open space at nearby Lochore Meadows. The Centre kickstarted plans to develop Lochgelly as an accessible active leisure cluster for residents and visitors and gave the sport a town-centre shop-window instead of obscurity on an industrial estate.

The £1.5 million Rockgelly Centre was delayed by Covid but will open later this year in the refurbished St Andrew's Church, run by a new community interest company – part of an astonishing rise in occupancy rates of local shops and offices. In seven years, Lochgelly vacancy rates have halved. The new OVHA business centre was 86 per cent let three years ago and the refurbished Miners Institute 70 per cent let. An eloquent riposte to naysayers who predicted the new units would sit empty forever.

And there is a blizzard of projects on the go. The Community Shop sells affordable clothing and homeware and provides a place to blether, volunteer and overcome social isolation. The Connect Project links would-be volunteers with local vacancies and the chance to gain qualifications. There are proposals for a Happy Lands Heritage & Visitor Centre – located in the area that gave its name to a 2012 film depicting life in Scottish mining communities during the 1926 General Strike. Heritage trails and guided tours are starting up, featuring the restored Miners Institute and the birthplace of Jennie Lee, the Labour MP who became the youngest woman elected to the House of Commons in 1929 and helped launch a million careers by creating the Open University (against stiff opposition) so that education could become a route out of poverty for anyone.

In 2016 all this hard work was finally rewarded when Lochgelly won the title of Scotland's Most Improved Town in the annual Scottish Urban Regeneration Forum Awards. According to Helen Ross, 'I was the proudest person in the world that night.'

So what's their secret?

According to Hazel Cross, Lochgelly's success is down to strong partnerships, trust, honest and animated discussion, ambition for the town and a realisation that change doesn't happen overnight.

Yip, it's almost as disappointing as 'friendly people'.

But how many more examples are needed before we accept that Scots are more capable than anyone has given us credit for – able to run communities and well able to run Scotland?

While journalists have watched the Parliament, they've taken their eye off an equally important arena where ordinary Scots have taken over assets deemed too complex, too remote and too unlikely to make a profit by private landowners, millionaires, councils and quangos. Scots have been saving Scotland quietly for decades.

Without politicians. And it's been done in a cooperative, deliberative and impressive way.

How would all this be possible, if the average Scot wasn't pretty savvy – and some community leaders, pretty special?

Special 'ordinary' people

Allan Macrae from Assynt was a man who made history. So was Tommy Riley in Drumchapel. They both died in June 2013. Allan and Tommy never met. But in many ways they were gentle brothers in the same fight for expression and dignity. They left a mark on their communities. They believed in the folk around them when no-one else did.

And meeting them changed my life.

Against all the odds, 30 years ago, Allan Macrae, Bill Ritchie and John MacKenzie led the Assynt Crofters to the first community land buyout in Scottish history. A big achievement for a wiry wee crofter, happier shifting sheep around the hill than dealing with difficult people. And yet Allan was full of surprises. He was eloquent in the manner of an old-fashioned orator – declaiming rather than speaking and belting out fiery words and inspiring ideas at a volume that defied his slight frame and shy manner. Allan let fellow crofters and the rest of Scotland know that being bought and sold like so many deer or sheep on the land was completely unacceptable.

When Lord Vestey carved the North Lochinver Estate out of his massive northern domain and put it up for sale in 1992, provocatively advertising the land as 'an unspoilt wilderness' – he drew up boundaries that coincided with the local Assynt Crofters Union branch. So people living on this 'new' parcel of land already knew and trusted one another and had a shared history of practical deeds, land management, complaint mediation and action. If Vestey had doubled the acreage, he might have brought in new faces and weakened the crofters' resolve. As it was, the main obstacle the Assynt crofters faced was themselves, and that negative inner voice constantly muttering in the ear of any Highlander – dinnae get above yourself.

Happily, Allan was not a man plagued by such inner doubt. He was a firebrand – and attributed a lot of that to his mother. Allan proudly introduced her after a radio programme I presented for Radio Scotland in the Culag Hotel in Lochinver just after the buyout. I was (evidently) astonished when she started speaking with a broad Cockney accent. Allan smiled and said, 'Hybrids are the strongest plants.' They are. Whatever differences of opinion existed, whatever obstacles were hurled at him, Allan kept going in his own idiosyncratic, thrawn and independent way,

Buying the North Lochinver estate was one thing – reviving

the communities' fortunes was another. I first met Allan through my friend and Assynt Crofter Issie MacPhail. I remember watching the two of them trying to herd sheep into a fank in a Force 8 gale. Somehow Allan was reading a well-thumbed paperback whilst gathering the sheep, rolling a cigarette (with one hand) and staying upright. He was only the second person I'd ever seen reading Paolo Freire's *Pedaogy of the Oppressed*. In this unsnappily-titled book the radical Brazilian suggests that living without power or control is an art to be cultivated – not just a set of aspirations to be repressed. And like any artform, practitioners must employ and refine their skills. 'Inferiorism', as Freire called it, is a skillset that stops marginalised people 'feeling free' or 'taking responsibility' or 'thinking big', even when circumstances improve. Skills like spending next to nothing, making do with second, third or fifth best, leaving instead of speaking out, and above all discouraging potential troublemakers and children from showing defiance or ambition. Freire's contention is that behaving like a second-class citizen or inferior is so deep-seated and almost instinctive that it must be consciously un-learned. 'This man is right,' Allan muttered when he finally came inside, rustling in his ancient waterproofs. I spotted the cover-free paperback again some years later in his car. After the historic Assynt buyout in 1993, Allan came across to Eigg to advise islanders there, trying to psyche themselves up for a more difficult buyout battle. His advice was simple. Buy everything. Buy all the rights. Don't be fobbed off. Get everything – go for gold. I wonder if Allan ever realised how influential his words and support had been. A few years later islanders were in precisely the position he foresaw – offered 49 per cent control of the island by Lottery funders. It was a heck of a lot more control than they'd had under absentee landowners like Keith Schellenberg – but with Allan's powerful advice ringing in their ears, they refused. Later – when Eigg islanders bought the whole island lock-stock and barrel, Allan came over for 'Handover Day'. Walking around with him was like walking with God.

This smiling, unimposing man was known by reputation in every house on the island. His presence was the ultimate validation of the bold buyout decision – a baton of confidence and belief passed from an existing land pioneer to the next. I remember persuading him to wear my gold lame jacket for just one picture. Buoyed along by the euphoria of the day, he wore it. If only Allan could have met Tommy Riley. He was a founder of the Drumchapel Men's Health Group in 1993 – the architect of a minor social revolution in one of the hardest, most macho parts of Glasgow with the highest rate of chronic illness, suicide and premature death amongst men in Europe. Tommy set up the Danny Morrison Health Clinic (with others) which was funded for one glorious year by Glasgow Health Board before they took fright, cut the money and left Tommy and the others back on the street where they'd started. Some of the guys picked up and got jobs – not Tommy. He didn't drink before the project began, but the pressure of trying to win respect and support for the broken men around him changed all that. Ten years ago, I tried to find Tommy to write about his experience in a book called *Blossom*.

When I eventually found Tommy he was in a very bad way. He had COPD and was an alcoholic – clear-eyed, honest and broken by a system that had used and crushed thousands like him. Brave men who tried to face down the macho stereotypes of generations to care for their own health and their children. Amazingly, despite the amount of column inches spent on men's health in Scotland , no-one had even recorded his incredible experience building (probably) Scotland's first purpose built men's centre.

But even without affirmation from the great and good and despite all the difficulties, Tommy like Allan, always saw a much wider picture. We often talked about the raw deal working Scots have faced in cities and on the land. He envied my trips to Norway – it was like the Promised Land, he said – an equal country without slums. He'd love to see it but knew he wouldn't get there.

Neither he did.

So, in memory of these two great men – standard bearers for countless thousands of other folk who've helped to save their communities – here's the thing. We can continue to apply sticking plaster solutions, as if our people aren't ready for profound change. Or we can build an equal society and watch astonished (or actually not) as all communities blossom. Capable men and women have been ignored as engines of change for too long. And yet leadership and the capacity to transform Scotland exists everywhere.

We are not sitting walled up inside a hopeless case in Scotland.

We should appreciate what we've got – and who we've got.

Because across the world – and especially in the Faroes – everyone else already does.

Different, but different enough?

So, you think you know about Scotland – then the door is flung wide open, on the top floor of the Geology Department at the University of Iceland. I was there in 2018 to interview Professor Pall Einarsson, for a film about the country, after many visits left me acutely aware that volcanoes have totally shaped its history. What I didn't realise was that those Icelandic volcanoes have also shaped Scotland.

According to Pall:

> 50–70 million years ago Scotland and Greenland sat side by side – the Atlantic Ocean hadn't yet formed – and the Iceland hot spot was creating volcanoes in Greenland and Scotland. So Scottish volcanic areas like Skye and Iona are the first signs of the Iceland hotspot in action. Most ideas about how volcanoes operate on the inside come from Scotland. Scotland is really the cradle of vulcanology.

Interesting though this is, how do volcanic links with Iceland enhance the case for Scottish independence? Bear with me.

Like many Scots, I'd been aware of massive contributions by the 'Father' of Modern Geology, James Hutton and Hugh Miller. Dr Hutton lived in Edinburgh during the 18th century Scottish Enlightenment and was the first major figure to challenge the conventional view of the Earth as only 6,000 years old. Hugh Miller, a stonemason from Cromarty, lived a century later and became one of Scotland's most influential palaeontologists. But Pall's news about the hard-wired volcanic connections between all the North Atlantic islands – Iceland, Greenland, the Faroes, Skye, Mull and Iona – was new to me. In a fascinating piece published by the Geological Society of Glasgow, it seems:

> The plume of hot rock that sits beneath Iceland has long-reaching fingers – two of which stretch all the way to Scotland and Norway. This could help explain why the Scottish Highlands aren't submerged beneath the waves.[30]

Whit? It seems the earth's crust beneath Scotland and western Norway is unusually thin, meaning both regions should in theory be below sea level.

'Something else must be going on to explain why they're not,' observes Nicky White of Cambridge University, 'and that something else is the "hot fingers". This is because the hot rock is relatively buoyant, which could compensate for the thinness of the crust, pushing it up.'

Double wow.

Iceland only exists, breaking the North Atlantic waves, because of its 30 volcanoes. Perhaps the northern half of Scotland is only afloat for the same reason.

If that's a bit mind-blowing, there's more.

According to Alan McKirdy and Roger Crofts:

> Scotland has drifted across the surface of the planet

---

30 https://geologyglasgow.org.uk/headlines/scotland-floats-on-iceland039s-mantle-plume-44/

like a great Ark, constructed of rock rather than wood, and driven not by the tides and winds, but by the movement of plates on the Earth's surface. In the distant geological past, Scotland travelled towards the South Pole and wandered the southern hemisphere, before drifting to its present latitude. In the process it passed through all the Earth's climatic zones. The landmass we now call Scotland carried an ever-changing cargo of plants and animals, many of them now extinct. For its size, Scotland has the most varied geology and natural landscape of any country on the planet.[31]

I have no suitable expressions of surprise left.

Scotland's astonishing geological restlessness explains phenomena like the ancient, orange 'desert' rocks at Yesnaby on Orkney and Lewisian Gneiss – some of the world's oldest – which appear across much of the northwest Highlands.

In her own, long and varied geological life, Scotland has been a bit of a migrant.

As regards Britain, until 410 million years ago, Scotland was separated from England by an ocean wider than the present-day North Atlantic. The two countries – each part of a larger land mass – collided and squeezed up mountains in place of the vanished Iapetus Ocean. As McKirdy and Crofts explain:

A mountain range perhaps as high as the Himalayas was created as a result of the Scotland – England collision.

Erosion has cut those colossal mountains down to size, and the two countries, originally an ocean apart, are now joined at the Iapetus Suture – a line which runs almost parallel to Hadrian's Wall.

31 https://www.scottishgeology.com/wp-content/uploads/lfbg/ LandscapeFashionedbyGeology-scotland.pdf

Who knew?

Well, ok – geologists.

But Scotland's incredible life story is not something taught to many of us and perhaps explains why basalt is so revered in Iceland that the stunning new concert hall Harpa is built of five storey-high, glass columns modelled on basalt, while in who-really-knew-about-volcanoes Scotland, basalt is simply the columnar stuff you get on Staffa.

But maybe knowing a little more prompts fresh curiosity and admiration for this ancient, well-travelled country, the same way revelations about astonishing, vigorous earlier lives can transform our perception of the aged.

Scotland is not just another country politically speaking – but once upon a time, sat on another continent as well. But can a different location 50 million years ago make a big contribution to the independence debate today? Perhaps.

Alasdair Gray opens his 1997 book, *Why Scots should rule Scotland* with the words

> my argument is not based on differences of race,
> religion or language but geology. Because landscape
> is what defines the most lasting nations.

He goes on to argue that the isolation caused by bands of high mountains, poor soil and a colder climate, left Scots less prone to attack and more in need of cooperation to survive than folk in England, whose relatively flat, fertile plains invited invasion and produced, over time, a defensive rather than a cooperative outlook. Essentially, he thought, national temperament is shaped by geology.

It's a brilliant though broad-brush theory that doesn't quite account for the Viking invasions of Scottish islands or the mountains, bog, loch, marsh and moor that cover large parts of England. Still, his observation that folk from fertile areas become defensive – a typically provocative bit of Alasdair Gray thinking – does translate quite neatly onto the voting map of Scotland, especially the fertile (former) Tory seats of Aberdeenshire, the Borders, Perthshire and the Lothians. But then the rise of the SNP turned even the productive farmlands yellow (politically speaking) and Brexit turned England's northern uplands True Blue.

It seems geological strata can be overlaid by human formations, after all.

But away from the slightly shaky ground of politics, Scotland's different geology has had a massive and obvious ecological impact on our lives. The pioneer of Scottish Environmental History, Professor TC Smout, observes a very real ecological border between Scotland plus the North of England and everywhere south of the Midlands – which escaped the ice cap that covered our own 'natural region' 22,000 years ago. The ice sheet, which covered all of Scotland only started to melt 11,500 years ago – the blink of an eyelid in geological time.

That ice-laden past gave us profoundly different landscape and soil structures, different flora and fauna to southern England and ironically, a better chance of escaping the sea-level changes produced by climate change today. It seems those parts of Scotland most firmly compacted by huge ice sheets and three-mile-thick glaciers are recovering vigorously enough to protect the coastline from rising seas. This process, known as isostatic rebound, could see land rise by nearly four inches across Scotland – a huge mitigating force against flooding that's missing in areas that were historically ice-sheet-free – like the south of England. There's other good news for Scotland. Our Scots pine forests are remnants of the ancient, much larger Caledonian forest that covered most of Scotland until trees were lost to a wetter climate, over-exploitation and advancing agriculture in the medieval period. But recent research suggests Scots Pine populations are nonetheless as genetically diverse as their continental cousins, which suggests that despite huge losses, the last fragments of the Caledonian Forest in Scotland still harbour the genetic variation that could regenerate future populations.

So, Scotland is different, beneath our feet, around our glens, across our lochs, in our forests and beneath the seas that connect us with Iceland.

Impressive. But while ice-sheets melting 22,000 years ago produced a different landscape and even a distinctively Scottish outlook, they don't exactly clinch the case for independence today.

Are there more modern, more human differences?

Not really, say supporters of the union. Present-day Scots speak (roughly) the same language, watch the same TV programmes and laugh at the same jokes as everyone else in Britain. End of.

Really, these folk should get out more.

If a shared language is the test for membership of the UK, then Iceland, Norway, Sweden, Denmark, most of Finland, the Netherlands, parts of Poland, half of Belgium and of course the whole of Canada, America, Australia, New Zealand and big chunks of the entire world should be queueing up to join.

The degree of fluency in English across the planet and the Nordic countries in particular is unnerving and almost annoying. After taking three Norwegian courses at Edinburgh University and then in Oslo for research on a PhD, I still found every conversation in a shop or street switched instantly from my stumbling Norwegian to their seemingly fluent English. No Norwegian misses an opportunity to perfect their English since it became the world language and a better aide to mobility and personal advancement than an Irish blinkin passport. Forgive the bitterness. I still can't accept that despite ten formative childhood years in Belfast I was born in Wolverhampton and thus cannot apply. If there is a God, he must be Derek Dougan (one for the teenagers).

Anyway, an excellent dinner with one Norwegian academic and his wife revealed such a sophisticated command of English and haute cuisine that I was completely floored.

'I always have a problem in London [where he was Visiting Professor] distinguishing between hake and cod.'

I had no idea how you could tell the two apart in any language.

'I think hake has a milder taste, softer texture and smaller flakes than cod. Is that roughly right?'

Fa kens. Scots are generally more acquainted with the difference between battered and breaded haddock in the classic fish supper.

Similarly, my stumbling Swedish advanced not one iota during a fabulous two month winter stay at the Visby writer's centre on the island of Gotland. Tucked up with one Finn, two Swedes, a Lithuanian and two Norwegians, I was sure my fledgling knowledge of at least one language would blossom. Not a chance. Since we were able to join the university library (yip, a university on an island of just 58,000 people), each night was spent watching my companions' favourite English language films and pausing on bits they'd never fully understood for a proper explanation. The most challenging was a film about Irish painter Christy Brown, born with cerebral palsy who learned to hold a paint-brush with his left foot. Hence the title of this Oscar-winning film which included bravura performances by Daniel Day Lewis as Christy and Brenda Flicker as his gutsy mother, Bridget. Christy becomes suicidally depressed after realising the woman who'd encouraged his artistic talents doesn't reciprocate his deeper feelings. Witnessing her son's despair, Bridget goes out to the tiny postage stamp of a garden behind their terraced house wearing her pinny, gets down on hands and knees and starts assembling rocks and bricks to construct a ramshackle extension – a room for Christy, who was sharing a bedroom at the time with his three fully-grown brothers. Her tool-free, makeshift efforts are determined but amatuer – coaxing even the distraught artist outside to help. Finally, the men of the household return – they work on a building site – and laughingly complete Bridget's hard work.

Pause.

'So why did the mother not go to the council and explain she needed a bigger house?'

Jings. That question could only be asked in well-provisioned and for many years, semi-socialist Sweden.

'That's not how 1950s Dublin operated – the point is there was no other way for the mother to show her love.'

That had everyone stumped.

'But if they were entitled to a better house, why didn't she just ask?'

Where to start?

Sharing languages often just highlights the profound social and political differences that lurk beyond. And interesting as these evenings were, they hardly constituted a relaxing night off.

My point is that there's near total fluency in English across Northern Europe, and a huge interest in English-speaking culture without anyone accepting the deep-seated inequality that curses every bit of the UK past and present – or wanting to join. Indeed, on his 'divorce tour' in 2011 John Cleese headed straight to Norway, where Monty Python has always been as popular as it was here in decades past. Imagine my surprise, for example, on a trip to Arctic Finnmark where I discovered my guide, Tore, could recite several sketches verbatim, just like myself.

Nobody expected to be walking the frozen streets of Karashok hearing the Spanish Inquisition sketch recited by a 70-something Norwegian, in fact those that did...

It was a fabulous, delicious moment of shared culture. Mind you, Tore also loved the deeply Irish Father Ted.

I relate all this not just to revisit memory lane, but to suggest that neither fluency in the English language nor an interest in English culture constitutes a desire for constitutional assimilation or political union with England. Obviously.

Norwegians have long admired Britain and England in particular, since their royal family spent the Nazi occupation of the Second World War living in London, broadcasting vital messages of support to the resistance.

But that doesn't make Norwegians want to be English any more than their obsession with Upstairs Downstairs represents a desire to ditch Europe's most equal and democratic society in favour of Britain's ludicrous and antiquated class system. Or watching every episode of Borgen makes English viewers want to pack in first past the post, adopt proportional voting and embrace coalition government like Denmark. Ochone.

In fact, the near universal ability to speak English across Northern Europe serves only to question the importance of linguistic difference in defining the imagined communities that constitute nations.

Now I'll grant you that language – along with ethnicity and religion – were once the nation-determining King-Pins. When Norway became independent in 1905 there was near unanimity about quitting Swedish control, but such disagreement over language, that four were created (there are still two) along with 18 official dialects.

But times have changed.

The main cultural difference between Norway and Sweden today is not their (whisper it) almost inter-changeably similar languages or equally declining adherence to Lutheranism but the size of their Muslim populations – almost three times larger in Sweden than Norway because of the former's liberal asylum policy. Another difference – the dispersed population in Norway sustained by its oil and gas reserves and maintenance of fishing outside the EU.

But generally, most European states are now more ethnically diverse, less religiously devout and pretty effective English speakers. But none of that diminishes the strength of their own national identities.

Strange then that some Scots believe national difference must be as stark as two primary colours or as non-negotiable as the old Iron Curtain before a country can hope to justify 'secession'. Perversely, many Scots demand whopping cultural differences of Brazil v Uganda proportions before being able to take our own claims for nationhood seriously.

Essentially, the connection between the English language and the case for the union is not its unifying force, but its vindication of Britain's uniqueness. After all, why would the world pay us the ultimate compliment of making our speech their language unless its originators – us – were not very, very, very special indeed? Like linguistic Lords of the Manor we expect our idiosyncrasies and verbal tics to be known and understood across the world, without knowing more than a few beer-ordering words of any other lingo. The ubiquity of English has swollen Britain's already guid conceit of itself – when in truth it is American that has conquered the globe.

Actually though, if we set language aside for a minute (after noting that Gaelic and Scots are most definitely diverse, indigenous languages) Scotland has some whopping differences with England that don't exist in Wales or Northern Ireland.

Not just the way we vote – but the way we live.

Unlike all the other home nations, most urban Scots (579,000 families) do not have front and back doors, a roof over (just) their own heads, their own garden or the conceit that their homes are castles. Tenements are to Scotland what terraced houses are to England, Wales and Northern Ireland. Urban Scots have traditionally built upwards whilst the rest of the UK built outwards. So at least a million Scots live in four-storey, eight-household, stone-built tenement flats without a Corrie style terraced-house in sight. Flats in Scotland are normal. In fact, look around when you're abroad. English terraced housing is Europe's odd relation. That of course is not the view in Albert Square, Coronation Street, Westminster, Number Ten or Broadcasting House. 56 million people can't be wrong.

Perhaps though, 5.5 million people can beg to differ.

Kings, queens, currencies, wars, inventors, languages, geography and latitude all command great attention in discussions of national identity. Yet people are shaped by the way they live. And at least a fifth of Scots live relatively cheerfully one on top of another, not side by side, sharing access, common services, roof-repair bills, stair-cleaning responsibilities and very often family ties in refurbished, centuries-old, stone tenements. The closeness of that life has sometimes been suffocating, sometimes life-sustaining – often both. But almost all Scots have been touched by the experience. Tenements housed unsanitary, overcrowded slums 60 years ago but after the stone-cleaning, insulation and renovations of the '80s, they have helped create Scotland's trademark dense, compact, popular world cities. For better and for worse, for five centuries at least, in sickness and in health, and quite uniquely in the UK, Scots have been wedded to our sturdy, stone tenements.

Two other distinctive aspects of housing have also helped shape Scottishness – the tendency to rent (not own) housing and the likelihood of being a council (not private sector) tenant. Put all those trends together and you have a population which, until recently, was reliant on the state not the private sector for decent housing, ready to vote Labour in gratitude, use public transport (since dense cities make stops closer) and share parts of their living space like common stairs. Might any of that explain the Scots' fondness for public ownership and the belief there certainly is 'such a thing as society'? And then there's law, education, culture, banks, religion. You name it – Scotland has different systems to those operating south of the border.

Take law. You can be the hottest kid on the block in London legal circles, but that gets you nowhere in Scotland, without spending time and money to complete further qualifications. The Law Society of Scotland cheerfully points out that English solicitors need only pass seven extra exams – for some nationalities it is 11. Scotland's legal tradition is based on the European model which emphasises the role of legislation passed by Parliament whilst the English legal system emphasises precedent – one of the important ways conservatism is built into the fabric of English life.

Our education systems are also subtly different – Scotland favours a generalist approach, turning out 17-year-olds with five or six Highers for university, while England rapidly specialises to produce 18-year-olds with three A levels. English students graduate with specific Bachelor Arts degrees after three years, while Scottish students graduate with general BAS after four.

So what, you might think – not different enough to hang your hat on. Ironically, professionals themselves disagree. Commentators like Professor John Bryden have speculated that the separate status given to lawyers, teachers and even their unions and associations in post 1707 Scotland was a cunning move designed to detach professionals from wider Home Rule movements. After all lawyers with their own Scottish 'closed shop', doctors with their own Royal Colleges and teachers with their own Scottish trade unions like the EIS, have already achieved a measure of independence. How much do they need? By contrast, Norwegian professionals had no special status under Danish or Swedish rule – and that brought professionals into the wider movement for Norwegian independence.

It's also worth pointing out how unproblematic these longstanding, cross-border professional differences have proved to be. Where there's a will…

Of course, you could write a book about Scotland's very different cultural traditions. Two generations back few Scots observed Christmas, some started the new year on the 9th of January and Hogmanay was the really big festival. First footing was a thing – Easter was not. Scotland has traditional sports like shinty and curling, but unlike Ireland, largely confined to the Highlands and a diverse, growing and world-renowned musical heritage which is rich beyond the dreams of avarice.

So of course Scots are different – shaped by institutions that predate the Union. By an education system that has always sought breadth, not specialism. By a legal system based on statute, not precedent. By a Kirk not led by the Head of State. By a housing policy not historically based on sale and inheritance, but (for better and worse) on tenancy and rent. By an economy based (since the war) on state activity not private enterprise. And by an endless quest for kinship and connection in lieu of the social democratic state, Scots have lacked the opportunity to build.

But all that most Britons notice about us is that we wear

kilts – who doesn't these days – have two public holidays at Hogmanay and free prescriptions.

In fact, we do many things differently north of the border but since we don't quite understand why, there's no reason anyone else should. As a result, Scots are often propping up what doesn't matter and ignoring what does. Occasionally we catch the scent of a blossom that has been taken from the room – like Hugh MacDiarmid's little white rose of Scotland that 'smells so sweet and breaks the heart'.

The scale of this 'differentness' is largely overlooked on both sides of the border with all sides in the Scottish constitutional debate wont to concentrate exclusively on our old friend, language.

Which means it's worth pointing out that the languages spoken by our nearest and deeply independent Nordic neighbours differ only by shades of grey – except for the Finns.

Languages in Northern Europe	
Scots	A quine and a moose are loose aboot the hoose on a braw bricht moonlicht nicht
Norwegian	En kvinne og en mus er løs om huset på en bra klar månelys natt
Swedish	Kvinna och en mus är lost om huset på en bra och tydig månbelysta natten
Danish	En kvinde og en mus er løst omkring huset på en god lys mane lyser nat
Dutch	Een vrouw en een muis sjin los over het huis op een goede helldere maannacht
German	Eine Frau und eine Maus sind locker über das Haus auf einem guten hellen Mondacht
Finnish	Tyttö ja hiiri ovat lötsät noin talo kaunis, kirkas kuutamoyönä
Scots Gaelic	Tha boireannach agus luch ma sgaoil air feadh an taighe air oidhche bhrèagha ghealaich

In practice, Scotland's 'high bar' of distinctiveness is not louped by many European states who've been independent for some time and are yet awfy like their neighbours. The Low Countries have pastel-coloured borders. Yet try suggesting the Netherlands and Belgium, Norway and Sweden or Spain and Portugal should merge. Try and stand well back. In mainland Europe, slight but important points of cultural distinction form the cornerstone of each nation state.

So, the question arises again. Is a very different history, different institutions and a different voting record for the last century enough to justify the creation of a different state, here in Scotland? Of course it is.

Some distinctive nations choose to go it alone, but others do opt to remain within larger states. Former parts of Denmark are now within Germany, the population of the United States of America contains more Spanish speakers than Spain, Russia straddles five time zones and the single state of Brazil is physically larger than the 50 states of Europe. Enormous diversity can remain within single states (though generally with autocrats or proper federalism) whilst other nations depart from remarkably like-minded states as soon as war, occupation or revolution permits.

Ideas of what's 'different enough' do vary.

But if Scotland fails the usual difference test on language, religion and ethnicity – that may actually work in our favour.

The Catalan parallel

In 2018 I was invited to Barcelona by BBC World for a televised debate the day before the Catalan Declaration of Independence. I was backing Amadeu Altafaj, from the Catalan Government, whilst a constitutional expert, Professor Ricardo Gosalbo Bono, was seconding the Spanish Foreign Minister.

Did the Catalans have a strong case for being different to the rest of Spain?

Yes, obviously.

Catalonia has its own judicial system, civil law and police force. In fact, it was recognition of Catalonia's strong case for limited autonomy by the left-leaning Second Republic in 1936, that triggered the coup by General Franco and the horrors of the Spanish Civil War. In 1939, Franco imposed a policy of limpieza, (cleansing) and executed hundreds of political dissidents in concentration camps, banning the Catalan language, flag, and national holiday, the Diada.

But the language did survive – today there are 10 newspapers in Catalan, two radio and one TV station plus books and Catalan literature. Newcomers can find themselves fairly frozen out if they don't take a deep breath and learn the lingo.

And there's another badge of difference. Literally.

The Creu de Sant Jordi (Saint George's Cross) was inaugurated in 1981 to recognise individuals who've helped protect the Catalan identity. It was awarded in 2019, to the captain of FC Barcelona, Lionel Messi and before that to world-famous cellist Pablo Casals, surrealist master Salvador Dalí, the Firefighters Department of Barcelona and the Institute for Catalan Studies – which survived underground during the Franco dictatorship. Somehow, this little nation, denied the right to self-determination by mighty Madrid, still operates its own distinctive honours system.

So different? Catalonia seems to qualify on a number of counts.

And yet, after the BBC World debate, Professor Bono came over to tell me – and I'm paraphrasing here – you must understand Spain has no really big problem with Scottish independence, because you are not like any of the other independence campaigns in Europe. You speak the same language as your neighbours. You practice roughly the same religion or lack of it. You don't claim a different ethnicity. There are none of the usual distinguishing features that make life hard for incomers in other breakaway states. Things that make the prospect of their independence seem scary. And unlike Catalonia, your country is a nation and was once a state.

'Scotland,' he declared, 'you are a one off, because you are genuine civic nationalists.'

That stopped me in my tracks.

Now of course, every imperial power will devise prescriptions for legitimacy that just happen to disqualify their own 'troublesome secessionists'. And of course, the Spanish still insist Scotland must have a lawful referendum, or they'll veto EU membership – to further distance Scotland's example from the Catalans.

As my mother would say, no flies on buttons.

And although Scotland is supposedly in a voluntary union – unlike Spain's constitution which absolutely outlaws independence – we are nowhere nearer the exit door.

But still, the point is that even Spain acknowledges Scots are a special case.

It's ironic. We spend a great deal of time, trying to accentuate the level of difference between Scotland and England to justify going our separate ways. Yet Scotland's strength in the eyes of the international community is precisely our reluctance to create cultural, ethnic or linguistic chasms. We want independence because we are an outward-looking, viable, social democratic nation stuck within an insular conservative country and since most trappings of our former state are still intact, we're clearly good to go. Scotland becoming a country doesn't make other people unwelcome or create second-class citizens. It just finally puts our own genuinely unique democratic heritage centre stage.

It's a difference that's been clear to constitutional experts for a very long time.

Since 4 April 1320, to be precise.

For, as long as a hundred of us…

The Declaration of Arbroath, or letter fae the Barons as it was less pompously known, 'was the earliest European assertion of the right of a nation to self-determination,' according to historian Dr Fiona Watson. Medieval specialist Dr Tom Turpie has called it 'one of the most significant documents to come out of the British Isles, if not Western Europe in the Middle Ages.'

And, of course, it was the first medieval document to define a nation as the sum of its people, not just the property of its King. The first conditional framing of monarchy.

Special. And a totally different conception of sovereignty to that emerging in England.

The letter's big objective was to persuade the Pope – supreme adjudicator of international disputes – that Scotland should be recognised as an independent Kingdom with Robert the Bruce its lawful King. In 1320, that was a tall ask.

The Pope had excommunicated Bruce three times – once for killing a rival – and had summoned him to face the music, in person, several times, in vain. As a result, the whole of civic Scotland was facing a papal interdict that would stop official ceremonies like marriage. Another factor was pushing the warrior Bruce towards peace. His brother Edward had died in battle, leaving King Robert without an obvious heir – exactly the same kingship crisis that prompted English incursions 30 years earlier. Suddenly, Scotland might be up for grabs again.

So, despite the victory of Bannockburn, King Robert had to turn to the Scots clergy, relatively under-acknowledged actors in the Declaration story, to provide the words and diplomatic guile to mollify an infuriated Pope.

Three letters were written but only the last remains, now known as the Declaration of Arbroath. Written in Latin, it carried the seals of Scotland's barons to give an impression of unanimous support and the following memorable pledge:

> If he [Robert the Bruce] should give up what he has begun, seeking to make us or our kingdom subject to the King of England or the English, we should exert ourselves at once to drive him out as our enemy and a subverter of his own right and ours, and make some other man who was well able to defend us our King; for, as long as a hundred of us remain alive, never will we on any conditions be subjected to the lordship of the English. It is in truth not for glory,

nor riches, nor honours that we are fighting, but for
freedom alone, which no honest man gives up but
with life itself.

Of course, the latter part of that powerfully crafted clause
grabbed all the limelight – thanks in no small measure to
Mel Gibson. But the earlier part is fascinating. A declaration
by the barons, freeholders and abbots (though admittedly
not the common folk) that they would rise up and choose
another King if Bruce bottled it or tried to cut a deal for the
English crown.

A very different stance to the Divine Right of Kings, that
prevailed in England.

Now of course, there are stories within this story.

The Barons had no desire for democracy and King Robert
no intention of being usurped. The Declaration was a cleverly
worded statement of intent – an argument intended to win
peace where war had failed. And it worked.

In 1324, Pope John XXII recognised Robert as king and
four years later peace terms were agreed with the English.

Importantly, it was not Bannockburn that delivered peace and
freedom. Bruce realised he couldn't beat Edward into submission,
so words came to the rescue. The Declaration sealed the deal,
adding an important extra dimension to Scottish identity – canny
peace-makers, shrewd persuaders and eloquent writers, as well
as fierce fighters. And – whatever the framers' real motives – the
first powerful advocates of popular sovereignty.

According to Tom Turpie, the Jacobites initially used the
Declaration to justify their royalism:

They used it to say that all states need monarchs. But in
the 19th century people on the left began to use it, from
the angle of popular sovereignty, suggesting Scotland
has a long tradition of democracy. For the last 300
years [the Declaration] has taken on a life of its own.
Did it influence the American Declaration of Independence?

There's no direct proof of a connection, but the us Congress hold Tartan Day on April 6th, because they believe Scotland's Declaration helped shape their own. As Billy Kay points out, many of those American framers were of Scots descent and the Declaration of Arbroath was published in more than a dozen books in the run up to the American Declaration in 1776.

Today, those historic words about liberty, freedom and the people's right to self-determination still inspire folk around the world and underpin Scotland's modern civic identity, which is not overly worshipful, not impressed with airs and graces, not slavishly devoted to royalty and not happy that a British Prime Minister can veto the exercise of self-determination by the Scottish nation. It's not that everyone can recite the Declaration verbatim. We don't have to. It has enthused and infused the works of so many others since 1320:

> Ye see yon birkie ca'd a lord,
> Wha struts, an' stares, an' a' that,
> Tho' hundreds worship at his word,
> He's but a coof for a' that.
> For a' that, an' a' that,
> His ribband, star, an' a' that,
> The man o' independent mind,
> He looks an' laughs at a' that.

'A Man's a Man', Burns' paeon to the emptiness of inherited power, was written towards the end of his life in 1795 and sung by Sheena Wellington at the state opening of the new Scottish Parliament in 1999. It epitomises Scotland's independent-minded democratic outlook. So did the Claim of Right – a document crafted by the Campaign for a Scottish Assembly, which declared that all signatories

> Do hereby acknowledge the sovereign right of the
> Scottish people to determine the form of government
> best suited to their needs.

This echo of the Declaration of Arbroath was signed in 1988 by almost all Labour and Liberal Democrat MPs including future luminaries of the No campaign, Gordon Brown and Alistair Darling. Ahem.

The point is that Scotland's case for difference as a nation is ancient and profound – we think differently about sovereignty and vote differently, we believe in the Common Weal and public ownership of vital assets. We are a friendly, outward-facing social democracy stuck within an isolationist, backward-facing Conservative state.

And though that's less obvious, measurable or dramatic than the usual distinguishing features of a different language, religion or ethnicity, those civic differences are real, yet create fewer antagonistic waves towards neighbours and incomers.

Glory be.

We were once a nation state and though we shared the kit with neighbours, we kept the box. We have all the components of statehood, and want to get going again. It's no more complicated than that.

And ironically, this kind of civic reasoning is the one that sits most easily with Europeans because it promises a new country will be inclusive and not hostile to large minorities like the English – of which I am one by birth. Indeed, Scots are very uneasy about ethnic distinctions. Look at the basis upon which the independence referendum was held. With the Scottish Government in charge, the voting register included everyone living in Scotland, at the time, regardless of where they were born. By contrast, the Brexit referendum – run by the Westminster government, two years later – was ethnically based, enfranchising only those born in Britain or Commonwealth countries and Ireland.

No-one argued about the residency premise behind the indyref franchise, even though it papped oot Sir Sean Connery – the world's most famous Scot – who lived in the Bahamas and many other Scots working and living abroad. Lest anyone thinks this was a ruse to exclude likely No voters, the inclusion of non-Scots on the indyref register basically scuppered independence.

A majority of voters born in Scotland said Yes to independence in 2014.

But nearly three-quarters of people from elsewhere in the UK voted No.

And yet I've come across no Yessers who think we should have excluded No voters who made Scotland their home on grounds of ethnicity. We want to win fairly and inclusively – and that's an incredible strength.

Perhaps countries campaigning to become states need to be inclusive and upbeat, whilst those grimly defending what they've got define identity more negatively.

There is a theory about nationalism which classifies two main types – defensive and aspiring. Defensive nationalism tries to protect what already exists. It includes the unionists in Northern Ireland, the Israelis and apartheid South Africa. It tends to be a bit thudding, but has cash, institutional control, high-profile supporters (including other heads of government) and the support of the establishment.

Aspiring nationalists are trying to create something new. They include campaigners for a united Ireland, the Palestinians, at one time the ANC in South Africa and obviously independence supporters in Scotland. They tend to have the best tunes, the poets, the culture and the high hopes because they don't have the cash or the clout.

It can seem like a very uneven battle, but eventually the folk with the tunes tend to succeed.

New Commonwealth republics

Take the independence of Barbados declared in 2021 after decades of painstaking constitutional work behind the scenes. No armies. No battles. No confrontation. And no highly paid Inner Temple lawyers.

Yet their achievement is very relevant for Scotland. It wasn't a desire to keep being ruled by Her late Madge that kept Barbados inside the Commonwealth with the British monarch as head of state – it was the difficulty cutting through a deep thicket of constitutional law that has embedded the British sovereign at the centre of many ex colonial legal systems. Even large, formally independent and mature democracies like Canada and Australia are finding it nigh on impossible to unpick that final and apparently most innocent measure of British control. And that's the big reason 15 Commonwealth realms with the British monarch as head of state, didn't immediately follow Barbados, dump the British monarch and elect a President. Not grudging respect for King Charles or even an enduring fondness for the late Queen, but the massive difficulty of unpicking Britain's monarchy from their own constitutions despite dispensing with colonial rule last century.

Barbados actually became independent in 1966, but it took another half century of painstaking constitutional work to finally and completely jump ship. Now Jamaica has embarked on the same patient path of constitutional unpicking. And the Prime Minister of the Bahamas – directly after signing the Queen's book of condolences – declared his intention to hold a referendum on turning his nation into a republic as well.

Before that, Jamaica will have to comprehensively review its original 1962 constitution, analysing charters that relate to fundamental rights and freedoms before electing a head of state. It's already created a new Ministry for Legal and Constitutional Affairs to handle the task. But when the legal work is complete, Jamaica must hold a referendum, scheduled for 2025, where at least two-thirds vote in favour, to finally become a Republic — just another of the hurdles built into the country's original constitution by Westminster.

The Australian central bank has announced that a portrait of Queen Elizabeth II on its $5 note will be replaced by a piece of Aboriginal artwork – not an image of King Charles.

Canadian public opinion is also drifting away from the British monarchy. Polling in 2022 showed 51 percent of

Canadians want a republic and 77 percent feel no attachment to the British monarchy. But removing the Crown would require the approval of several state legislatures and a massive constitutional overhaul. Most treaties with indigenous peoples were signed with the British Crown, not the Canadian government. As observer Jonathan Malloy puts it, Canada went down this road in the '80s and '90s and the country nearly collapsed amidst all the competing demands.'

Other failed republic referendums include Australia in 1999, the Bahamas in 2002 and 2016, St Vincent and the Grenadines in 2009, Grenada in 2016 and 2018, plus Antigua and Barbuda in 2018. These bids for total independence all shared the same basic problem – the prospect of massive constitutional upheaval and the fear that unscrupulous politicians might exploit that unrest.

What's the point of all this?

The enduring presence of the British monarch as head of state in former colonies has less to do with admiration or sentiment and more to do with difficulties of departure, hardwired into Commonwealth constitutions by canny Brits. Anyone hear a bell ringing?

Still, if tiny Jamaica does the legwork to remove the British monarch as head of state, it will re-ignite debate in larger democracies. Especially if the Royal Family embarks on another charm offensive like the one that recently backfired, when Will and Kate's 2022 Caribbean tour went down like a lead balloon. From photos of the young royals shaking hands with Jamaican children through wire fences, to the military parade in which the pair stood, dressed in white, in an open-top Land Rover, the visit was seen by local politicians as a throwback to colonialism.

Can King Charles turn this around?

It probably isn't up to him. If an individual could reinvent deference, the late Queen Elizabeth would probably have managed. Yet quietly, amongst the former sugar and slave plantations of the British Empire, efforts to remove her as Head of State were progressing all the way though her apparently popular and friction-free reign.

Getting shot of Britain may not be easy, but that doesn't make supplication acceptable for nations trapped within the British realm.

According, to Jonathan Malloy:

> Commonwealth Realms face incredible challenges to leave the British monarchy. [That] is not mainly the result of current actions by the British monarchy, [but] structures of governance, directly attributed to the British Empire which still have deep ramifications for former colonies.

So, it's not just Scots battling an unwritten constitution which gives 'the world's most powerfully devolved parliament' no lawful route to an advisory referendum.

But it's worth being reminded about the reward for breaking free. According to Prime Minister Mia Amor Mottley, her nation's laws are no longer signed off by people neither born in Barbados, nor living there, nor able to appreciate the daily realities of its citizens.

Simple and powerful.

It's classic British nonsense to leave a former colony independent, yet not independent; able to leave Britain's control, yet not able to leave. To be part of an apparently smiling and contented Commonwealth and a real world of forced, rictus grins, with legions of lawyers working behind the scenes to cut ties that have constrained more than they have bound.

In the end it amounts to this.

If Scotland wants to join the 65 countries that have claimed independence from the British Empire or United Kingdom, we are different enough to qualify.

It's the hope that kills you

Ok, by now there may be grudging acceptance that a rain and wind-rich country is not such a bad bet after all, that

Scots are no more innately argumentative than anyone else, that our country's settled will is different enough to justify independence and that the best resolution for any Caledonian 'head/heart' divide is to stop facing two ways in one blinkin country for another confusing second.

But there's still one last dollop of poisonous mythology tangled round our national propeller.

When all else fails and there's no option but to accept that Scotland could make a perfectly good go of independence, there's always one reliable, gloomy old trope to fall back on.

It's the hope that kills you.

Now admittedly, that generally applies to Scotland's sporting efforts, but those who entered polling booths believing Yes might win in 2014 also know the pain.

How to respond? Well, you could join the cynics, divorce yourself from the collective efforts of folk all around, disassociate from troublesome hope-mongers, deploy gallows humour and *Trainspotting* 'Scotland is crap' levels of cynicism, settle down, give up and embrace quiet despair in the sure and certain knowledge it's better than entertaining vain hopes of change. We all know the script. But really?

The radio commentary before Scotland's February 2023 rugby match against Wales –after a second successive victory against the English at Murrayfield – was in another league of perverse pessimism, even for Scots. Because it was pretty obvious we were going to win.

Brilliant, straight-talking Irish-born commentator Tom English actually apologised for predicting that Scotland would beat the mighty Welsh, as if the merest whiff of hope and confidence would seal our collective fate. The Scots in the commentary booth groaned with theatrical, learned or genuine horror (hard to distinguish) as the veteran Irish commentator ploughed on, pointing out that Scotland on paper was infinitely the better team, even though they'd lost to Wales in the last three encounters.

Don't say it! Don't say it!

Ah, you've jinxed us.

It's like *Macbeth*. Ah no, look what you've made me say, now. We're all doomed.

Cue, much nervous laughter and a semi apology for his offensive optimism by Tom English... who went on to be 100 per cent right.

Savour again the headlines:

Six Nations Guide: Finn Russell shines as Scotland turn on the style to hammer Wales

BBC: Scotland blow away Wales to end Gatland hoodoo

Guardian: Russell and Steyn shine as ruthless Scotland flatten Wales in Six Nations

Scotsman: Finn Russell masterclass as Scotland storm past Wales to make it two wins out of two in 2023 Six Nations

Yip, it was suddenly good to be Scottish.

So why all the uneasiness about success?

It matters because it mirrors our continuing lack of confidence about independence.

On paper, we are dancing.

But in reality – we fear, we believe, feck it, we know – that everything will go wrong.

'Little we complain, though we suffer much', says the Gaelic proverb. And the Galloway-born essayist Alastair Reid (who spent much of his life in Spain and the States) captured the seemingly endless Caledonian capacity for gloom in this 1978 poem entitled 'Scotland':

Walking into town, I saw, in a radiant raincoat,
the woman from the fish-shop. 'What a day it is!'
cried I, like a sunstruck madman.
And what did she have to say for it?
Her brow grew bleak, her ancestors raged in their graves
as she spoke with their ancient misery:

'We'll pay for it, we'll pay for it, we'll pay for it!'[32]

Grim. Mind you, Reid's *Guardian* obituary in 2014 observed that:

Towards the end of his life, spending lengthy periods
of time in Scotland, Alastair was pleased to observe
that his poem was less relevant than it had once been.

Still.

There's a saying – the lighthouse attracts the storm. It's
not possible of course, but it can seem as if lighting a beacon
of hope invites the very threat it guards against. Certainly,
decades semi-following the men's national football team tends
to reward pessimism. And even that short mention, prompts
'Costa Rica' to spring to mind almost unbidden. For the
young or forgetful, Scotland was beaten by this tiny central
American state 1–0 at the start of the World Cup in 1990,
before staging a comeback with a spirited 2–1 win against
Sweden and competing well against Brazil, only to lose by a
late goal.

According to Maurice Malpas:

The Sweden game was a typical response from
Scotland. We had our backs to the wall, nothing to
lose and everything to gain. So, we went out and did
it. I think people might have preferred it the other
way round – if we'd beaten Costa Rica, they could
have accepted a loss to Sweden.

Strange old sausages aren't we?

How different the spirit in a tiny country a thousand miles
further north. Seven years ago, when Iceland beat England
in Euro 2016, the world witnessed a sub-Arctic nation of
just 330,000 out-perform a former footballing 'great' of 60
million. Two years later, the Icelanders qualified for the World

---

32 *Weathering*, Canongate Books, 1981.

Cup in Russia and came away from their opening game against twice (now thrice) World Cup winners Argentina with an astonishing one-all draw.

Iceland had a football world ranking of 130 in 2014, but leapt to 30th after that match – their first major tournament, and the smallest country ever to reach a major football final. By the way, there are only 21,500 registered football players in a country with 160,000 horses and 200,000 sheep.

So what's the secret of the Icelanders' success?

It isn't the terrain – 'a cacophony of sweeping volcanic hills, dried lava plateaus and ominous mountain ridges' means pitches are sand or gravel flatbeds of dried volcanic magma.

It isn't the climate – snow-laden winter months mean the Icelandic national team couldn't play on grass until 1957.

It's partly the growth of indoor stadiums in every village… and the phenomenal local support. One-eighth of Iceland's population travelled to France for Euro 2016 and 99.8 per cent of all Icelandic televisions were tuned in to watch. Icelandic fans are called 'Tólfan' ('The Twelve') because their unswerving support creates a twelfth player on the pitch. But the Tartan Army's equally remarkable dedication hasn't given such a lift to the Scotland team, so something else must be happening.

It is.

I got a whiff in 2018, walking past the national stadium in Reykjavik one night whilst in Iceland making a film. The full stadium, full car park, buses from distant towns like Akureryi (five hours drive away) and the roar of the crowd suggested it must be World Cup related. It was the Iceland Women's football team qualifying for the Women's World Cup by beating Slovenia in front of a packed stadium. When I asked an excited steward for the secret of the Icelander's success she said, 'the water' and winked. The fact women footballers are paid the same bonuses as the men, clearly helps.

But something even more fundamental happened to change the motivation of Icelandic teenagers more than 25 years ago, when a young researcher at the University of Iceland, called

Inga Dóra Sigfúsdóttir examined American research about addiction. It revealed clear differences between the lives of kids who took up drinking, smoking and drugs, and those who didn't. A few factors emerged as strongly protective: participation in organised activities – especially sport – played three or four times a week, total time spent with parents during the week (not just weekends), feeling cared about at school, and not being outdoors in the late evenings.

Other nations probably saw that research too. But Iceland put it into action. A new national plan was introduced called Planet Youth. It became illegal to buy tobacco under the age of 18 and alcohol under the age of 20, and tobacco and alcohol advertising was banned. Parents attended talks on the importance of spending time with their children every night, not just weekend 'quality time' and of keeping kids at home in the evenings. An outdoor curfew was placed on 13- to 16-year-olds after 10pm in winter and midnight in summer. It's still in effect today. State funding was massively increased for organised sport, music, art, dance and other clubs, so kids could feel part of a group and experience the power of natural highs. In Reykjavik, a Leisure Card gives families £250 per year per child to spend on recreational activities.

The results have been stunning.

Twenty-five years ago, Icelandic teens were among the heaviest-drinking youths in Europe. Today, they top the European league table as the cleanest-living. The percentage of 15- and 16-year-olds who've been drunk in the previous month plummeted from 42 per cent in 1998 to 5 per cent in 2016. Cannabis use fell from 17 to 7 per cent. Daily cigarette use plummeted from 23 to just 3 per cent.

Has this impacted on the outlook of Iceland football squads – men and women? You bet.

After the Euro 2016 encounter, Iceland coach and part-time dentist Heimir Hallgrimsson said:

What's changed for us? Our coaching, our facilities,

the way we train. There's an explanation for all of it. Scotland is a traditional football nation but that's maybe what keeps you down. Tradition.

Hallgrimsson is right in more ways than he could possibly know.

There's nothing magical about Iceland's success or Scotland's general ability to get so far and no further. Iceland jettisoned the traditions of elite sports when it decided to give priority to the whole life experience of youngsters in Iceland. Footballing success was almost a by-product of something far more important. Societal change.

By contrast, football in Scotland has traditionally been a male affair with an exclusive culture that stands apart from – and generally above – the interests of wider society. That's too narrow a focus.

We need a planned, financed, coordinated and politically endorsed programme that gives every child a brilliant after-school experience – be that football, swimming, judo, table tennis or a non-sporting option. That's what the Icelanders have quietly been doing for quarter of a century and it's worked. The World Cup qualifying teams of 2018 were the girls and boys of 1998 who pioneered the Planet Youth approach. They are the first fruits of Iceland's sporting turn-around.

The Iceland model is currently being tested in Scotland at 13 secondary schools across five council areas. Hopefully it will survive the current climate of cuts in public spending just as Reykjavik council continued funding Planet Youth throughout the near bankruptcy of 2008.

Mind you, if we learn something from Iceland it would be kinda payback, because the memorable chant of Iceland supporters during the 2018 World Cup – a 'Hú' clap with the rhythm slowly speeding up was 'borrowed' from Motherwell fans, and featured in an award-winning Coke ad, produced by Iceland's part-time goalie (and filmed by two Icelandic film crews) thereby reinventing the slow hand clap as a powerful Viking tradition. Just as Australian Mel Gibson spotted the story of William Wallace and invested cash, face-paint and some historically impossible meetings to have an international hit. Ownership may be nine-tenths of the law, but energetic, imaginative use can trump everything else.

But, the main takeaway from this Icelandic tale isn't the need for more energy, taking back our chant or puckering up. Confidence doesn't work like that. The lesson from the Icelanders is that organisation and practice win the day. Disappointing, eh?

But key.

Self-belief is self-generated, not attached by well-meaning others. Scotland won't generate self-belief by a modern version of the Highland Charge – running hell for leather in the hope that noise, determination and a strategically-timed musket volley will disperse the opposition. Effective (and well-organised) as the Highland Charge once was, the advent of firearms demanded a different approach and the confidence to abandon old ways and seek out new forms of organisation.

On the eve of independence, here we are again.

Simply put, the lack of self-belief that bedevils many Scots, arises from lack of experience. Remember Malcolm Gladwell's ten thousand hours thesis? Who in Scotland – until the trade unions of last century and the community buyouts of recent years – has spent ten thousand hours in charge of anything?

Our forebears lived on land owned by someone else.

The language they spoke was banned by someone else.

Their ability to stay was decided by someone else.

Their children were saved from urban squalor by council houses – owned and managed by someone else.

And today we live in towns, villages and islands with a degree of remoteness from power that is unique in Europe – all run from somewhere else.

A nation of active, confident, connected sporting teenagers will do more for national morale than the biggest single victory at Murrayfield or Hampden. Of course, victory by elite athletes does inspire. But only if the watching masses are already active and eager to improve. Sadly, we're not.

A 2016 study of 38 nations saw Scotland's children ranked joint-last for physical activity – amongst the least active in the world despite having the 'very best' environment for playing outdoors. Admittedly, that was seven years ago, but a 2021 report by health experts was no better; 'Despite a decade of favourable policy, physical activity and health of children and youth has not improved.'

Against this 'stuck' backdrop, an inspiring performance by a great Scottish team just accentuates the gap between the healthy, motivated, organised elite and the spectating, isolated, passive masses.

The golfers Arnold Palmer and Gary Player are credited with the quote 'The harder I practise, the luckier I get.'

Maybe we could adapt that. The more we practise anything – and experience for ourselves how to take decisions and get organised – the more easily we accept responsibility and realise that almost anything is possible with teamwork.

Norway starts its kids early on this virtuous circle, with affordable kindergarten (often outdoors) from the age of two so that only children (now the majority) learn to share and take care of smaller bairns from the outset. We need to follow suit.

The kid goat's leap

I remember visiting the Bukkespranget Outdoor kindergarten in Tromsø, five years ago. The word means the 'kid goat's leap' and describes the small but adventurous physical steps children are encouraged to take every day. Sitting in the early morning darkness at 'drop off time' around an open fire (wearing a borrowed, all-in-one snowsuit since I was too daft/unprepared for the outdoors to have one of my own), I was chatting to kindergarten owner Turid Boholm when one of the kids clambering on a low climbing frame behind us fell into the snow with a soft thud. Almost on autopilot I was up, but on a faster auto-pilot Turid sat me down again. One of the slightly older children – maybe five years old – came over to help the younger bairn. There was no damage done – the team take care to remove stumps and stones so there are only 'small learning accidents' – and play continued with the children cheerfully sorting themselves out. Staff are constantly watching but they leave space for children to care for one another. So learning is a constant feature but not learning the three 'R's – that comes later, at the age of six or seven when children are ready. The kids at kindergarten are learning something far more important – confidence built through plenty of small, shared adventures.

Doing. Not just watching the elite.

As a fairly headstrong and taller than average lass, I didn't understand the hesitation caused by too much watching till an encounter on the fabulous, boulder-strewn beach of Rackwick on Hoy in Orkney. The only way across was to run, skipping skilfully from foot to foot and rounded boulder to boulder without stopping, thinking about it too much or worrying. That's what I generally did until Rackwick, when my boyfriend set off just ahead of me. Suddenly, coming second, I had a profoundly different experience – watching as he nearly fell, nearly missed his footing, nearly had too large a gap to skip before the next boulder. All I could see were problems and the multiple ways he might fall – all he saw was the next step, which he took successfully time after time. The difference between us – he was doing, I was watching. In life, you need a mixture, otherwise danger seems to be lurking all around.

Watchers become worried, hesitant and keen to overprotect and regulate. Doers get frustrated because left to their own devices, solutions so clearly offer themselves up.

I remember climbing the Sutherland peak of Suilven – there's a long walk in and I had started late (as usual), so arrived a bit knackered at the foot of the near vertical-looking mountain with its famous domed top. I couldn't see any path up at all, which was a bit discombobulating. I would probably be the last one up that day, climbing solo on a mountain with a very dodgy, narrow summit ridge.

So, I didn't want to be on a path less travelled. This was an oft climbed hill, so there had to be a way to follow in others' footsteps. After a wee while walking backwards and forwards and consulting the map, I took the first step up the hill and there, suddenly in front of me, was the next. Nothing more by way of a path – until I took the next step and so it went on, one step at a time, all the way to the top.

Which was indeed one of the narrowest summit ridges I have every crawled along, humming 'Buffalo Soldiers' by Bob Marley for courage and distraction. Ahem.

Solutions present themselves when you begin.

Or as Goethe put it, 'Whatever you dream you can do. Begin it. Boldness has genius, power and magic in it. Begin it now.'

Unfortunately, Scots have experienced far too much watching and not enough beginning, stuck indoors at the premature age of five and even four, unlike 82 per cent of the world's countries whose schools start at six or seven when children can control motor functions, sit still and concentrate on formal learning. Our early starting age, shared by kids across Britain, is a relic of the world's earliest Factory Acts, which let women be put to work in factories and provided school as a place to stash their children. That's why other countries with a starting age of four and five are generally British colonies. Only one country has never cared about the evidence on developing confidence amongst children.

We live in it.

Happily, Scotland has finally dusted down its collective thinking with the last SNP conference adopting six/seven as a school starting age – a pivotal moment in Scottish politics and public life. If that pledge gets delivered, with better pay and training for staff, local organisation and plenty of parental involvement, we will be a lot further forward in every aspect of young lives – including football.

Not relying on hope, courage or bravado amongst the

next generation, but producing better organisation of their early years.

Let's encourage our kids to become the best participants they can be in any sport and at any level – even if that means our elite teams are initially mediocre by world standards and don't win medals or even entry to European competitions. Let's develop the activity, skills and potential of the whole population like Iceland and leave some other poor sods to produce the world's most watched club football, watched by an unfit, sedentary home population forced to pay through the nose, simply to look on.

Then it won't be the hope that kills us, because far less will ride on the performance of elite teams and if they lose, we know our young folk will learn and progress.

So, we can hirple on as we are, with all the frustration and anger generated by a life on the sidelines – or we can do something about it.

Scots have been made civic bystanders by political structures that centralise power while offering communities the unpalatable choice between stepping up to become buyout superheroes or having no say whatsoever in their local domain.

Community councils (average budget £400) are utterly ignorable while regional councils – the largest in the developed world – do everything. *Blossom* devotes a great deal of space to this problem, but it's pretty clear central control has robbed Scots of the vital, confidence-building experience of running communities which in turn has hollowed out confidence in our ability to run Scotland.

There's not been nearly enough practice, experience, ownership, control, empowerment and recovering from mistakes – the most powerful way to learn – to laugh that doubt away.

Perhaps that's why so much seems to turn on the identity and capacity of one person – the First Minister. If the mass of people are deemed incapable of heavy lifting– or expect to be left on the sidelines – the very hard work of delivering independence will fall on a tiny pair of shoulders. Why?

When you look at Finland, Iceland, Norway and Estonia – countries that became independent over the last century – they built on powerful local government and widely dispersed land ownership. Essentially, the local independence they already experienced generated the drive for national independence.

Scotland is experiencing precisely the opposite.

In sport, in life and the political domain, exclusion makes Scots pull their punches, undershoot, underimagine and ultimately, underperform. It is the ultimate vicious circle. But can it be circumvented?

Well, the answer is there in every community buyout.

And on 11 Feb 2023, the answer was there on the pitch at Murrayfield, when Scotland beat Wales 35–7. As predicted.

But what happened next?

A small amount of joy and a lot more anxiety because success had just created yet more troublesome hope, including the harder-to-handle possibility that Scotland might now win the Six Nations – yip, the ENTIRE SERIES. Nightmare.

The thinly disguised terror and chittering nervous laughter provoked by this possibility was harder to bear than watching the match.

But after the stunning victory against Wales, that relentless, negative, collective inner voice became almost audible. Star players Kyle Steyn and Duhan van der Merwe aren't really Scots – they're South African-born and only qualified by playing for Glasgow and Edinburgh clubs. Jings, if three months made folk Scottish enough for a vote in the indyref, what's un-Scottish about joining the gang after living here for three years? And by the way how many Irish fans were moaning when the late Jack Charlton steered their country to World Cup success through his 'flexible' interpretation of the Granny Rule?

But if you suspect – if you know that your team is going to lose – it takes something beyond bravery to keep watching.

And that's what the prospect of independence feels like to

many people. They share the same deep-seated conviction that despite our good form on paper, all the oil, all the windpower, all the whisky, indeed the whole damn barrel-load of advantages, somehow Scotland will feck it up. It's impossible to gainsay this argument with statistics or fill such a confidence vacuum with facts and figures about Scotland's potential.

Consistent success may transform the outlook of new generations. But they still have us oldies to reckon with. The folk who know Scotland is not designed to win.

Why?

Because we know what winners look like – Old Etonians who come ready fitted with brassneck and the cavalier, entitled approach of folk who don't need to try too hard in this world.

Measured against them, and living in their competitive, dog eat dog world, we know that we don't have what it takes. No killer instinct. No ability to muscle everyone else off the park, or talk ourselves up like airheads. Yes, there are occasional toe-curling bouts of nervous boasting. Yet the Scottish Cringe and the Scottish Brag are two sides of the same coin. They speak of an endless anxiety about performance. An inability to just be. And unless we confront the origins of this damaging lack of confidence, we will continue to undermine ourselves, whatever the constitutional set up.

We all know where we are in life when Scotland comes second. We know what it's like to have a potential that never quite gets realised. Because that's where we are in the United Kingdom. And that 'also-ran' status won't change until our ideas about success are radically overhauled. What does real confidence look like – the dogged, determined and sometimes unsuccessful Andy Murray or the swaggering leaders of Britain PLC?

It's high time to reassess.

Real confidence doesn't have to be right all the time. It can admit mistakes. Can take the lead without dictating to everyone else. Can be flexible – embarking on journeys without every i dotted or t crossed. Can be generous. But can also work very, very hard in pursuit of a vision.

If confidence is redefined as something different to the blustering Downing Street model, we might discover that many Scots already have it in quiet, modest spades, just like our European cousins.

I remember being part of a marine energy consortium based in the Netherlands which tried to locate tidal turbines at key sites around Scotland's coastline. The Dutch guys were no slouches. Their turbines are placed in almost every river system in the Netherlands, cleverly located on sluice gates along the Isselmeer, which makes them easier to remove for maintenance and repair. Yet when it came to bidding within the UK system they were floored.

We don't get any work – the director complained – because we simply don't know how to brag. We don't know how to oversell ourselves wildly. We don't know how to exaggerate and manufacture claims we cannot back up. We're not used to lying. We're used to making small incremental progress over a period of time – not promising the Earth.

Across Europe, modest, collaborative realism tends to outperform noisy, self-important bragging every time. It just cannot win contracts in the Anglo-Saxon world.

Is that really the domain Scots want to inhabit? One that sees the loudest mouths win – where our own natures put us at a permanent disadvantage?

What version of success do we hug towards us? The kind we cannot deliver – locking in glorified failure for another generation – or the kind we can deliver easily. The kind every other culture manages. The kind you get competing on a level playing field without embarrassing, inflated claims of inherent greatness. The kind you work for and deserve. The kind that blew Scots oot their chairs the length and breadth of the country on 11 February 2023, when the jinx finally ended and Scotland beat Wales by a thumping margin.

C'mon.

Let's tilt the scales in our own favour, get decision-making power decentralised so control is experienced as widely, locally and early in life as possible.

Let's have the hope, feel the fear and do it anyway.

Like everyone else.

PART TWO

The State of the Kingdom

SO, WITH BAGGAGE hopefully semi-parked, where are we on the vexed question of independence and the union?

Obviously, it'll take time to see how the departure of Nicola Sturgeon, John Swinney, Peter Murrell and the old guard pans out and Humza Yousaf settles in with his new cabinet.

But one thing's certain.

Irrespective of SNP leader, around a half of Scots can visualise a radically different future, despite daily media 'critiques' of the Scottish Government, independence and nine long, frustrating, campaign-free years.

That's not a failure – it's a minor blinkin' miracle.

No matter how many googlies have been bowled or difficult questions raised about the process of creating a new state, half of Scotland's population hasn't slacked off.

Perhaps that's because there's been seismic change in the relative strength of the constitutional players involved in our future – the nation of Scotland, the Kingdom of the UK and the cool, wee neighbours to the west, north and east of us, especially Ireland.

Back in 2014, Scotland was only seven years into life as a 'government' not an 'executive' – a small but significant change in the name and aspirations of the Scottish Government made by Alex Salmond. That year, the hated bedroom tax had only been mitigated by Holyrood for a few months and the suite of welfare powers that currently shield the vulnerable from Westminster did not even exist. The idea of a Scottish Child Payment targeting help at poor families was a pipe dream. And of course, the idea of independence as a popular option was very new. It's hard to remember a time before the constitutional issue became the main predictor of voting intentions. That's how much Scotland has changed. We're not arguing about the ends any more, we're arguing about the means.

Belief in Westminster – abandoned

Over a decade, the nation of Scotland has continued to develop a social democratic outlook that's completely at odds with Westminster past, present and foreseeable future. Westminster itself has seen a total collapse in standards of governance, public services, trust and GDP, forcing Labour onto the most right-wing, 'centre' ground this country has ever seen. Meanwhile, Scotland's small, same-sized neighbours have moved from the hazy, underexamined background to the foreground as positive examples of what life might be like for Scots after the UK. That includes Ireland, avoided completely during the first indyref because of its vexed history of partition and violence but drawn into the debate wholeheartedly now – partly because of Brexit but mostly because of the extraordinary, problem-solving abilities of the Irish themselves.

In short.

Over the decade since the first indyref campaign, Britain, Scotland and Ireland (plus our go-ahead Nordic neighbours) have changed position on the starting grid. When the chequered flag falls again – as one day it will – Britain will not automatically occupy pole position. That's quite a result, and explains why no mainstream political party will easily countenance another referendum. They know they'd likely lose. It's this changing constellation of forces that's the real driver of independence. As journalist Neil Mackay wrote in the *Herald*:

> How can anyone who loves Britain support what the Tories have done? Why support 'Britain', if the British Government is killing the very notion of what it means? Why not imagine a new country where the old ideas of what made Britain great can be protected or reconstructed?

Quite.

The collapse of everything precious about the post-war settlement would leave Scots as depressed and rudderless as the rest of the UK, if we hadn't been building an escape route for the last decade – a new state of our own. As psychological surveys in conflict zones show, people can thole almost anything if they have a shared goal that seems attainable and worthwhile.

Unionist politicians can't make a fresh start for Scotland look worthless, so they've concentrated on making it seem unattainable. But many unattainable things have come to pass.

Nelson Mandela was eventually released by an apartheid government that handed over power peacefully.

Despite a lifetime's enmity, the Rev Ian Paisley and Martin McGuinness made power-sharing work. And when Stormont resumes there will be a Sinn Fein First Minister.

After hundreds of years controlled by absentee lairds, the people of Eigg doubled the population in 25 years as owners.

Stuck things do release.

It may take time, luck, unexpected events, friendships and special personalities.

But change does happen.

So will Yes-leaning Scots keep the faith or eventually forget the offensive, blustering nonsense of Boris Johnson as PM and the ludicrous charade of Liz Truss at the helm. Will we conclude our lives are safe in their hands again? Can we unsee what we have seen or un-dream a better country? Do we think a Keir Starmer-led government can tackle the fundamentals, turn the clock back on decades of privatisation and put things right within one term in office, before the Tories bewitch English voters again as they always unaccountably do?

In a word, no.

Some things have changed profoundly and irrevocably since 2014.

Ask any Scot if they have confidence in the Westminster Government, and you'll find no-one, except the odd card-carrying Tory. That's a seismic but silent revolution in political attitudes. Confidence has been detached from Westminster, though not completely attached to the idea of independence. Not yet.

Still, that's step one in the change process.

Of course, some think Keir Starmer might get things working again, if he wins the next election.

But that wildly optimistic outlook overlooks the deeply-embedded nature of the decisions that have locked Britain onto its current, unequal, isolated, scapegoating path. It didn't take a year or even a decade to get to this sorry pass. It won't take a year or a decade to reverse out of it. Especially when a sizeable chunk of the English electorate thinks nothing much is actually wrong.

Consider the roll call of ministers who've screwed up, got caught out but carried on. How is that even possible?

A judge found Matt Hancock had broken the law by concealing Covid contracts awarded to chums who were ten times more likely to be fast-tracked and successful. But the former Health Secretary survived to 'star' on *I'm a Celebrity* – encouraging such delusions about his own popularity that he handed WhatsApp messages to an anti-lockdown journalist co-writing his biography, who promptly published them. Hancock had already decided not to stand again as an MP, since the Tories are clearly going to be whauped and he's not that dumb. But the revelation he spent hours salvaging his ministerial career after being caught snogging a colleague should halt any invitations to board the consultancy gravy train. I'll bet it doesn't. In short, there's no getting rid of Matt Hancock from English public life.

Ditto former Home Secretary Priti Patel – found guilty of bullying.

Or the whole DWP, judged to have acted unlawfully over Universal Credit.

Or the comeback kid Robert Jenrick who unlawfully fast-tracked a Richard Desmond property deal, saving the Tory Party donor £40m in community charge payments and gaining a new job as Immigration Minister, into the bargain.

Or Dominic Cummings with his almost forgotten regulation-busting trip to Barnard Castle. Or Boris Johnson, whose lying to parliament, partying through lockdown and unlawful proroguing of parliament torpedoed what was left of Britain's international reputation.

Bending the rules, breaking the rules, chancing their arms and sacrificing one another when the going gets rough – it's all par for the course and even provokes a bizarre grudging respect from Tory voters.

To gain Alpha Male credentials in the Nasty Party, serial rule-breaking is the order of the day. If you won't run rough-shod over procedure, make it up as you go along, insist white is black, black is white and stab the next guy in the front, then you aren't right for the Inner Circle. Look at the wee smirks when they're caught red-handed.

Governance, for the English ruling class, is a game.

Governance for Scots has always meant so much more.

John Smith used 'settled will' to describe the consensus behind home rule and devolution at the Labour Party conference in 1994. But in the quarter of a century since Holyrood re-opened for business, that consensus has deepened to become a collective Scottish belief in social democracy – made easier to discern by the stark contrast with successive sell-yer-granny Conservative and even occasional Labour governments at Westminster. Scots can almost see their kind of country now. They vote for it at every election. And are infuriated when over-budget ferries and outcomes 'only' equal to the UK average blot that fast-developing Celtic copybook.

That's step two in the change process – the outline of an alternative state is now clearly visible.

Of course, unionist parties insist a social democracy can still thrive within a centralised conservative state.

I suppose in a hesitant way, it can.

Using our precious time and energy to battle right-wing ideologies, it's possible.

Without any warning of sudden, international law-breaking

wheezes by the unelected (by us) occupant of Number Ten – I guess.

Without forewarning or consultation about future budgets.

And for so long as glacial progress feels like some kind of result – of course.

But is that thriving or just ticking over? And which are Scots aiming for today?

The truth is hard to avoid.

Scotland and England – two different countries

They were different states whose leaders papered over the cracks to create one union.

Over the last 20 years of devolution, the cracks have reappeared.

When Scots have had the slightest chance to decide, we have opted for:

No academy schools.

No three-star hospitals.

No Virgin-run health trusts.

No privately owned water companies.

No privately owned rail companies.

No tuition fees for higher education.

No prescription charges.

What is this, if not another country?

Ah well, critics might respond, the United Kingdom is a union of equal but different...

Dinnae wind me up. Why is Scotland so different from the rest of the UK?

Well, are you really so different...

Son, 63 per cent of MPs in England are Tory. 10 per cent of MPs in Scotland are Tory.

But that's because...

Scotland is another country. Always has been, always will be.

Seriously, what other explanation is there?

These differences once described the shape of Scots'

simmering resentment. They now describe the shape of our settled will.

It's an expectation across all Scottish parties including the Scottish Tories, that key services and natural assets should stay in public ownership. Political debate here revolves around how best to finance, maintain and extend that – not whether public services are a good thing.

After all, Scotland gave birth to the trade union movement and the Labour Party, so public ownership is in our political DNA. But since no one lives simultaneously on both sides of the border, Scots cannot realise how different things have become south of the border, where the privatisation of the English health system has all but destroyed it.

In 2010, the English Health Secretary, now British Chancellor Jeremy Hunt, presided over the biggest ever collapse in NHS spending in 2010, when the usual 4 per cent above inflation increase was slashed to 1 per cent. Some English health trusts went bankrupt as a result, others took out loans and some essentially handed control over to private companies like Virgin Care. Junior doctors went on strike, removing emergency care for the first time in NHS history when Hunt ended overtime payments for weekend work – hastening today's crisis where tens of thousands of doctors' vacancies remain unfilled. Indeed, Jeremy Hunt's semi-privatised health trusts ran up such crippling levels of debt that £13.4 billion was quietly written off during the second week of lockdown. Nice work.

But you can bet your bottom dollar you'll never hear any of that mentioned in the customary, flailing BBC interviews about problems in the NHS. Or Virgin Care's decision to sue NHS England in 2016, because its three-year £82 million healthcare contract was not renewed but awarded to a group of in-house NHS providers and a social enterprise – as it blinkin' well should be. Unfortunately, to avoid the high costs of legal action, the six Surrey clinical commissioning groups caved in and agreed an out of court settlement with Virgin, which has never disclosed the amount it won.

Maybe Virgin used the ill-gotten gains to set up the kitty that financed their next legal challenge three years later – suing the British Government for being stripped of the lucrative West Coast rail franchise. This time though Sir Richard Branson lost. But dinnae fash. According to the *Sunday Times* Rich List, that year Dickie was worth around £4.5bn.

Would it not just be simpler to have a publicly owned railway? The break-up of British Rail in 1997 was meant to introduce healthy competition between private British companies to lower prices and improve services for passengers. Instead, rail ticket prices in the UK are amongst the most expensive in the world. The public ownership pressure group We Own It says passengers currently pay five times more for tickets than our European neighbours (as a proportion of salaries), even though Westminster subsidies to the rail sector have almost doubled since privatisation.

Meanwhile, these private rail companies have shelled out £1.2 billion in dividends to shareholders over the last five years, during which time 50 per cent of trains in the north of England arrived late. It is almost criminal.

The East Coast rail service though, has done pretty well. Taken into public ownership for five years, it generated £1 billion for the public purse, only to be re-privatised in 2014 and then re-nationalised in 2018. The Northern Rail franchise has also blossomed after being taken back from the German-based Arriva Rail.

But still the dogmatic, Tory government thunders on with its disastrous private ownership model. And here's the kicker. In 2019, only a fifth of train operating companies were owned and operated by British private companies or British government authorities. Four-fifths were owned by European state-owned companies like Nederlandse Spoorwegen, Deutsche Bahn, Trenitalia and the French state railway SNCF.

Taking back control. It would be funny if it wasn't so tragic.

Meanwhile, last year ScotRail was taken back into public ownership for the first time in 25 years. And despite Kate

Forbes' taunt about the poor performance of trains on Humza Yousaf's watch, punctuality has improved and the Scottish Government has quietly electrified lines across the central belt of Scotland and up to Perth and Dunblane in keeping with its climate change objectives.

There's a pattern here.

A private free-for-all in England v publicly-owned systems in Scotland.

But you'd need to be psychic or hovering across the border to get a fair comparison of the two. No interviewer or politician south of the border will acknowledge the fuel poured onto that privatised bonfire of the utilities by Brexit and the painful, pointless Osborne austerity experiment that stimulated no growth and did nothing to reverse Britain's abysmal productivity record.

The Tory philosophy – whether it's one nation, 'compassionate' or just Liz Truss – none of it has worked.

It's against the slow car crash in services south of the border that Scotland's new thinking and better systems should be judged – many of them like free personal care and Single Transferable Voting for council elections, actually introduced by Labour First Ministers.

Departures from UK norms by unionist leaders are significant because they prove Scotland's settled will exists far beyond the nationalist community.

Indeed, consider the recent rammy over Westminster's decision to block Holyrood's Gender Recognition Reform Bill (GRR). Most SNP and Green politicians were furious, obviously. But Scottish Labour MSPs were also beeling.

BBC Scotland's political editor looked stunned when Glasgow Labour MSP Paul Sweeney told him: 'It feels like a politically malicious act and I think it's about time Viceroy Jack got back in his box.'

A shocked Glenn Campbell responded: 'Viceroy?!'

Sweeney replied 'Yes, I think it's a deeply unusual act that's an affront to the parliament and this democratic institution.'

Sweeney was backed by Labour colleague Monica Lennon MSP who said Keir Starmer's expression of 'concern' about the bill was unhelpful, uninformed and undermined Scottish Labour; 'He didn't follow the evidence as we did.' And more recently, joining a chorus of protest against Labour's attack ads that claim Rishi Sunak won't jail child sex abusers, Ms Lennon said she wouldn't bow to pressure and, 'wheesht for a Labour government.'

Jings.

Indy supporters thought it was only us who (once) did that.

Still, nobody crosses their party leader in the run up to a general election unless something more important is at stake. And of course, it is. Not just the GRR bill but the authority of Scotland's parliament, and perhaps – even on this fraught issue – the country's settled will, which has generally had the energy to tackle thorny issues (and new ways of thinking) before dyed-in-the-wool Westminster gets around to it.

Anyway, whatever the public made of the GRR Bill, two thirds of MSPs backed it, including some Tories, whose UK Government then produced the Section 35 cosh to whack it o'er the heid – for the first time in the history of devolution.

This was not a boring, predictable bust-up between two political parties or even two governments, but between two parliaments with members of ALL parties in Holyrood defending a collective decision – whatever backtracking took place during the SNP leadership contest.

That level of agreement between erstwhile rivals is a settled will in action.

Even the Scottish Conservatives have supported the Scottish Child Payment which, once again, helps mitigate the cruelty of their own Westminster government. Scottish Tory leaders Ruth Davidson and Douglas Ross openly attacked Boris Johnson when he was the darling of the English right – and banned him from attending Scottish conferences or 'helping out' during their election campaigns. Of course, Johnson was massively unpopular here in ways neither he nor his London acolytes could fathom. But Davidson and Ross understood the Boris problem instantly and intuitively. Johnson was an arrogant chancer and a classics-spouting toff. If Scots couldn't thole the pompous Donald Trump – and they couldn't – Johnson stood no chance.

How could Davidson and Ross have understood that unless they were on a different political wavelength to their London bosses? More like pragmatic, welfare-state-supporting Nordic Tories and less like doctrinaire, state-dismantling Westminster 'colleagues' like Jacob Rees-Mogg who famously described the Tory Scottish leader as a 'lightweight'.

Sure – Ruth Davidson hated Boris so much she accepted his offer of a gong and a seat in the House of Lords, claiming £25k in expenses in one year despite making only four speeches. And Douglas Ross was so ready to axe Boris that he blotted his Scottish copybook for all time by suggesting Johnson might usefully stay until the Ukraine conflict has been resolved.

Ross might have private fantasies about turning Edinburgh into a Singapore-on-the-Forth-style tax haven. But we'll never know. That idea would get wild applause at the party's English conference and sink like a lead balloon in Scotland, because policy approaches within each unionist party differ so markedly north and south of the border.

For Westminster Tories, proportional representation is a Very Bad Thing and for Westminster Labour Not a Priority. But for Scottish Tories it's the only reason they got ANY seats in Holyrood for the first 15 years and for Scottish Labour it's the system they embedded in each devolved assembly, going further in Scotland with STV for council elections in 2003, at a time UK Labour was hopelessly split over a far less proportional system of Alternative Voting for Westminster.

Scottish Labour has never recovered from Johann Lamont's Tory-sounding talk of Scotland's 'something-for-nothing society' and her revelation about being treated like leader of a 'branch office' by her own party. But UK Labour feels no fear as it draping itself in the Union Jack, cuddles up to conservatism, and mimics Tory slogans and policies – Starmer's ridiculous 'Take Back Control Bill' is the most toe-curling example – even if that leaves Anas Sarwar working hard to represent Scotland's pro-EU majority as his London boss 'moves on' from Brexit.

To be fair, Labour is not just straining to find agreement between Edinburgh and London.

Let's hear it for Mark Drakeford

In 2021, Welsh Labour leader Mark Drakeford said the United Kingdom was 'over' and called for a new 'voluntary association of four nations' instead. Jaws at Labour's London HQ hit the ground as the Welsh First Minister called a spade a bloomin' shovel, and parliamentary sovereignty a redundant notion. 'The idea that sovereignty is held only in one place and is handed out to other places, but always on a piece of string so it can be pulled back to the centre at any moment when the centre requires, I think that is over,' he said.

Amen.

'The European Union but potentially also Canada, Australia, or the United States, are examples of what I'm talking about, where sovereignty is dispersed amongst its component parts and pooled back together for central purposes.'

Yip – the f-word federalism again. The concept totally and utterly ignored when Gordon Brown's long-awaited damp squib of a Constitutional Commission was finally unveiled in December 2022.

Unionist parties have no bright ideas about the future of the UK. But whilst the path to independence currently looks stuck, the growing strength of the country's settled will is something to behold.

When Scottish political leaders go agin it, they come a cropper.

When crazy right-wingers offend against it – generally in the Commons – they are dismissed as political aliens.

And ironically, its power is underestimated in Scotland

precisely because it is so rarely challenged – unless an ill-advised quip on a rare Scottish visit by a scared Westminster leader sharpens focus. Suddenly, with the dull clack of a clumsy confrontation, Scotland's own way of doing things becomes clear again. Like reflective armbands, picked out by headlights, even on the darkest night.

Westminster helps Scots locate, test and rejoice (quietly) in our own governance systems. We know now, they do things differently down there and they always will. Heavens, they elect Jacob Rees-Mogg.

So, here's the thing.

Can Scotland – a social democratic nation – thrive in an isolationist conservative state, intent on axing Human Rights laws, hellbent on further privatisation and determined to steamroller away the standards of the EU (still adhered to in Scotland) in the forlorn hope of swinging a few more miserable trade deals?

Of course, we can tick over, try hard to escape the race to the bottom and the pointless competition hard-baked into every British default over the last century. But thrive?

With political control scattered across two such radically different outlooks – governance in Scotland is often like pulling fruit out of a currant bun.

Messy and knackering.

Any number of recent events provide proof.

The Supreme Court in November 2022 decided Holyrood doesn't have the power to hold its own lawful advisory referendum. Nor will a Holyrood or Westminster election result persuade Westminster to gie us a loan of their Section 30 powers, as they did in 2014. The 'Mother of Parliaments' and the courts have decided the union is Hotel California so Scots can check out – but never leave.

And since independence supporting Scots will never stop trying, London's 'computer says no' approach means energies that should be expended on a green transition will now be spent strategising for another lawful vote. It will eventually be worth it – but what a colossal waste of time.

Even house-trained poodles have more room for manoeuvre than the Scottish Parliament.

So, should we just settle for what we've got? After all, different nations exist within other states that function as relatively united kingdoms or republics. But that's generally because they've done what Mark Drakeford suggests and embraced truly powerful devolution and federalism, decades ago.

Belgium has three 'regions' as autonomous as the American states and three official languages: Flemish, French and German.

The Faroe Islands have been able to sign international treaties since 1946, and opted out of EU membership (and the Common Fisheries Policy) when 'mothership' Denmark joined in 1973. That's powerful devolution.

The mighty Republic of Germany consists of 16 states within a federal structure created in 1949 to distribute power and prevent another wholesale Nazi-style takeover. Ironically, British civil servants were in the lead. But having turned Germany into a model of distributed power via a federation that soon became an economic powerhouse, our guys came back to Britain, cracked open the Pimms and let the sluggish, centralised state of Britain moulder on.

Basically, some states can adapt to contain multitudes.

Britain is not one of them, mostly because parliamentary sovereignty will not allow Westminster to be 'undermined' by a competitor parliament – be that Brussels, Belfast, Cardiff or Edinburgh.

So, Scotland's settled will is at odds with the archaic British default.

That was the case long before the vote in 2016.

But Brexit proved to be the tin lid.

The Brexit effect

Don't worry. This is not a blow-by-blow re-enactment of the most perverse, often tedious and self-harming political decision of recent times. Nor an unadulterated paeon of praise for Brussels. Just an invitation to consider what the Brexit vote on 23 June 2016 actually laid bare – in black and white voting figures and in the full glorious, technicolour of identity and political belief.

The day after the EU referendum, the 'United Kingdom' ceased to exist.

Like land after an earthquake, a political fissure appeared at the border. A rupture that's grown deeper and more unbridgeable with time.

On either side – two different countries. Poles apart.

And I'm not talking about the Irish border, since, in general terms, Northern Ireland and the Republic agree. Whatever the hysterics from out of step Ulster Unionist leaders, the bulk of NI citizens voted Remain, chiming conveniently with neighbours and long-standing EU members, Ireland.

No, the Brexit chasm occurred along the older land border between England and Scotland. Agreed – it wasn't of great interest to a stunned UK media at the time, adjusting suddenly to the unexpected reality of life outside the EU. Nor was it the subject of mass protests by Scots who'd grown wearily accustomed to voting one way (left) and getting another direction entirely (right) for most of the last century. But nonetheless, an astonishing thing appeared on 23 June 2016. A Brexit voting cliff-face. Look at the map. Is it really a United Kingdom?

This map of voting by council area – produced by the douce BBC – reveals a revolutionary truth.

Given the same exposure to the same propaganda, the same slogans on the side of a bus, the same false promises and the same hysteria about 'Brussels rule' – Scots voted Remain while English folk voted Leave. Ditto Wales while Northern Ireland voted Remain.

But Scotland was the UK's democratic outlier – gobsmackingly unanimous at council level and nearly unanimous at ward level – with the exception of six wards in the fishing towns of Banff and Buchan, the Isle of Lewis and the Shetland islands of Whalsay and South Unst, where skippers had been fined for breaking EU fishing quotas. Without any great fandango, campaign or debate, Scots in all 32 council areas rocked up to vote Remain.

Even in councils dominated by fishing. Even in Tory wards right beside the border. From the Yessers of Glasgow to the

Figure 1: Remain/Leave voting by council area, June 2016

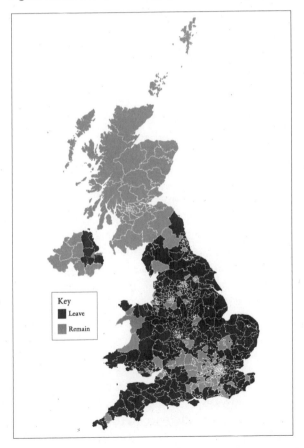

Key
Leave
Remain

No voters of leafy suburbs – every single council in Scotland went the same way. For EU membership. Together.

I'm sure John Smith would recognise this as another outing for Scotland's settled will. But that will has no way of being realised inside the United Kingdom – as the intransigence of the intervening seven years in Downing Street and the mealy-mouthed, cowering acceptance of Brexit by His Majesty's Opposition have amply demonstrated.

Scotland's vote went against the flow of voting in England.

But England doesn't really do dual controls, or any compromise with its smaller neighbours.

Unless, of course, a history of violence has helped produce an international peace agreement, taken so seriously by Joe Biden, there was no chance of a US trade deal ever happening, until Britain devised a 'Windsor Framework' to give Northern Ireland the best of both worlds – the deal the whole of Britain had until Rishi Sunak et al backed Brexit.

Still, every nation in the UK now has what it voted for in 2016.

Every nation except Scotland.

For us, it's either EU or UK membership. It cannot now be both.

Which is slightly weird.

Our views on Europe may not be the most important political difference between Scotland and England.

But it's the difference that happened.

The one that made world headlines.

The one with precisely measured dimensions.

The one that animated most European neighbours.

And the one with the highest-profile protagonists.

Unsurprisingly, Boris Johnson's blinkered determination to 'Get Brexit Done' remains as vivid in Europe's collective memory as Nicola Sturgeon's reasoned, dignified search for an alternative and her message to panicked European citizens in the immediate aftermath of the Brexit vote assuring them Scotland would always be home, if they wanted it to be.

No-one missed that difference in tone.

Including Remain-voting English neighbours.

Did our European neighbours understand why Scots wanted independence in 2014?

Probably not.

Do they understand now?

In a heartbeat.

All because of Brexit – the prism through which the rest of the world understands Scotland's democratic dilemma.

England is essentially a conservative country – currently favouring a kind of right-wingery that wouldn't be out of place in Poland or Italy. And though there may be occasional Labour interludes – during which privatisation, cronyism, anti-union laws, nuclear weapons, arms sales and inequality are half-heartedly discussed, but not tackled – the pendulum always swings back towards a party, outlook and vision most Scots have emphatically rejected since 1955.

True, the Conservatives were the official opposition at Holyrood until 2021. But that was an anti-independence vote rather than a ringing endorsement of their austerity, corruption and destruction of the welfare state.

Scotland is a social democracy trapped inside a conservative country.

Devolution hasn't the power to fix that – and that slowly dawning realisation has chiselled a political ravine between Britain's two biggest nations, clearly visible in voting behaviour the year before Brexit gouged the final gully.

Look at this map and tell me it's a 'United Kingdom'?

Brexit is just the tip of the political iceberg separating Scotland and the UK.

And more political and cultural difference is being uncovered each passing year.

But there's another fascinating quirk about Scotland's defiant Remain majority in 2016.

It was a near total reversal of our previous Euro vote.

Why Scots dumped Euro-scepticism

In 1975, Scotland contained the only 'No' voting regions in the British Isles – Shetland and the Western Isles. What are we like? Evidently, thrawn is too small a word.

So why the big change in 50 years? Many books and academic papers have been written on this subject.

But here's a thought.

It was Ted Heath, a Tory premier, who took Britain into the trading mechanism of the EEC in 1973. The referendum on his deal was delivered two years later by Labour's Harold Wilson, looking for voter endorsement of a mini renegotiation, not a whole new enthusiastic phase of Europeanism.

Popular English lefties Tony Benn and Michael Foot campaigned for a No vote and trade union leaders described the EEC as a 'boss club'. The SNP campaigned for a No vote after parliamentary leader Donald Stewart said the EEC 'represents everything our party has fought against: centralisation, undemocratic procedures, power politics, and a fetish for abolishing cultural differences.' Winnie Ewing said a vote for the Common Market would be like signing a 'death warrant.' Yip – the same Winnie who later became a celebrated MEP.

Bygones.

But maybe Scots were lukewarm about the EEC in 1975 because it looked like London/corporatist/ anti-trade union Tory wheeze.

It may have been a relatively unsubtle rule of thumb.

But in the days before Scotland had its own parliament, that thumb was all we had. It helped shape voting behaviour in Scotland for long leaderless decades, so dinnae knock it.

Of course, in 2016, Remaining in the EU was a Tory position – officially anyway. But Prime Minister David Cameron's lacklustre campaign was rapidly side-lined by the virulently anti-European Murdoch press and far-right actors like Nigel Farage. It rapidly became clear that Brexit opinion was right-wing opinion.

Figure 2: Election result, 2015

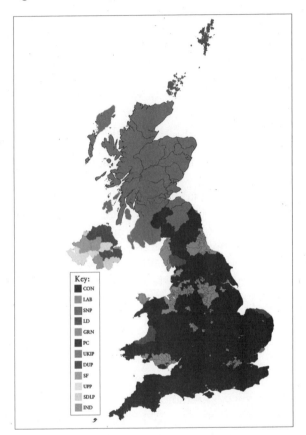

So, Scots once again exercised that rule of thumb.

With the far right gathering behind Leave, Scots were given the strongest possible motivation to vote Remain.

And so, in 2016, Scotland's collective thumbs up to Europe almost precisely mirrored England's collective thumbs down.

Of course, voting wasn't 100 per cent on either side. There was a large Leave minority sprinkled across the country – 38 per cent of the overall vote. Not large enough, to tilt the uniform yellow of Scotland's Remain result by council area.

Though to be fair, seven of the top ten Remain voting councils in the UK were actually in London (Lambeth, Hackney and Haringey with 75 per cent support, compared to 74 per cent in Edinburgh) and Belfast West. But the capital's overall 59 per cent didn't trump (sorry) Scotland's 62 per cent Remain vote.

1975 and 2016.

Are the Scots just a lot contrary and ready to support anything opposed by frothing English Tories? Or is the change in Scottish thinking about Europe deeper – is EU membership now part of our settled will?

Well there was the long, warm afterglow of watching deprived areas (and the whole of the Highlands and Islands) become beneficiaries of EU funds in the '70s and '80s.

Britain didn't seem to care – indeed Margaret Thatcher personally created the Proclaimers' list of precious, broken Scottish places – but the EU did. Its frameworks gave the marginalised special treatment. Whether that was 'less favoured area' status for hill farmers or the Committee of the Regions – a platform that gave 'sub-national' authorities a direct EU voice. As English planning academic Richard Williams observed, 'UK local authorities are accorded a stronger constitutional role within the institutions of the European Union than they are within the constitution of the UK.'

Indeed. And though Scotland only bagged three of the 24 'local and regional' seats, a prominent Scot – the late Charles Gray, Labour leader of Strathclyde Region – led the whole UK delegation.

The Committee of the Regions brought 'subsidiarity' to a sceptical and relentlessly top-down UK. It meant EU decisions had to be taken at the closest practical level to the citizen – not Whitehall – which caused successive Tory and Labour 'command economy' premiers to choke on their cornflakes. But it also had a specific impact here.

The same month Charles Gray headed the British delegation to the first Committee of the Regions in 1994, his local authority took on and defeated Margaret Thatcher with a postal referendum of Strathclyde residents on the privatisation of water and sewerage services. Seven out of ten voters returned voting papers – a whopping 1.2 million people – and 97 per cent voted against privatisation.

Now that's a result.

Two years later, an infuriated Margaret Thatcher swung the axe, abolished Strathclyde and replaced it with 12 smaller councils.

But Scotland's three water authorities remained in public hands and merged in 2002 to create Scottish Water – still a publicly owned water authority owned by the Scottish Government, in stark contrast to the privatised free-for-all in England where foreign investment firms, private equity, pension funds and businesses from tax havens own more than 70 per cent of the water industry.

Does that very different ownership model explain why only 14 per cent of rivers in England and Wales are in good biological health compared to 66 per cent of rivers in Scotland?

Fa kens. And Scottish Water is far from perfect.

But here the resource is in public hands – like most countries which regard water as too precious to be owned by private interests. Even in the US – whose agents travelled the world urging privatisation upon developing countries – water supplies rest safely in public hands.

In Scotland, we have Strathclyde Region's clever and feisty referendum to thank for being able to follow most of the world, not Thatcher's England. And quite possibly, Charles Gray had the Committee of the Regions to thank for finding the confidence to act. In Scotland, without our own parliament, Westminster Tories ruled the roost. In Brussels though, Conservatives were a relatively small grouping compared to Social Democrats and Gray's fellow council leaders either owned or managed their own water resources.

Did that empower the leader of Strathclyde Region?

Sadly, since he died in the winter of 2022, we'll never know for sure. But after his experience of saving Scottish water, Charles Gray's politics began to change.

In 2013 – despite being a member of the Labour Party from the age of 16 – he announced he'd vote 'Yes' in the indyref and urged all Labour supporters to do the same:

> I would appeal to all Labour supporters to grab this unique opportunity and vote for an independent Scotland so we can start to build the kind of country we want for our families and future generations based on social justice and fairness.

Amen.

Many older Scots also have warm memories of EU regulations acting as a shield to protect them from the worst excesses of Thatcherism. Speaking at events around Scotland in the last ten years, someone invariably points out they got overtime or paid holidays for the first time after EU membership, as Britain's grudging acceptance of the Working Time Directive finally gave workers here the same 'perks' that had become basic rights in mainland Europe.

The EU may well be the 'boss club' Scottish trade unionists opposed in the 1975 referendum. But the customary presence of proportional voting and thus negotiation and compromise (along with fully fledged welfare states and the odd revolution), all served to produce a slightly constrained capitalism at the heart of the EU and a boss class that maybe behaved better than the patrician fat cats of Britain. That's a sweeping generalisation, I'll grant you.

Perhaps it's fairer to say Labour and union figures felt happier in a European context where bosses expect to negotiate, not legislate strikes out of existence or cut opponents off at the knees.

Another factor explaining Scotland's Remain tilt was cross-party agreement in Holyrood about the need for more incomers not fewer, accompanied by a general distaste for the little Englander presumption that British culture is infinitely superior to everything else.

But of course, one of the biggest reasons for the pro-European stance north of the border was the 2014 indyref. Not just the broken promise that a No vote guaranteed continued EU membership, but the implicit message – agreed by both sides in the independence debate – that EU membership was in itself valuable and desirable. After all, why would the No camp sabre-rattle about independence ending EU membership if they didn't consider the EU to be a Very Good Thing?

Since the SNP's electoral platform was independence in Europe, the only debating point around EU membership in 2014 was whether it would still be possible after a Yes vote. I'd guess that universally endorsed presumption about the desirability of EU membership stuck with Scots – over two long years of indyref campaigning, two longer years of austerity and the meagre four months set aside for EU Referendum campaigning.

Scots were surrounded for this entire period with the heady scent of agreement across the Scottish political spectrum about the desirability of EU membership – even though not a whiff drifted south across the border.

So, in 2016, without a single pro-Brexit Scottish party leader, only two pro-Brexit members of the new Scottish parliament and UKIP polling just 2 per cent in Scottish elections, Scots were already politically primed to vote Remain.

It seemed like a no brainer. Which might explain the low turnout in Scotland, compared to England, where a very different, emotionally charged debate was taking place using Europe to explain the country's diminished post war status – all the EU's fault, of course. England was re-fighting 1066.

Scots were rubber-stamping the only thing agreed upon by all shades of political opinion in 2014 – the cultural, political, trading, research and employment importance of EU membership.

It was like two separate Brexit referendums – yet another indicator that Scotland and England are two separate countries.

Anyway, within the conventions that govern the UK, Scotland's very different Brexit result should have mattered.

Why?

A very short history bit.

A union of equals

The United Kingdom is based on the Treaty of Union 1707 which created a brand-new state, Great Britain, from the Kingdom of England (established 927 AD) and the Kingdom of Scotland, whose origins pre-date England by 84 years, ahem.

England absorbed Wales as a principality in 1536 (sorry). It did not absorb Scotland.

Thus, the flag of the new state combined the crosses of Scotland's patron St Andrew and England's St George. The Scottish Court of Session, the High Court of Justiciary, and the separate Scottish legal system all continued along with a Scottish Mint and Scotland's crown, sceptre, and sword of state remained at Edinburgh Castle.

There was a largely positive reaction in London where the Duke of Queensberry was seen as a hero. Sir John Clerk of Penicuik accompanied the Duke to London in April 1707 and recorded details of the enthusiastic reception the Duke received:

> From Barnett the ways were linned with the London
> Mobb, which (modestly speaking) cou'd not but
> exceed sixty thousand and by these we were welcomed
> and huzzad the whole way in such crowds that
> many of them were troaden to death & particulary a
> merchant of great substance who fell from his horse.

But on the streets of Edinburgh there was uproar and by 1713, the Union was so unpopular in Scotland that a motion was put forward in Westminster to end it, defeated by only four votes. Damn. Then followed the Jacobite Risings of 1715 and 1745 – and the brutal suppression of Highland culture after Culloden.

In 1801, another Act of Union combined the Kingdom of Great Britain with the Kingdom of Ireland. Partition after independence for the Irish Free State in 1922 prompted another name change – to the United Kingdom of Great Britain and Northern Ireland.

In fact, there have been 16 different states on these islands in the last 2,000 years.

But though Scots nobles were bribed and Scotland was coshed after the failed Rising by Bonnie Prince Charlie, Scotland's institutions were not subsumed lock, stock and barrel into the church, legal system, educational outlook, language(s) or legislative process of England. Separate bills have always been passed at Westminster to enact policy in Scotland, whilst poor old Wales was tacked onto the end of every Act passed in England. And as for Northern Ireland – it's been a branch of the Home Office for most of the last century. That's not to say Scottish bills were dramatically different from their 'England and Wales' counterparts. But the fact separate legislation was deemed necessary says something about the nation's enduring status.

Essentially, Scotland joined the union as a single country with most of its important institutions intact – as befitted a country that supplied a Stuart dynasty to occupy the vacant English throne. Scotland didn't join the union as a random bunch of one million – now 5.5 million – individuals. It joined as a country that had been a sovereign state in its own right for 864 years.

One more time – and at the risk of becoming extremely repetitive – the United Kingdom is a union of four nations.

A deck of four distinct suites, not 66 million individual playing cards.

That's why it doesn't matter if Scotland contains fewer folk than Yorkshire.

Scotland is a historic nation that helped create the modern United Kingdom (God love us).

Yorkshire is a region with a distinct personality but no constitutional identity within England or the UK (lambs).

Put bluntly, Scotland should have a union joker card.

Yorkshire – with all due respect – should not.

Or at least not until England catches a long overdue grip and stops being the most centralised country in Europe by genuinely devolving power.

But right now, Scotland is a constitutional player.
Yorkshire ain't.

And those are the Terms and Conditions which have been in force since the Treaty of Union and which were conveniently forgotten in 2016, when the Euro-friendly nation of Scotland was effectively told to shut it by the Euro-phobic nation of England.

And even though there is no special union warranty to enable a formal complaint, the rankling over Brexit is like the aftermath of 1707. With the difference that this time there will be no violent rising by Scots or advantageous trade deal from London to sweeten the pill.

Au contraire. Britain's post Brexit free trade deal with New Zealand contains none of the protections for local farmers included in the EU's trade agreement with the Kiwis, and Scottish farmers are steeling themselves for a deluge of imports. The British Government has agreed to allow 12,000 tonnes of New Zealand beef into the UK – that's four times the total allowed into all 27 EU members.

But hey, who cares?

Not former Trade Minister Penny Mordaunt, who responded to Scottish pleas for protection by announcing she'd axe all limits on imports in 15 years-time. Ok – she's as likely to be running the ship in 2037 as I am to be climbing Everest. Still, if you want to see livestock on Scottish hills – go see them now.

Chuck into this cauldron of Whitehall indifference, the Supreme Court ruling of November 2022, which prevented Holyrood from consulting its own citizens through a lawful referendum and suddenly, the heather was crackling.

The judges' verdict was presumed to be a massive setback for independence.

Whaur's yer indyref2 noo – snorted most of the Scottish press.

Whaur's yer voluntary union of equals – came the louder public retort.

Nicola Sturgeon's resignation, a fairly unedifying leadership contest and the election of Humza Yousaf as new SNP leader and

First Minister has seen support for independence fall – a bit.

And some weary Scots may be ready to give up and give in.

Maybe, this is just the way it is. Maybe might is right – England has 10 times our population, the UK has a take it or leave it attitude to everything – international law, parliamentary practice and Supreme Court judgements – we'll never get a referendum and without it we'll never get into the EU single market and become a new Ireland. Besides, Scots voted to stay in the UK, eyes wide open, in 2014.

Ah yes.

That famous, fateful promise that voting for the union would guarantee continuing EU membership whilst voting for independence would somehow guarantee exclusion. Of course, we quickly discovered the pledge was worthless.

But we should have seen it coming.

David Cameron was the architect of both polls – so the possibility of Brexit couldn't have crept up on him unawares. Indeed, he announced plans for an 'in-out' EU referendum on 23 January 2013 – 18 months BEFORE the indyref vote.

In short, Cameron was preparing to gamble away Britain's EU membership at precisely the time he was guaranteeing continuing membership to Europhile Scots.

Why wouldn't a compliant British electorate hop to it, do as they were told and vote Remain? Why would anyone believe the cigar-smoking, Enoch Powell-admirer Nigel Farage over a dapper Old Etonian? How could a generation of born to the manor Tories get beaten by a bus ad and a set of punky newcomers? Cameron's indyref promise to Scots about Europe was based on good old, lofty, public-school arrogance and was broken the minute English voters used the European vote to vent anger and despair over a stagnant, unequal society. Essentially the Scots voted on a pig in a poke in 2014, never imagining the English electorate – offered the chance to upset everything – would seize it with both hands and chuck Cameron, the EU and Britain's whole post '70s economic settlement right out the window.

That they did and that most Scots didn't see it coming

speaks of a certain naivety on our part and a stubborn refusal to accept that England really is a different country. But Brexit did more than just define different political cultures on both sides the Tweed.

It ushered in meltdown at Westminster as tough-talking Tory Prime Ministers found Brexit rather difficult to get done, with oven-ready trade deals eluding them and the economy quietly collapsing as banks and other businesses left for the Eurozone, red tape mountains accumulated for exporters, and the end of free movement meant staff shortages in every sector of the economy.

Perhaps waving a tearful farewell to Brussels didn't fire up independence campaigners as much as the horror show of government by a wounded Theresa May followed by an opportunistic Boris Johnson. But the effect of the Brexit vote is longer-lasting – next to no-one in Scotland has faith in Westminster.

It once seemed Britain was the template for everything; that other countries operated on a variation of British themes like the Sun supposedly circled the Earth. In this way of thinking, the vital and distinguishing characteristic of Britain – the sovereignty of Westminster – meant recognition of Scotland's different Brexit vote had to be avoided lest it undermine the whole sacred, irreplaceable, ancient edifice. Which it has, anyway. Presumptions of specialness and even competence at Westminster have so completely fallen away both at home and abroad.

According to *Le Monde* in December 2022:

> The British Conservatives are showing themselves to be prisoners of their glittering but quixotic promises on Brexit. Instead of the prosperity, sovereignty and international influence they claimed to bring by breaking with their European neighbours, they have reaped only a slowdown in their exports, the depreciation of the pound, the worst growth forecasts

of the developed countries (except Russia), and diplomatic isolation.

Évidemment.

Seven years ago, the Brexit vote didn't look like the last straw for the union – yet that snub to Scottish nationhood has made Scotland's departure inevitable. Why? Not just because of the damage to economy, employment, tourist trade, academic research and the freedom to move, love and live in Europe. Not just because of the ever-growing support for EU membership in Scotland. But because Brexit has become visible confirmation of the fact England and Scotland are two different countries, steadily growing apart over long, acrimonious decades. Brexit has simply been the tin lid. But what a lid. Shiny, light-attracting, heat-hogging, and in the eyes of every candidate for British prime minister – sealing splendid isolation back into British foreign policy, tighter than a jar of sour plums.

The European dream is dead in England. But not in Scotland – effectively now the only torch bearers left for the 14.5 million voters across the UK who voted Remain. No-one is advocating for them in British politics, or keeping alive their hopes of reintegration with the continent right beside them – even though UK opinion is finally swinging back towards the Scots' initial and automatic Remain position. What does that say?

It says we were right.

Intuitively right.

Not vulnerable to the lies told by the Leave camp. Not willing to thole Nigel Farage. Not living in the same country.

Remain-voting Londoners might feel some admiration for Scots and even a little envy. We voted Remain as a fairly united nation, whilst England has fallen apart. Indeed, Scotland is on the verge of acting out London's dream. If we can find a way to vote for independence we can stay connected with Europe, stay outward-facing, stay committed to tough European environmental standards and workers' rights, stay out of damaging trade deals, stay socially conscious and stay progressive.

We can divorce England – they can't.

The world is now watching, listening and understanding the case for Scottish independence – with Brexit as the cut-through issue that's given us fresh impetus.

We have the attention and sympathy of players who didn't even register the case for independence in 2014.

Maybe that's because the London-based press and media need a narrative to keep the turmoil of Brexit alive.

Or maybe, it's the hope an independent Scotland could provide a safe haven for hundreds of thousands of Remain-voting Londoners – many in the chattering classes – who can't stand the idea of a lost decade. Either way, 'how to move to Scotland' spiked as a search term the day after the 2019 election.

Scots didn't actually rate EU membership as a very important issue, compared to austerity, independence, the climate crisis and services like the NHS and education before 2016. So maybe that's why we under-estimate the impact our strong Remain vote is having now in London, Europe and the wider world, all of whom have finally registered that Scotland's voting patterns are the diametric opposite to England's.

Ye cannae choose which issue finally creates a spark and ignites the attention of others. For the Norwegians, the last straw was consular representation at fishing ports – hardly the biggest problem they had with the Swedish King. A bit like catching Al Capone over fluffed paperwork. So yes, the EU has shortcomings – some serious ones. Yes, the bureaucratic nature of its proceedings makes it an unsexy and even unlovely place to get worked up about. As Alyn Smith put it many years ago, the EU is more like a giant weights and measures department, with ambitions that might yet prove beyond its station. But this is perhaps the most fruitful battleground independence supporters will ever find.

Of course, more than that, a bit of our identity has been removed – and that always hurts. And we know EU citizens living in Scotland will henceforth be in a dodgier legal position than before, so solidarity and empathy drives folk too.

So, even though EU membership doesn't feel like the issue most Scots would choose to go to the barricades over; even though 'our' Prime Minister is intent on ignoring us, even though our slogans can feel like tedious repetition, we cannae give up.

Strange to relate, the London-based media don't see our present situation as hopeless, boring or doom-laden at all. What's old, familiar and repetitive to us, seems new, significant and newsworthy to them. Whatever – the biggest thing aiding the case for independence today is that fairly solid bedrock of 50 per cent support and the increased international visibility and sympathy Scotland enjoys thanks to losing the Brexit vote. Weird.

Is England irredeemably Conservative?

Perhaps though, it's worth waiting to see if folk in England finally catch a grip, disown Nigel Farage, cancel *Daily Mail* subscriptions in their thousands, tear up Tory membership cards and buy RNLI Xmas cards in gratitude for their excellent work saving desperate asylum seekers in the Channel?

It's not going to happen, is it?

If England is going through a hop off you frogs, loadsamoney phase, it's already lasted 40 years and counting. It's been more than two generations since the dreadful *Sun* headline and Harry Enfield's compellingly awful character encapsulated the greedy world of Thatcherism circa 1985.

Of course, dismissing a nation's political outlook as merely a passing phase is a patronising view that's normally reserved for Yes-supporting Scots. I suppose that's fair enough, in the sense that support for pro-indy parties has only surged to 50 per cent in the last 15 years. A mere gnat's bite in time compared to the four long decades enjoyed by Money Money Money and followers of the Blessed Margaret down south.

Clearly, in the eyes of commentators who don't generally live here, its Scots who are going through a rebellious teenage stage with a new parliament in its early 20s itching to prove itself by leaving home for good. No one asks in as many words but the question is always implied – when will you guys just calm down, accept the rules of the game, the limits of the country and the possibility devolution could give Scotland more room for manoeuvre (eventually) than you could ever conceive of (once upon a time)? In short, why won't you just go back to normal?

Ah normal. That ended for most of us in 1979, with the election of one Margaret Thatcher and the abrupt termination of the post war settlement Scots helped create.

It seems hard for academics, pundits and the great and good to accept that independence is not a temporary preoccupation that will blow over in the face of Tory intransigence. And that's partly because the bigger question about national character is never asked. Is England irredeemably Conservative or just going through a temporary, authoritarian phase?

Will 'one more push' by Scottish voters deliver a Labour government that is genuinely Labour in the eyes of Scottish voters and not just marginally less market-focused, flag-worshipping and migrant-blaming than the incumbents?

Is real change likely – and is it likely to last?

Or will the current pattern keep repeating itself – a couple of decades of Tory rule during which massive, irreversible constitutional changes are made (Thatcher's privatisation, Osborne's austerity and Cameron/Johnson's Brexit) followed by a few recovery years with a gentler but hardly transformational Labour government, before the tide turns again?

Optimists will point out that the Tories themselves once championed Scottish devolution through the 'Declaration of Perth' in 1968. Indeed, when Margaret Thatcher abandoned that policy stance by Ted Heath on becoming leader in 1976, leading Scots MPs like Alick Buchanan-Smith, and Malcolm Rifkind actually resigned. In theory, that could suggest the Tories current disdain for devolution is just the remnant of a

Thatcherite 'blip' and the party may one day finally return to its devolutionary roots.

Excuse me while I have a giraffe.

I'd suggest the whole period offers a different lesson.

Despite the genuine commitment of leading Scottish Tories to devolution, the policy was dropped like a stone, not to resurface for almost 40 years because a UK leader demanded it. The Conservatives under Thatcher were a party for whom Scottish home rule was neither a top priority nor a philosophical commitment. That party hasn't changed.

In fact, it's got more extreme, on all sorts of policy fronts.

Mrs T could only fantasise about the Rwanda deportation dream Suella Braverman is determined to make reality. And even Theresa May, who vowed to change the Tories' reputation as 'the nasty party' chucked that overboard without hesitation when she created a 'hostile environment' for migrants. Or did she think no-one would notice? Maggie didn't come up with a bedroom tax and benefit sanctions regime so vicious and inflexible that claimants have been driven to suicide. How many we'll never know because Work and Pensions Secretary Thérèse Coffey has refused to publish five reports, including one on the connection between suicides and welfare changes. And in January 2023, Ms Coffey confirmed that an independent review of the sanctions policy, proposed by her predecessor Amber Rudd in 2019, has been abandoned.

But hey, maybe that's for the best.

Maybe the shredding of data about 50 deaths after the loss of payments was purely accidental, as DWP officials claim.

Maybe a BBC investigation which found 82 claimants died after termination of benefits was malicious.

Maybe a Glasgow University study, terminated in 2022 after the DWP refused to release data, was indeed impossible because of legitimate DWP worries about the security of university storage facilities.

Aye right.

Maybe pigs fly.

And maybe DWP staff need pills to sleep at night.

The 2023 budget has indeed removed one 'rigid tick-box exercise' facing disabled people, but Jeremy Hunt has announced a more 'rigorous' enforcement of sanctions on folk deemed able to work who are unemployed – never mind whether employer prejudice about disability is the reason. No wonder the Tories don't want suicide studies published.

Even Margaret Thatcher didn't preside over state-orchestrated cruelty like this.

The unpalatable truth is that, each Tory tide is getting higher – eroding the remnants of community and solidarity, turning citizen against citizen (in England) and maybe one day reaching its zenith with a Singapore on the Thames-style Britain that finally scratches all those Tory itches by quitting conventions on human rights and privatising the welfare state.

It's grim and this is what Labour is up against.

Unless the party can win three terms in office to become a medium to long-term default amongst English voters – not just a one-off government and a temporary reprieve – Britain is doomed and Scotland is snookered.

So, what are the chances of a new Labour era, by which I mean a redistributive party, red or at least dark pink in tooth and claw?

Not high.

Look at what they're up against.

Not just Rishi Sunak – who at the time of writing is wildly excited about presiding over a 'stagnant' economy rather than a full-blown recession. Labour is up against the whole embedded conservatism of England.

The late Tom Nairn made a lifelong study of this, captured in excellent books like *The Break-up of Britain*, *The Enchanted Glass*, *Landed England* and a series of 1960s *New Left Review* articles co-authored with Perry Anderson – both heavily influenced by the alternative tradition of Marxism established by Antonio Gramsci.

This summary of the Nairn-Anderson theses by the *New*

Statesman's Rory Scothorne is spot on:

> Nairn suggests Britain, rarely defeated throughout its
> history, has for centuries been in a kind of cold war with
> modernity itself. The world-conquering force of English
> capitalism was such that it never had to 'modernise'
> in the way every other competitor did. Instead, [it]
> preserved itself in a kind of 'transitional' aspic, neither
> pre-modern nor fully modern. Those on the receiving end
> of enclosure, clearance and proletarianisation may have
> found their worlds turned upside down, but [that] was
> never enough to radicalise national politics.

Nairn suggested that Britain's working class – created by the
world's earliest industrial revolution – developed too early
to benefit from the formative influence of Marxism, settling
instead into Labour's blend of quasi-religious moralism and
liberal 'empiricism'. So,

> the self-delusion of popular Britishness remains
> crucial to understanding Labour's contemporary
> failures: the party simply could not tell a positive
> story about membership of the EU, for that would
> require justifying the considerable limits of British
> power to a culture primed for dreams of maritime
> greatness. Efforts to triangulate by claiming Labour
> could 'lead' Europe were no match for the... history-
> proof ideology of 'muddling through' that renders the
> national spirit impervious to defeat.

Forgive the lengthy quote, but Scothorne, drawing from Tom
Nairn, has put his finger on the very crux of Labour's dilemma
in conservative England:

> The God-given authority of the monarch was
> smuggled into the modern world under parliamentary

disguise. Westminster is thus empowered – via Crown-in-Parliament – to act as a sort of corporate deity, making and unmaking laws and structures as it pleases, with the royal family sticking around to inject what Tom Nairn called 'the glamour of backwardness' and an aura of timeless familial stability into the arrangement.

Argue with that if you can.

Except to say Scots have historically made a better stab at questioning the modern 'corporate deity' at Westminster.

It was the SNP MP and KC Joanna Cherry who led the successful challenge to Boris Johnson's arbitrary suspension of parliament in 2019 at the Court of Session in Edinburgh.

It was Ms Cherry plus five other Scots politicians – Andy Wightman MSP (Scottish Greens), Ross Greer MSP (Scottish Greens), Alyn Smith MEP (SNP), David Martin MEP (Scottish Labour), Catherine Stihler MEP (Scottish Labour) along with Jolyon Maugham QC from the Good Law Project who established, at the European Court of Justice, that Britain could unilaterally revoke Article 50 at any time during the long, drawn-out Brexit negotiations. There is no MP who has tackled the arbitrary power wielded by England's modern Henry VIII more effectively than this tenacious Scottish lawyer/legislator.

But beyond electing unslavish MPs, Scots are also relatively impervious to the siren attractions of the monarchy.

Monarchy v republic

Rory Scothorne suggests the royal family are not just regal eye-candy but:

indicate to subjects that Britain is not like other states, and thus need not be held to similar standards. By proving that we do things differently here, they help us avoid the realisation that we actually do

> things worse. It is royalty, above all, that makes
> Britain's conservative constitution popular.

Maybe, in England but not with Scots.

Shetland Council – alone in the UK – voted against giving staff a bank holiday for the King's coronation, because national holidays in Scotland are for councils to decide. But in Westminster-run Northern Ireland, local elections were postponed by two weeks to avoid a clash. Yip, a month after celebrations of the Good Friday Agreement and its democratic breakthrough 25 years ago, local democracy had to take second place to the coronation of an unelected head of state.

Maybe that's par for the course in an archaic British state. Maybe that's why most Scots are itching to reform it.

A Panelbase poll in December 2022 found 55 per cent of Scots would prefer an independent Scotland to be a republic rather than keep King Charles – a result which suggests Scots align with most of Europe where 21 of 27 EU member states are republics with elected heads of state. Even amongst the six European monarchies, Britain is out of step – it's the only one with an actual coronation ceremony. European monarchies have either replaced them with simpler events (like Denmark) or never practised coronations (like the Netherlands and Belgium). Indeed, most monarchies today just require a simple oath taken in the country's legislature.

But hey Britain – simple?

No way.

King Charles' 'scaled down' event consisted of just one new gold carriage and two new thrones – one each for himself and Camilla – with London papers suggesting she should get plaudits for re-using Queen Mary's crown.

Meanwhile, Charles is chuffed that the whole affair cost a mere hundred million quid and lasted 90 minutes instead of the three hours spent on Queen Elizabeth's ceremony in 1953.

If that's what constitutes an austerity coronation, you hesitate to think what would have happened in days of plenty.

Still, while the British press and English councils trilled about the chance for a moment of coronation togetherness, Scotland stood with one eyebrow collectively arched.

A month before C-Day, Scots had far fewer street parties planned than the rest of the UK – though of course, unofficial spontaneity may have kicked in. There was also a march and rally through Glasgow, calling for an end to monarchy on the big day itself. Meanwhile, in 2022, just 14 events were held across Scotland to celebrate 70 years of the Queen on the throne.[33]

Across the whole UK, there were 16,000.

When it comes to the cowed reverence and Union Jack emblazoned excitement that accompanies royal events, Scots tend to back the Bard; 'The rank is but the guinea's stamp, The Man's the gowd for a' that.'

That's not to say there aren't supporters of the monarchy – Panelbase found 45 per cent would keep the monarchy in an independent country. But I suspect that's a vote for a seriously pared down European-style monarchy – which clearly ain't what 'frugal' Charles plans, even if some of his 11 royal residences (10 castles, 56 cottages and 14 ancient ruins) are opened to the public.

Anyway, this is the obsequious, forelock-tugging reality Sir Keir Starmer's Labour Party must tackle or meekly endorse. Which is it to be?

We already know the answer. Ditto with all the big issues.

What chance of a return to public ownership beyond railways that are already halfway there, and the bantamweight arrival of Great British Energy to compete on the sidelines while the billion pound profit-making BP and Shell rock on? None.

What chance of a return to the EU or at least the single market? None

What chance of an end to the ramped up anti-immigrant rhetoric that fuelled the recent attack on an asylum seeking hotel? Some, but the virility test for the Labour leader will be keeping the horrific Rwanda deportation route open and

---

33 https://coronation.gov.uk/events/

stopping more boats on the Channel.

What chance of the same wages and investment as our European neighbours when it comes to the health service?

None. The Labour leader has put too much distance between himself and crazy 'socialist' high-taxing Jeremy Corbyn to backtrack any time soon. So while Britain has only a third of Germany's hospital beds and NHS spending per head 30 per cent less than Germany with the sixth fewest doctors per head in Europe, Labour will have to ignore the need for higher taxation and join the desperate Tory search for 'efficiencies' instead.

Of course, some Scots, weary of waiting for independence and disenchanted with the rancorous SNP leadership contest, may be considering a Labour vote next time.

I wonder how many remember what happened last time the party had a big say in Scotland's government. That was the Smith Commission to establish a better deal for Scotland in the wake of the 2014 independence referendum, when Labour – not the Tories – took key powers off the negotiating table.

One draft included proposals to devolve income tax personal allowances, employers' National Insurance contributions, inheritance tax, and the power to create new taxes without Treasury approval.

But they never made it into the final deal.

According to the BBC, another draft included a LibDem proposal to devolve the power to vary Universal Credit.

Think how many folk would have been saved the misery of negotiating a system so badly conceived that most claimants wait six weeks before getting any cash, hoping not to fall into rent arrears, debt, homelessness and unemployment in the meantime.

But devolving Universal Credit was blocked by the UK Cabinet.

Other proposed new powers included the creation of a separate Scottish Health & Safety Executive; 'greater Scottish involvement in BBC governance beyond one Trust member', and putting the Sewell Convention, by which Westminster doesn't normally legislate on devolved matters without Holyrood consent, 'on a statutory footing'. That, on its own, could have stopped all Boris Johnson's post Brexit power grabs. Instead, its existence was simply 'recognised' and the other proposals just went walkabout.

What a sell-out.

As Kevin McKenna observed, in a typically provocative 2014 *Herald* article:

> Scotland's [new] spending status is about equal to that of a child saving up for the new Xbox (you're not getting it all at once because you'll just spend it on sweeties).

There were qualifications throughout the Smith Commission report and genuine anger amongst those watching Labour's conduct during the final negotiations.

> Seeing all welfare powers being taken away at the last minute and Labour argue against devolution of the minimum wage are things I don't think I'll ever forget,

McKenna was told.

> In the last hours of the Smith deliberations, the Tories were getting direct input from Westminster government departments and cutting deals with Labour to avoid anything that might affect English votes for English laws [EVEL].

How utterly depressing – because you know what happened to EVEL?

After all that grandstanding and righteous nonsense from David Cameron about ending the 'unfair' practice of Scots voting on domestic English legislation (something the SNP had chosen not to do for a decade), the EVEL mechanism was abolished by a Tory government motion in 2021. Michael 'Flashdance' Gove explained its demise:

> Ultimately, it's a convention which arose out of a set of circumstances after the 2014 referendum, where you had a coalition government... We've moved on now.

Meaning...?

Still EVEL's short life did serve a purpose – it showed angry English Tory MPs and voters that Jocks had been punished for daring to leave the UK.

So, thanks Labour.

Thanks for suckering voters.

Thanks for leaving Scotland with a worse post indyref deal than we should have had.

And good luck.

Labour is the second party of Scotland, having wrestled the Tories back into third place. But an estimated 40 per cent of its members back a second indyref, and if its ranks are swollen by any 'returning' SNP supporters, that proportion could soon reach the magical 50.1 per cent. At which point, it'll be very hard to stop indyref-supporting candidates from being selected as candidates. Indeed, newspapers suggest the Labour Party fielded 25 independence/indyref2 supporting candidates in the last council elections. Yip, that is just a drop in the ocean. But survey the demographics. The majority of the working age population supports independence, and there's no getting away from the impact that will finally have on a party that needs to win youthful support from the SNP and Greens and must square the circle of its support for self-determination all around the world – including Northern Ireland – but just not here.

So, the blueish tinge to Keir Starmer just confirm it.

England's going through a Tory phase and it's been a gey long one.

PART THREE

The State of the Nation

LET'S GO BACK to the starting line-up for indyref2.

Westminster has gone from being a safe pair of hands in pole position, to a den of corruption and economic mismanagement where a lettuce managed to outlast the last Prime Minister.

The union has gone from a 'safe' economic option within the EU to a surly, isolated and isolationist power, whose dwindling credibility should attract as many robust questions as the option of independence.

So, how has Scotland fared as part of the crumbling UK?

Maybe things haven't really been so bad?

Yes – they really have. And nothing demonstrates Scotland's predicament and under-performance within the UK than the area of energy.

Picture the scene. It's minus 5 in November 2022 amidst the worst energy crisis to hit Europe in generations.

It's Iceland – whose name neatly summarises its sub-Arctic location and capacity for producing real, card-carrying amounts of cold. I had come off the flight at Keflavik wearing thermals, layers, a bunnet and the thick, long-length puffer jacket I generally reserve for Nordic exploits.

But by the time I reached the student accommodation in Reykjavik, I was boiling – forced to turn off radiators and open windows to cool down. And those windows stayed open all night long. In Iceland I felt truly warm for the first time in months.

How come?

How could I be over-heating in freezing Iceland?

Given its northerly latitude, non-stop mini earthquakes. regular volcanic eruptions and near bankruptcy in 2008, this country should be empty, on its knees and pretty damned cold indoors with heat banks galore as folk struggle to survive.

But it isn't.

How come?

Iceland is remote, treeless, isolated and so barren that Icelanders were forced to remain part of Norway for centuries just to get supplies of wood. It's the only country where Viking settlers terrorised no indigenous people – because there were none there already – and settlers famously landed three times before any opted to stay. That's why 40 per cent of Iceland's matrilineal DNA is Celtic – those early settlers captured women from Ireland and Scottish islands to populate their colony. And did I say the population is tiny? Just 355,000 – about the size of Aberdeen and Dundee combined.

Yet Iceland is toasty thermometer-wise and supported by other small countries across the world for helping them in their moments of need. Iceland was first to formally recognise the independence of the Baltic Republics despite threats from the Soviet Union to cut oil and trade supplies. Iceland stood by these small nations, sending its foreign minister Jon Baldvin Hannibalsson to the Lithuanian capital Vilnius in January 1991, amidst Russian attacks that had left 14 people dead and hundreds injured. He formally recognised Lithuania as a state and stopped the clock ticking for long enough to allow larger nations to follow suit, tanks to withdraw and Lithuania to join the United Nations, along with Latvia and Estonia. Why did he do it?

'Iceland is a small country. It's in our interests to have other small countries in the world.'

You've got to love Iceland and its far-thinking world view.

And its irrepressible and crazily creative people.

And its fish.

And its cheap energy.

Cos there's wadges of it.

Why Scotland is colder than Iceland

Sitting astride a geological fault line means Iceland is cursed by earthquakes, lava slides and eruptions but also blessed with natural geothermal power. Wells drilled to a depth of over 2km extract hot water vapour, which is separated into liquid water and steam and used to power turbines which produce electricity.

Cheaply.

Iceland has the most affordable house heating in the Nordics, roughly 80 per cent cheaper than Helsinki and the UK. So it's no wonder this frozen country is thriving. Naebody's cold.

Geothermal energy heats nine out of every ten Icelandic homes, the hot water pipes melt snow from pavements, heat swimming pools, power fish farming, food processing and greenhouse cultivation.

Cheap, homemade, renewable, geothermal power is the main reason student flats are permanently warm.

The other is district heating – hot water distributed via pipe networks at relatively low cost, so that nobody freezes. It's been a common practice across Northern Europe for centuries and means Nordic householders don't carry the vast cost of buying and maintaining hundreds of thousands of individual boilers, or replacing them with prohibitively expensive greener models.

One council-run central boiler – many pipes.

That's how it works in Iceland and most of Northern Europe.

Many private boilers, no pipes and and sky-high energy bills – that's how it works in Britain.

And that's why Icelandic homes rapidly became too hot for this Scot accustomed to wearing five jumpers and a bunnet indoors from November to March of every year.

It's also why the Icelanders can illuminate absolutely everything – including graveyard tombstones – at New Year. It's why you can opt for a bathroom stop at the remotest point on their famous Golden Circle bus tour – safe in the knowledge that the 'conveniences' will not be damp, freezing or generally minging as they would likely be back home. It's why thousands of Icelanders have well-paid jobs producing geothermal energy and exporting their know-how and technology around the globe.

It's why the Icelandic Government subsidised the use

of geothermal technology to heat and irrigate greenhouses when the financial crash in 2008 made imports unaffordable, converting a food-insecure nation of importers into a nation of home-grown tomato producers. One glasshouse farm at Fridheimar, east of Reykjavik, produces 370 tons of tomatoes throughout the year – 15 per cent of Iceland's total tomato market.

It's why the jewel in the crown of Iceland's burgeoning tourism industry is the Blue Lagoon even though it's NOT naturally geothermal but a crafty mix of freshwater from the nearby Svartsengi Power Station and seawater. Cute.

And it's why that pricey spa now has competition from a myriad of natural geothermal hot springs – at one you can put foil-wrapped dough into the earth and eat baked bread by the time you come out.

All because of geothermal energy.

All because of the island's volcanic nature.

And all because Icelanders recognised there were advantages to life on a gigantic volcano and stubbornly refused to see their island home as ithers saw it – a hopeless, barren, sub-arctic desert valued only for its sulphur mines.

Indeed, sulphur might have remained Iceland's biggest industry, if 121,000 folk hadn't seized the moment and declared independence from Denmark in 1944, when the 'mothership' was occupied by Germany.

What was their motivation? After all Iceland gained near total autonomy in 1918, when a referendum, approved by 92.6 per cent of voters, made Iceland a sovereign state with its own parliament, stuck only in 'personal union' with the Danish King.

No-one can really tell you now. One of the beauties of independence – all those old grievances just fade away. But the consequences?

Some good – some challenging. And some totally epic.

Like the transformational development of hydro and geothermal energy.

The 1970s oil crisis had encouraged Iceland to subsidise small geothermal projects by farmers and councils. But it was hard to build big. The country was emerging from centuries of crushing poverty and foreign rule, lacking basic transport, financial infrastructure, knowledge about geothermal's potential or experience of delivering big energy projects. Indeed, the UN Development Programme classified Iceland as a developing country with such a sparse and dispersed population that establishing an interconnected energy grid would be almost impossible.

But of course, it wasn't. And whilst you could argue that energy self-sufficiency helped fuel a cockiness that eventually led to the collapse of Icelandic banks and livelihoods in 2008, it also put the economy back on its feet. Thanks to its never-ending green energy resources, Iceland will always be 'investable'.

Energy, indy and economic success

It was the same combination that transformed Norway after independence in 1905, when Scotland's Nordic Twin was judged 'one of the worst performing economies in the western world'. But the Concession Laws of 1906–9 effectively turned that around as the newly independent Norwegian state effectively nationalised rivers that had been snaffled up by foreign (often English) industrialists and investors.

Thereafter, income from hydro dams flowed directly to county and municipal councils rather than private coffers or central government. And when North Sea Oil was found in the '70s, it followed the same 'hydro' template of public ownership, leading to the creation of a Sovereign Wealth Fund which let Norwegians put oil income beyond the reach of their own governments. Now the world's largest state pension fund has over $1.19 trillion in assets, and is worth about $250,000 per Norwegian citizen. It's driven disinvestment from tobacco and fossil fuels and the interest has modestly bankrolled the world's most successful democracy.

In case you need reminding, that didn't happen here – on oil or hydro.

Hydro development began later in Scotland than Norway thanks to opposition by private landowners until WW2 allowed the visionary Labour Scottish Secretary Tom Johnston to force through change. The North of Scotland Hydro-Electric Board was formed in 1943, delivering electricity to the Highlands for the first time. Scores of hydro dams and power stations were built, and workers at St Fillans in Perthshire set a world tunnelling record in 1955, grinding their way through 557ft of rock in just one week. By the mid 1960s, Scotland had 56 dams connected by over 600km of rock tunnels, aqueducts and pipelines. A bit like Norway.

But in 1979, something very unNorwegian happened. Britain (and an unwilling Scotland) disowned public ownership of energy and all other state assets with the election of Margaret Thatcher and 18 subsequent years of Tory control, during which the Hydro Board was privatised and merged with the Southern Electricity Board to become SSE PLC.

Since the 1960s SSE has built one new large-scale hydro power station, Glendoe and has plans for another whopper at Coire Glas near Fort William – a 92 metre-high dam and two reservoirs in the Scottish Highlands that would double both SSE's own hydro portfolio and the UK's energy storage.

In short – game-changing.

It'll cost £1.5bn to construct, create 500 skilled full-time jobs and let Britain finally transition from gas dependency by generating enough renewable energy to power three million homes in just under five minutes.

Can you feel the but coming?

Well, it seems the UK Government (in charge of energy decisions) hasn't provided the long-term financial guarantees needed for SSE to go full steam ahead – though Finance Director Gregor Alexander puts it more delicately:

Whilst Coire Glas doesn't need subsidy, it does

require more certainty around its revenues and it
is critically important the UK Government urgently
confirms its intention on exactly how they will help
facilitate the deployment of such projects.

The idea this could yet fall through is nothing short of
criminal. Yet it points to an inconvenient truth for supporters
of the union. Scotland's hydro expansion, energy security and
contribution to net zero relies entirely on the whims of a UK
Government that has banned onshore wind development in
England and re-opened a coal mine – all to please NIMBY Tory
voters and MPs.

It's an utter travesty that can only end with Scottish control
of Scottish resources.

Meanwhile, Scotland got 71,500 jobs from the extraction
of our North Sea oil and gas, plus buoyant local economies in
Aberdeenshire and Shetland, along with the highest electricity
prices and rates of fuel poverty in the UK. 'Our' oil and gas is
sold to the highest bidder on the international market, helping
Shell and BP to record profits of £30 billion plus at a time when
four 4 in ten Scots aged 50 and above were in fuel poverty.

Meanwhile in Norway, state-owned Statoil profits flow
into their sovereign wealth fund – exactly what should have
happened here.

What made the Norwegians so enlightened?

Perhaps the introduction of proportional voting in 1919
(80 years before Scotland) which ended the mismatch between
votes cast and seats won by the fledgling Norwegian Labour
Party and thus averted the revolutions witnessed in Russia and
Finland. The same year legislation limited the working day to
eight hours with excess work paid as overtime – something
that didn't happen here until Britain joined the EEC in the
1970s – and 115,000 industrial workers in Norway gained
the legal right to a week's paid annual holiday – something
that took Britain another two decades.

Nonetheless, there was a bitter General Strike in 1935 that

has a profound and positive impact. Two pivotal agreements were struck by the country's first Labour government – made possible by that PR voting system – helping end the confrontation between employers and workers that still rages in Britain. Well, end is perhaps putting it too strongly. But confrontation was replaced with negotiation. And workers got a pretty good deal.

The Main Agreement, established rules on wage negotiation, collective agreements and forming unions. The Crisis Settlement delivered large scale state investment in land clearance, industrial development, roads, railways and – crucially – hydro-electric power stations. And the local, state-owned control over the hydro energy resources, set the pattern for oil.

I know. It's all so damn logical and fair.

But there's more.

Negotiation not domination

In Norway, the idea of negotiation spilled over from these seminal agreements into other areas of governance, while Britain went down an entirely different combative road that made compromise, conciliation, negotiation and public benefit seem like dirty words.

So, the gains available to rational, negotiated economies have been denied to Britain and, until recently, union membership has been on the slide. Trade union leaders are rightly suspicious of overtures that might result in capitulation or co-option. And us v them drains batteries. It's been safer for workers to stay united, wary, at arms' length, on high alert and not ready to give an inch. A workers' version of the Viking Shield Wall. Impenetrable.

And absolutely right. Without such solidarity, many Scots today would still be living in single end slums.

But can Scots follow Norway a century on, and undo the industrial conflict of recent centuries? Negotiated settlements between the Scottish Government and public sector unions have been encouraging and contrast with the strikes, acrimony and eventual government backdowns south of the border.

Still, let's not miss Norway's most important lesson.

The country's hydro energy revolution was made possible by its political revolution.

Independence first – energy second.

If Scotland had opted for independence ten years ago, we could have been in the proposed green 'North Sea polo' grid, exploring subsea connections with Iceland to offset our intermittent wind with their baseload geothermal energy.

But as part of just-in-time Britain, energy security in Scotland – the Saudi Arabia of renewables – is as ropey as it is across the whole country.

Maddeningly, it's too late to emulate Norway's energy savviness because renewables will never match their massive dividends.

The oil and gas has almost gone and the remaining reserves must stay in the ground. If Humza Yousaf opts to reverse Nicola Sturgeon's planning veto on Cambo field drilling, the Treasury will gain some oil revenue, the highest bidder will eventually gain some expensive oil and gas, the planet will gain some climate-warming and Scotland will gain the reputation of being a country that understands the imperatives of climate change but cannot resist the siren attractions of oil.

That's why the experience of another Nordic neighbour has relevance.

Kicking our fossil fuel habit

In 1973, 92 per cent of Denmark's energy consumption came from imported oil, till the OPEC crisis delivered a seismic shock and a bold new energy strategy emerged, backed by every Danish political party.

When world oil prices finally dropped, there was agreement to keep prices high, at 1973 levels. Car imports were taxed to the hilt, public transport was made more affordable and reliable and cities like Copenhagen were turned into cycling cities.

Like every other North Sea state, Denmark did expand natural gas production but made an even bigger shift into district heating and wind energy. Now 42 per cent of electricity comes from wind and Vestas, headquartered in Aarhus, dominates the world's wind turbine production. Yet Denmark's wind resource is only a fraction of Scotland's in strength and constancy. That world leader in wind should have been us.

But Danish politicians saw the energy crises of the 1970s as a wake-up call and took bold, collective action to phase out oil-fired power plants – the British Government didn't. And the Scottish Government – didn't yet exist.

Denmark does import some hydro and nuclear from neighbours but has gone from 100 per cent dependence on imported fossil fuels in the early '70s to the OECD's most energy secure and sustainable country today, cutting emissions and improving the competitiveness of Danish manufacturing as the oil price steadily rises.

Despite changes of government in the last half century, that basic energy strategy hasn't changed – a function of the steady, predictable, consensual government that comes with a century using proportional, not combative, first-past-the-post British voting systems.

Meanwhile, the UK Department for Energy and Climate Change has presided over cuts to onshore wind, solar and community energy, scrapped tax exemptions for renewable energy, scrapped Carbon Capture and Storage (CCS) projects in Scotland, sold off the Green Investment Bank and celebrated the first anniversary of COP 26 in Glasgow by announcing plans to open the first new coal mine for 30 years in Cumbria.

The UK no longer even has a Secretary of State for Energy and Climate Change. Why bother, when policy is effectively made by the oil and gas giants?

That's why Britain will not emerge from the current energy

crisis but will simply mitigate, postpone and endlessly repeat it. And Scotland will be dragged along, unless we learn the lesson from our small, Nordic neighbours and take political control of our energy resources – on land and sea.

The great advantage of Norway and Iceland is that hydro and geothermal are baseload energy – constant sources available at the flick of a switch, which can even out the intermittency of renewables like wind.

In Scotland, hydro has provided baseload energy, but flooding land is ecologically damaging, so we may not see more new hydro dams. Happily though, Scotland has yet another watery string to its bow in the form of tidal energy.

Ok, I'm biased.

My mother's Caithness family grew up beside the Pentland Firth and the strongest tidal currents in the northern hemisphere. So strong, that sailors on the Caithness-owned island of Stroma were pilots not fishermen. My mother used to recount their grim warning to large ships foolish enough to reject their offers of expert guidance through the treacherous waters – 'We'll get paid one way or another.' Sure enough, the homes of Stroma were famously full of ships' clocks, heavy ropes on stairs and bells aplenty.

The tidal current there was so strong that annual summer holiday trips across the Firth to Orkney featured thrilling sideways ferry motion and even more marvellous tales about the power of the Swelkie – a whirlpool which features in the Icelandic Eddas, created by two female trolls turning a millstone to grind out the ocean's salt. The Swelkie's name comes from Old Norse: Svalga, meaning 'the Swallower'.

Respect.

So, did the folk of Caithness understand the potential of marine energy in the Firth? Yes, they did. Did they get the chance to develop it for local industry and the future of the planet? No, they didn't.

Because even though Pentland Firth tides have the potential to power almost half of Scotland – confirmed by a scientific paper to the Royal Society in 2013 – Caithness got Dounreay instead, an experimental fast-breeder reactor whose radioactive waste was allowed to leak for more than two decades and will never be completely cleaned up.

Nice.

It's what happens when energy decisions are made by folk in another country.

Tidal operators Nova Innovation are back in the North Sea with the world's first tidal energy array off Shetland, but progress is in danger of stalling, because Westminster has been slow to earmark development funds.

If Scotland was independent our parliament could ring-fence cash to stop this precious lead in tidal technology shifting to Canada or Indonesia, keep tidal manufacturing jobs here and enhance energy security with another baseload source of renewables to add to our fairly brimming energy kit-bag.

We've got the seas. We've got the scientists. We've got the companies. We've got the gap in our wind-dominated energy portfolio that only a predictable energy source can fill. But we haven't got control over energy. So, we haven't got tidal – not yet.

Energy is reserved to Westminster and they want nuclear to provide baseload energy instead.

It's crazy – and given the state of the climate crisis, it's criminal.

Using dodgy, expensive, slow and hard to deliver nuclear energy in renewables-rich Scotland is as daft as digging for coal in geothermal Iceland.

But that independent country can show uranium and fossil-heids the door.

Scotland cannae.

Now, I'll grant you, none of this made the heather crackle as a driver for independence, in 2014. It took the Ukraine crisis in 2022 to expose the terrible cost of Britain's lazy dependence on gas for heating. And the unfairness of charging regimes.

BBC analysis shows daily standing charges have increased

by almost 100 per cent in South Scotland, 83 per cent in North Scotland but just 38 per cent in London.

Why the big difference?

Analysts suggest that the advent of the price cap prompted suppliers to shift part of the unit price for energy onto uncapped standing charges. Cute.

But that still doesn't explain these glaring geographical charging anomalies.

It's hardly that the south of Scotland, South Wales and south-west England with 100 per cent standing charge rises, make the least contribution to green energy production. Au contraire.

Scotland is a net energy exporter and the wind-farm-covered south of Scotland helps keep lights on across the whole UK – yet its people are paying disproportionately for the privilege. London, by contrast, was ranked the worst city in England and Wales for renewable energy use in 2016 and green energy production is still negligible.

Perhaps Scots are being made to finance 'our' own grid improvements – even though those connections supply our green energy to the rest of the UK. Still, since no-one has mobilised politically over the scandalous fact that Scottish wind producers pay a higher fee to connect to the grid than producers down south, the British Government probably thought it could get away with short-changing Scottish consumers.

Whatever. The result is that Scots, with the bulk of Britain's wind and hydro energy also have the highest levels of fuel poverty, and the highest electricity standing charges in Europe.

Would this be tolerated for a moment in an independent country?

No.

It could only happen in Del Boy Britain.

Take the Western Isles – beautiful but steadily depopulating, because of the highest energy costs in the UK, the highest proportion of damp homes, a sluggish economy and perceptions of marginality bolstered by a collective memory of forced migration during the Clearances. Yet, in any energy arm-wrestling competition, the Western Isles could beat Iceland hands down (ok, definitely hold its own), thanks to its incredible wind resource and yet to be exploited marine potential.

There has long been just one big snag.

Lack of investment in subsea connectors by the Westminster Government.

To make money in the UK energy system, a wind farm must be connected to the National Grid. But the Western Isles currently uses a cable that's only just big enough to take energy from yer Maw's three bar electric fire. I exaggerate for effect.

And it isn't even working right now.

The crappy, old, utterly inadequate subsea cable to Lewis and Harris currently has a fault. So, the island chain that could outdo Iceland to become the renewables hub of Northern Europe is being heated by an old diesel-powered station while its teeny-weeny cable is fixed. It's tragic. And much the same story in renewables-rich Shetland and Orkney.

But let's stay west awhile.

Finally in December 2022, Ofgem took the plunge and backed a 1.8 gigawatt subsea cable to run from Lewis to Ullapool and then onto Inverness which should be completed by 2030 – just three decades late. The Western Isles have been waiting for a decent-sized connector to let them throw six and transform their islands, lives, population-base, health and economy. Waiting for Westminster approval because Westminster controls energy.

Investing not waiting

I cycled the length of the island chain in 2006 for a book and Radio Scotland series and met folk from Pairc Trust (on the Lewis side of the great Clisham divide) trying to buy land on behalf of 400 crofters and residents. It took another ten long years and the first hostile land buyout against an 'unwilling buyer', before the struggle finally ended in 2015 with an 'amicable' sale. As Professor James Hunter wrote:

> The innumerable obstacles and complexities
> [the people] encountered were so difficult and
> time-consuming... it would have been perfectly
> understandable if Pairc's land ownership ambitions
> had eventually been abandoned.

Those ambitions included a causeway to slash journey times to Stornoway, a state-of-the-art old folks' home to stop local pensioners having to retire to the mainland and writing off student loans for young people who made the peninsula their home.

Impressive. And possible – in 2006 – because of the prospect of a steady annual income from the Muaitheabhal Community Wind Farm Trust (MCWFT), part of the larger Eishken wind farm.

But in 2015, just as the land buyout was being concluded – the wind farm bid collapsed. The problem wasn't the much-hyped objection about the safety of eagles but the sub-sea connector the British Government had promised but failed to provide.

In 2021, French firm Engie energy reluctantly abandoned plans for the £200m wind farm at Eishken, which would have been the largest in the Western Isles generating power for 100,000 homes (ten times local demand). Without the cable to the mainland there was no way to export their wind energy and therefore no way to make the windfarm profitable. To their credit, Engie didn't cut and run. They paid almost £3 million to the community – as promised. If only the British Government had acted as honourably.

It's been a maddening catch 22 for the whole Western Isles where wind and marine projects have become stranded assets for the want of cables which were installed decades ago by Swedish and Danish governments on their islands, despite far lower wind speeds.

Maybe this time, the subsea connector really will be built.

Or maybe a future Prime Minister will change their mind again – as successive Tory PMS have done with carbon capture off Peterhead.

Certainly, future income from renewables will be taxed and siphoned off by Westminster, just as it taxed and frittered away our oil and gas income in the '70s.

Meantime, the waiting and under-development has taken its toll, sapping the energy of dynamic people, crushing island confidence and feeding that deep-seated, self-destructive Scottish belief that nothing ever happens because – essentially – we are crap.

All because Margaret Thatcher decided to flog off the family silver, privatise the energy industry and put strategic decisions about long-term, energy investments into the sweaty paws of private companies whose short term perspective and gut instinct is to 'let the market decide' we should stick with gas.

Even if that means supplies are imported from France.

Yes, our own North Sea gas is being flogged back to us by the French because The Market supported by a succession of *laissez-faire* Whitehall dullards thought buying supplies 'just in time', would cost less than building storage facilities here and would further boost the profits of Shell and BP oil executive chums.

But thanks to Putin's invasion of Ukraine, forcing oil and gas prices through the roof, that wheeze has failed. And even though Rishi Sunak plans new oil and gas exploration licences, they'll take years to come on stream, provide supplies for the highest bidders and keep Britain ploughing the wrong, climate-destroying fossil-fuel furrow.

Nuclear love-ins at Westminster

That's also why the UK Government is banking on nuclear, encouraging foreign state-owned companies like the French EDF to invest in Sizewell C because home-grown capital in the City of London took one look at the nuclear financial proposition – decades to build, most expensive renewables by a country mile, plus enduring problems with Fukushima-style meltdowns and waste disposal – and thought, nope.

Yet, listening to the love-in during Prime Ministers Questions in the dog days of Boris Johnson's reign it became clear that Johnson and Starmer were still hooked on the power of the atom to tackle Britain's escalating energy crisis.

Johnson blamed Labour for cancelling nuclear power stations. Starmer counter-claimed that Tory nuclear plants had more starts than a dodgy apprentice but then listed nuclear in his own preferred energy mix.

Johnson proclaimed there is 'more joy in heaven over one sinner that repents' – no he couldn't quite remember the whole quote either – but his point was clear. Nuclear is supported by both main Westminster parties and fresh billions will be wasted in a bid to build new plants.

Even though no British money has gone into building nuclear power plants for decades.

Even though the Hinkley C nuclear power station is a decade late, wildly over-budget and won't come into service till 2036 – if the British Government finds new investors to 'ease out' Chinese state-backed group CGN.

Even though Sizewell C, if ever built, won't produce electricity until around the same time.

Even though the average nuclear plant takes 18 years in planning and construction, against a tenth of that time for renewables.

And even though the unthinkable happened again last year when Chernobyl was at risk of meltdown as war raged all around.

Despite all this Westminster hails nuclear energy as the green salvation of the world.

It's the same old story. Any threat to the status quo justifies more investment in the status quo.

But does Scotland need new nuclear?

No, we do not.

Quite apart from the untapped tidal resource in our northern seas, the Forth/Tay offshore wind project significantly exceeds Scotland's entire electricity demand – on its own. If some of that energy could be stored for use in transport, that field alone could satisfy nearly all of Scotland's energy needs. And supply England. Even when Scotland becomes independent, we will continue to green England with renewable energy at the best price they'll get anywhere and supply them with fresh fruit and veg produced in glasshouses, like the Icelanders, using a mix of our renewables in place of their geothermal energy.

With tidal and wave energy, heat pumps, local community grids and district heating for home energy, Scotland should be laughing all the way to the bank.

But we're not – because Scotland is caught up in Westminster's nuclear obsession and gas for heating laziness.

Which means no long-term subsidies and contracts for tidal developers and therefore no continuity for turbine manufacturers, low investor confidence in Scotland's marine energy resource and a timid price cap placed on the Scotwind North Sea licences.

As one expert put it,

> if you have a mindset that wants Scotland kept at heel
> politically, then you will want to see Scotland with
> nuclear and fossil energy, tied and locked in to UK policy.

This is madness.

Of course, nuclear has provided Scotland with baseload energy that kept the lights on and helped offset the intermittency of wind.

But so did coal.

So did gas.

And both are about to become history.

No energy solution should be on the starting line-up for our decarbonised future, just because it's done heavy lifting in the past. Especially when it needs endless taxpayer support. The German Institute for Economic Research examined 674 nuclear power plants built across the world since 1951 and found the average plant made a loss of 4.8 billion euros. Professor Naomi Oreskes from Harvard University wrote recently in *Scientific American*:

> The most recent US nuclear power reactors were started in 2013 and are still not finished. That's the problem with 'breakthrough' technologies. The breakthrough can be sudden, but implementation is very slow.

Nuclear construction costs have risen three-fold over the last decade whilst the costs of wind energy are almost three times lower and solar is five times lower.

But what about nuclear fission – according to Ms Oreskes that's 'a technology which has been just around the corner since 1943'?

Or small modular reactors (SMRs)? Rolls Royce says smaller reactors can be constructed cheaply, built in factories, transported in modules and fitted together 'like meccano'. Yet so far, the world's only SMR is in Russia, while Hitachi and Toshiba have both mothballed high-profile projects, prompting the Tories to pass a Nuclear Energy (Financing) Bill in 2022 to create 'a partnership between the public and private sectors' underwriting future nuclear construction. So our public cash is safeguarding their private nuclear plants. And Labour backed it to the hilt.

But neither party championed plans for a new Severn Tidal Barrage. Local councils in England and Wales are working together in vain to get electricity from the second biggest tidal range in the world which, if successfully harnessed, could generate seven per cent of the UK's total energy needs. Their 2022 launch was the 15th attempt to get backing for the scheme in 200 years.

What's the problem?

According to Cllr Huw Thomas, the leader of Cardiff City Council:

The UK Government has so far not lent its
support... due to a perceived requirement for high
levels of public investment and concerns over the
environmental impact.

Right.
Mr Thomas hopes the climate crisis, the Ukraine crisis, the
cost-of-living crisis and the energy crisis might nudge the Tories
on a bit.
But that won't happen.
Labour is already itching to counter-sign the next blank
cheque for 'new' nuclear, even if that means diverting money
from tidal research, community grids, district heating, heat
pumps, green hydrogen, demand reduction, better insulation
and the basket of other low-key, modest energy measures
that actually works, and tackling the crushing unfairness that
leaves renewables-rich Scotland paying through the nose for
the world's most expensive electricity.
Ofgem is letting companies fleece Scots because they can.
The answer is to 'take back control' over the whole energy
sector through independence so we can start asking the big
questions – should energy be re-nationalised and why do we
need supply companies if smart meters can be made to work
properly? Though thanks to another botched, Westminster-
led, £35 billion roll-out, that's a big if.
Rishi Sunak and Jeremy Hunt could abolish standing charges
on prepayment meters tomorrow and devise a new system
without unfair regional variations. But they won't. Nor will any
other part of the broken privatised electricity market fix itself.
Finally, if all of this isn't woeful enough, there's another
big danger in leaving Scottish energy in Westminster hands.
They are planning to siphon off renewable energy and
income, just as they siphoned off Scottish oil and gas revenues
in decades past.
In December 2022, Ofgem authorised more than just the
long-awaited Western Isles connector. It also backed two 2GW

subsea high-voltage direct links from Peterhead to England – to help ease the UK's energy crisis.

Why?

According to the *Digest of United Kingdom Energy Statistics* (DUKES) 2021:

> England's share of demand is larger than its generation share so it continues to transfer electricity from Scotland and Wales as well as import electricity from continental Europe.

In short, England needs Scotland's energy resources. Its reliance on Scottish energy is increasing, with Scotland exporting 39 per cent of its electricity to England and Northern Ireland in 2019.

If Labour wins the next election, that process will accelerate. Sir Keir Starmer has pledged to create the cringingly named Great British Energy to invest directly in renewables, alongside the current raft of private companies, who'll still be cheerfully raking in the profits. Like National Grid which reported a 19 per cent increase in pre-tax profits in 2021. Worse still, unless brave Sir Keir decides to tackle Britain's broken and fiendishly complex privatised electricity system, which allows the most expensive fuel (gas) to set the price for all the rest, customers will keep paying more for their electricity than the lower cost of renewable generation. Sweet.

But if GBE invests in Scottish renewables, they'll become British investments which must be negotiated back upon independence.

Seriously, this is a moment like the snaffling up of rivers in 1900s Norway, which prompted nationalisation. Except Norway had just become independent and could act to protect theft of its natural resources. Until we take the political plunge, Scotland cannae.

So, let's call a spade a spade.

England is facing an energy crisis.

Scotland would not be, if energy resources were owned and managed here.

The situation is grim – and should be one of the biggest drivers of independence.

Scotland must plough a green, nuclear-free furrow.

And take a leaf from our nearest Nordic neighbours.

Instead, we face Energy Groundhog Day.

Enough.

So why do countries become independent anyway?

ALTHOUGH THE SCOTTISH Declaration of Arbroath probably informed the American Declaration of Independence, let's be fair. The latter has been more lauded, repeated, analysed and used as a model for other aspiring states than our own. And of course, our Sensational Alex Harvey did write a great song about their Tea Party – the bust-up over taxes that that kicked off the whole Declaration (and inspired the only UK hit to mention George Washington's wooden teeth).

But the American Declaration is relevant to modern Scotland for two other reasons.

Firstly, far more countries have become independent by declaration than referendum. Since 1776, there have been 120 declarations of independence without the gold standard of either a referendum or election.

Most of these countries came into being from the wreckage of empires or confederations, including Spanish America in the 1820s and the Soviet Union and former Yugoslavia in the 1990s. Indeed, in the second half of the 20th century many countries used declarations to re-assert a sovereignty won earlier but lost through occupation (Estonia springs to mind).

After WW2, and Suez when Britain's ability to rule the waves seriously faltered, many former colonies became independent relatively easily, like Ghana in 1957. But no-one remembers them – just the hyper difficult independence struggles of Ireland and India.

Britain is in the *Guinness Book of Records* as the country from which most other countries have gained independence

– it did rule over a fifth of the world's entire population pre-1914. In 1939, Canada, South Africa, Australia and New Zealand were the first to be given independence within the Commonwealth. Since then, a total of 62 countries have gained independence from the United Kingdom – a greater number than France, Spain Portugal and the USA put together. That's not to say Scotland could just make a Declaration, cut and run. But it does put the obstacles faced by Scotland in context. It's not normal.

The second important thing is what motivated the men who drafted the American Declaration – nine of whom hailed from Scotland. It was frustration with London interference in local affairs, taxation without representation and centralisation of government. Ring any bells?

To be fair again though, the 27 grievances against King George III included some serious violations of liberty – Americans colonists were being press-ganged and forced to fight against their own people and the declaration asserted the British have 'plundered our seas, ravaged our coasts, burnt our towns, and destroyed the lives of our people.'

Still, it's striking that the bulk of the grievances are really to do with arbitrary governance by the King/ Prime Minister.

Just saying.

PART FOUR

The Cool, Cool Neighbours

THE KINGDOM AND the Nation have changed dramatically over the last decade. So has the visibility and relevance of our successful, resilient, wee Northern neighbours.

Scotland, like Norway, has important oil, gas, hydro and fish reserves and is pivoting away from fossil fuels to create a green energy future.

Scotland, like Sweden, has emerged from half a century of solid Labour voting; like parts of Finland, struggles with a legacy of bad diet; and like Denmark, has embraced wind energy, big time.

Scots have always glanced longingly at the vibrant Nordic democracies across the North Sea. Indeed, Labour MP Peter Shore observed in the 1990s that John Smith might not make the ideal UK leader because he was 'too Nordic to understand southern greed'. Since then voting patterns have proved him right. Just like our Nordic neighbours, Scots have created a social democratic consensus in which only the question that really divides opinion is the best constitutional way forward.

But over the last ten years, we've learned more about the mechanics of Nordic success and realised their world-beating performance in equality, local control and public ownership are the tough, high standards Scotland should aspire to reach.

So we know now there is a real choice for Scotland as a North Atlantic nation. Do we remain a 'remote', small, supposedly infertile, northern part of Britain, or become the most accessible, ethnically diverse, fertile, southern and second most populous part of the Nordic region?

No wonder many Scots want to reconnect with our friends in the North as an independent state.

But there's been another big change since 2014. During the indyref, Ireland was hardly mentioned by Yes campaigners since the country's experience of violence, civil war, partition and 'Troubles' has been such an unhappy one. That past cannot be erased. But since Brexit there are new stories to tell. Stories of resilience, economic recovery and the democratic triumph of peaceful, negotiated, citizen-led change to the constitution enabling equal marriage and abortion. Change no-one seriously expected to see happen - change that means Ireland is now at the forefront of Scottish thinking about independence. A modern country with a centuries-long attraction for fellow Celts.

The Irish Effect

The excitement was overwhelming.

At the age of 61 and for the first time in my life, I was boarding a train in Belfast bound for Dublin.

I know.

It's hardly bungy jumping off the Victoria Falls.

But it's the small, ordinary things that can produce the most genuine adventure. Try cycling on a country road at night without lights if you don't believe me.

Anyway.

Having been a bairn in Belfast and unable to go any distance on public transport without parents because of 'the situation', Dublin remained a mystery. Thereafter, living in Scotland, trips there were naturally direct. So, I was making a conscious and perverse effort to reach one Irish capital via another – simply for a train trip between the two neighbouring capital cities.

That meant a plane trip to Aldergrove (as Belfast International will always remain for me), an early morning wander on the Titanic quays gazing at the landmark Samson and Goliath cranes and lunch with an old friend masterminding the extension of new university accommodation in the New Lodge – a hitherto no-go zone after registering the highest number of deaths per square mile during the 'Troubles'. Finally, a short cycle on a free bicycle along the banks of the Laggan – a route best avoided until new flood defences raised water levels, thus submerging the muddy sleech and its terrible stench – to reach the station at Lanyon Place.

It was a beautiful, sunny, airy optimistic day.

And each part of it would have been unthinkable ten short years earlier.

All to discover what it's like to cross the Irish border by train.

A route that once meant crossing an iron curtain – in my young mind anyway. Obviously, the reality had always been different. Lots of folk had crossed backwards and forwards during long decades of shootings, abductions, bombings and murders. But others died near that border or – essentially – because of it.

So, what would it feel like to finally cross like everyone else?

The train whizzed through a flow of undulating, swathed, green countryside without signpost or interruption.

What did I expect?

An overhead sign?

A tannoy announcement?

Station names in Irish?

Tiny fields?

A change in air quality?

But that's the power of borders.

They never stop packing a virtual punch.

In Berlin they produced a book called, *Where was the wall?* because so many people who visited before reunification couldn't get their bearings till they relocated that old, murderous east/west divide. Maybe it's a ghoulish obsession – maybe it's just the enduring force of an old wound.

So, I thought crossing the Irish border should still mean something.

And of course, it does.

On the roads, remnants of the bad old days do remain, with massive petrol stations in the middle of nowhere facing each other across a border no longer pitted by fortified army checkpoints, long queues or controlled tension. Once the flow of cars was in one direction – from Northern Ireland into the Republic, where petrol was cheaper thanks to their weaker currency and economy. Now, the direction of travel has generally reversed, but oil companies hedge their bets by keeping a pump in both camps.

Obviously those checkpoints are ripe for re-activation should circumstances deteriorate – though with Sinn Fein poised to form governments on both sides of the border, it will be in their interests to make sure that can't happen on their watch.

Back on the train though, the Irish border is invisible.

There were no pre-boarding passport checks and even at the tail-end of Covid, no effort to check incoming visitors from the North.

And that's a mark of how much things have changed.

Folk from the north are no longer outsiders in the south. Not emotionally, socially or officially. And all of this matters enormously for Scotland.

Partly because a resolved border between NI and Ireland offers a handy template for England and an independent Scotland. Thanks for that Rishi.

But mostly because Ireland's bloody struggle for independence and reunification offered such a scary template for self-determination that our nearest Celtic neighbours were scarcely mentioned by independence campaigners in 2014.

That's all changed.

Since Brexit, an Irish passport has become gold-dust – a gateway to the good life. And in Ireland itself, Republican suspicion of the EU has melted away.

According to Dublin-based academic and businessman Frank Schnittger, writing in the online blog, Slugger O'Toole:

> Ireland's accession to the EU (then EEC) was the
> single most transformative event in our 100 years of
> independence. Indeed, [our] history could be neatly
> divided into two periods – pre and post EU.

Responding to a Euro-sceptic article by his old social policy lecturer, Schnittger makes a staunch defence of Ireland's EU membership:

I don't recall the last 50 years replicating the centuries of repression, dispossession and famine experienced under British rule prior to 1922. Apparently, membership of the euro zone forced Irish banks to engage in the reckless credit expansion of the 2009 financial crisis. But there is no mention of the complete failure of our own regulator to police their actions. Now, it seems we must consider 'Irexit' to accommodate the 'Britishness' of northern unionists, even though a large majority there voted against Brexit and see continuing membership of the EU as the most attractive feature of a possible united Ireland.

There's a complaint that 'we are now net contributors to, rather than beneficiaries from, the EU budget' – but that's the result of economic success due to EU membership.[34]

The rest of the article is similarly spirited and the online discussion engaged and informed until... Scotland's 'tolerance' of Brexit is mentioned. Schnittger suggests England must have beaten Scotland militarily in the 1700s to force such an utterly crap Brexit deal upon the country now.

Ouch.

Now I mention that not to be critical, but to note how completely pecking orders on these islands have changed. Ireland was once perceived as a hopeless rural, bog-strewn basket case, whilst Scotland enjoyed an Enlightenment, housed the 'workshop of the world' on the Clyde and was blessed with a surfeit of doctors, engineers and a skilled literate workforce.

If any history was worth knowing even 30 years ago – it wasn't the history of poor famine-struck Ireland.

But knowledge follows use.

And few academics in modern Ireland need to know much about Scotland. So, they don't.

---

34 https://www.sluggerotoole.com/2023/01/03/eu-membership-has-been-the-making-of-ireland/#more-143326

It should be extraordinary that such a well-read man is unaware of Scotland's story. But that mirrors my experience elsewhere – especially the Nordic nations – where (with notable exceptions) most folk think we are independent already or just the northern part of England. Outlander helped raise the profile slightly, but Scotland is still generally invisible – even with our devolved parliament. And actually, that should come as no surprise.

How much does anyone know about the truly powerful federal Länder of Germany? There you go then. A constitutional miss is as good as a mile and nothing short of independence will let Scotland throw six and become a respected player on the international scene like Ireland, which has transformed itself over the last decade, managing to turn the colossal disruption of Brexit into an economic opportunity and a stronger case for reunification.

Consider. In May 2022, more Irish passports were issued in Northern Ireland than UK passports – for the first time ever.

Her Majesty's Passport Office in London confirmed 48,555 citizens in Northern Ireland applied for a UK passport – 356 fewer than those who opted for an Irish passport the same year (48,911).

Obviously, that choice is a fairly pragmatic one, since an Irish passport allows the holder to travel freely within the EU. But it also signals a new fluidity in national identity. The Good Friday Agreement gave citizens of Northern Ireland the right to be British, Irish or both. Now Irish citizenship confers EU citizenship and a European identity as well. Once upon a time it could confer a hospitality box at Ibrox for life – no self-respecting Prod would touch it. Yet now, unionists are literally queueing up for Irish passports. It's a vote of confidence in the Irish Republic and its different political path that would have been inconceivable in 2014.

There's more.

Apart from being entitled to a UK border poll every seven years – a shorter 'generation' than seems to be operating in

Scotland – the European Commission has said citizens of the North will automatically re-enter the EU if they vote for reunification. In short, a future Border poll will also be a de facto EU referendum.

No such guarantee has been offered to Scotland – the most EU-friendly nation in the British Isles. But fair play to Northern Ireland. Their accelerated route back into Europe is possible because they can join an independent, popular European country.

And a modern, secular one.

While Scotland was preparing for the first indyref, Ireland was also making democratic strides.

In 2013, a Constitutional Convention met eight times to produce outline legislation on equal marriage. It echoed the public mood so well that its proposal got 62 per cent backing at the subsequent referendum. In 2016, another randomly selected Citizens Assembly was convened to revise the eighth amendment of the Irish Constitution, which hitherto banned abortion in almost all circumstances.

Ninety-nine assembly members were chosen at random to reflect the population in age, gender, social class and geography. The group included pro-lifers, pro-choicers and undecideds and they heard from people on both sides of the abortion debate, including medical, legal and ethical specialists, and folk with personal testimonies. Members had the chance to discuss amongst themselves, listen and reflect over five weekends between November 2016 and April 2017.

Louise Caldwell was totally honest about her motivation for joining in 2016:

> It was the end of the summer and I'd just spent three months with my three children. Then this guy comes along and asks if I want to go to a hotel in Dublin every weekend for five weeks and I'm like – yes! Adult conversation, sleep, no children – I'll be there!

But Louise went on to describe how she and her uncertain, non-activist colleagues were transformed into the focused democratic team that resolved the most emotive and taboo issue in Ireland.

> At the start, maybe 10 per cent of us were definitely pro-choice and 10 per cent definitely anti-abortion – the vast majority were in-between. What made us certain of our final recommendation was working together through evidence presented from a variety of perspectives. We were all changed by the evidence.

Yip, the irony screams out at you. If only such a trusting deliberative process had been engaged by David Cameron before the fateful Brexit referendum, which instead launched Britain on a porkie-packed, evidence-free path to disaster.

Anyway, despite fears the Citizens Assembly had gone too far, 66.4 per cent of the population backed its recommendation to remove the eighth amendment, proving that ordinary voters can successfully resolve issues regarded as intractable by politicians.

You may not remember the details.

You will remember the massive crowds of Irish youngsters, celebrating on the streets of Dublin and beyond. People power has helped modernise and secularise Ireland, improving the country's democratic credentials and boosting the case for reunification. Ireland is not the charming but hopelessly conservative country depicted by outsiders. It's now ahead of the democratic game, because it managed to do what Britain will never do. It trusted citizens to hear evidence and recommend change on emotive, pivotal moral issues. And as I'm writing, in early 2023, their Citizens Assembly is set to boldly go where most governments absolutely fear to tread – considering whether to decriminalise drugs for personal use.

What does that say about parliaments in Edinburgh and London?

Maybe it says we elect fair-minded folk who rapidly get scared off sensible solutions by the constant lobbying of vested interests. In the Irish Citizens Assembly, lobbyists are banned. Maybe British politicians have an unshakeable mistrust of the public – devolved parliaments included. But that just means departure from elite control would have an even more seismic impact here.

What would politics be like if grannies, 16-year-olds, drug users, head teachers, truck drivers, wheelchair users, fishermen, long term unemployed folk and jannies, Highlanders, Lowlanders, Sikhs, cleaners and priests all sat down together to work through land reform, a citizen's income, the use of nuclear weapons, the Gender Recognition Reform Bill – or how to run another independence referendum? It would be revolutionary.

The Irish can testify that well-facilitated groups of randomly chosen citizens find popular solutions to thorny problems – and confer upon them a sense of civic legitimacy, generally absent from the formal political arena.

So that's what the Irish were doing while Boris Johnson was boasting of oven-ready trade deals, attempting to prorogue parliament and preparing to break international law by unilaterally ditching the Northern Ireland protocol.

In 2016 one country in these islands was acting like a group of responsible adults, while its neighbour was behaving like a bunch of spoilt, Old Etonian, right-wing brats.

Which country chimed most strongly with Scottish attitudes?

The progressive 'minnow' of independent Ireland or the bully boys of mighty Westminster?

It really is a no-brainer.

But after these democratic breakthroughs, the Irish then had to cope with the curved balls thrown their way by Brexit. And they did, creating 32 new ferry routes that bypass the 'land bridge' of England. Rosslare Europort in Co Wexford has seen European freight increase by a staggering 370 per cent compared to 2019. In contrast, trade through the UK is around 20 per cent lower.

The decline in sea services to Wales and Liverpool has also given a Brexit dividend to ports in the North – including Larne, Belfast, and Warrenpoint – with freight volumes hitting 'unprecedented highs in 2021'.

The Irish Maritime Development Office says there's been a doubling of roll-on, roll-off cargo using direct routes to EU ports, like Le Havre, Cherbourg, Zeebrugge in Belgium and Dunkirk in France.

Ah Dunkirk.

A port with special emotional significance for Britain – the scene of a defeat turned into victory of sorts by a flotilla of small boats rescuing stranded British soldiers.

But today the not-so-small boats approaching Dunkirk are expanding trade routes with Ireland, a country viewed by the French as an 'underestimated' market. The port authorities are planning stronger links with Dublin Port and Rosslare Europort, whilst also creating new routes for the first time with Cork and Waterford.

'The decision to have a direct service between Ireland and Dunkirk has been pushed by Brexit for sure,' says the deputy chief executive of Dunkirk. 'I think that we all underestimated the market, the volume of cargo, leaving Ireland for continental Europe and vice versa.'

He says Dunkirk is pitching itself as 'one of the best places to land' for Irish companies distributing to Northern Europe, thanks to a strong road network connecting with the port. Meanwhile, the head of Rosslare Europort says, 'there is no denying the switch we've seen in the supply chain which has allowed Ireland to become France's nearest EU neighbour' to the west.

In short, far from being cut off and broken by an isolationist England, Ireland has sparked a bidding war amongst French ports eager for its trade.

Fortune favours the bold.

And the independent.

Scotland, read and weep.

And on top of all this, the Republic of Ireland has quietly demonstrated that it cares about Northern Ireland by demonstrating solidarity with practical help. Quite apart from extending that sought after Irish passport to anyone with a Northern Irish granny, parents or birthplace – pensioners living in Northern Ireland have been able to use their British travel cards to get free travel throughout the Republic since 2007 as well. For 15 years, all elderly Irish citizens, north and south, have had a pan-Irish 'right to roam' – extending the opportunity of travel and prejudice-busting experiences to the part of the population usually most resistant to change.

The Irish Transport Authority estimates the cost of that is £1 million a year. And despite the 2008 financial crash, austerity and hostility between the UK and Irish Governments over Brexit, this little act of generosity has neither been curtailed nor reversed. Pensioners from the fiercely loyalist Shankhill Road can travel to Cork and back for nowt courtesy of the Oireachtas (Irish legislature) – and tens of thousands have.

No wonder perceptions of life in the Republic have changed so dramatically that military historian and former *Telegraph* editor Sir Max Hastings wrote recently

> in Ireland as in Scotland, demographics and time are on the side of change. As old instinctive Unionists die off, the young favour a different agenda. Within a generation, I believe, Scotland will vote for independence and Northern Ireland for reunification with the South.

Why are the young in Northern Ireland so keen for change? It's not just the burgeoning economy but the way Ireland has harnessed people power to tackle difficult moral issues like abortion, reaping a very substantial reward in the process – the creation of a modern, secular Irish state in which religion is finally and visibly a matter of private conscience not state policy. Northern Ireland, unable to agree even on a Language Act – never mind abortion law or equal marriage – has been hopelessly left behind as the tectonic plates of competence, identity and allegiance have shifted at lightning speed, along with the economy – Irish GDP is currently the highest in Europe. Of course, there have been swings and roundabouts and quibbles about the usefulness of GDP as an accurate marker of real prosperity. Still, in the eyes of most academic commentators, Ireland is somewhere in the middle of the league table of European living standards.

Losing a colonial master – finding a continent

In the 1920s, unionists insisted 'Home Rule for Ireland' would lead to 'Home Ruin' because a protectionist government in Dublin would cut business off from its main export market in Britain. They also raised concerns over the quality of governance in an independent Irish state, warning that the nationalists' lack of expertise would lead to extravagant and unsustainable public expenditure. Some of that reckless spending did come to pass, but only after 40 years of almost over-strict fiscal control. And lessons were learned.

But one thing's for sure. 'Cutting businesses off from Britain' or less emotively, 'finding other trade partners' did happen thanks to the foolishness of England not Ireland – and it's been a great success. Fifty per cent of Irish exports went to Britain in the 1970s – just 10 per cent by 2020. The academic verdict is that 'The diversification of Irish trading partners, particularly with respect to the countries of the EU…[is] the foundation of modern Irish prosperity.'[35] (See Figs 3 & 4 overleaf.)

So, the Irish economy, identity and cultural self-confidence are rising together, in contrast to the combined falling stock of its former imperial masters.

---

35 https://www.economicsobservatory.com/irelands-economy-since-independence-what-lessons-from-the-past-100-years

Figure 3: Ireland's trade with the EU, 1924–2020

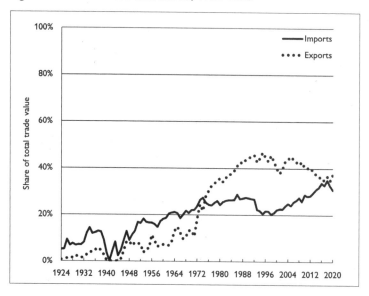

Figure 4: Ireland's trade with the UK, 1924–2020

British citizenship is hard to come by thanks to the backlog of asylum claims, abhorrent threat to deport refugees, closure of legal asylum routes to Britain and Theresa May's original hostile environment. By contrast becoming Irish is something of a doddle, which irritates some locals who think citizenship should have more to do with Ireland's unique culture and heritage than 'keeping employment options open.' But there's a plus-side to the wave of wannabe Irish – the confidence of the Emerald Isle has been rising steadily since the post-2008 financial doldrums. As Irish commentator Amanda Coakley observes:

> Perhaps claiming Irish citizenship is straightforward because we, the Irish, never thought our nationality would be in vogue. Think Irish and what used to come to mind? The decades of exodus to the US and UK, and those who created the music, writing and theatre shaped by loneliness and poverty. The truth is that 50 years ago no one wanted to become Irish.

That's all changed.

Through its knee-jerk hostility to Europe and all forms of immigration, 'Cool Britannia' now stands revealed as backward-looking and utterly archaic while Ireland looks thoroughly modern – the first country in the world to legislate for equal marriage as the result of a popular vote authorised by a gay, mixed-race Taoiseach.

That's had a huge impact on a Scottish independence debate from which Ireland was previously excluded – beyond the pale because of its violent independence struggle, the ongoing grief of Northern Ireland and the terrible economic crash of 2008.

But today the Irish stand revealed as a nation with far more than money on their side.

Are the Irish weeping at the loss of trading and cultural contact with Britain?

They're far too polite and diplomatic to say so, but are they heck.

Ireland has lost a colonial master and found a continent.

The last ever Scottish press trip to Brussels in 2019 offered ample evidence.

Of course, the big EU states of France, Spain and Germany still call most of the shots, but quite evidently, Ireland punches so far above its weight in the EU that it's inspiring and depressing all at the same time. Cos once again, that should be Scotland.

Take Ireland's Commissioner to the EU, Kilkenny man Phil Hogan – who resigned a year after our visit for breaching coronavirus rules during a golfing break in Ireland. But until 2020, Hogan ran the EU's vast Trade portfolio and his colleague Tom Tynan – originally from a dairy farm near Kilkenny – was responsible for technical barriers to trade, biotechnology, agriculture, maritime affairs and fisheries, research & innovation. Tynan also oversaw EU trade relations in Korea, Turkey, Singapore, Iran, Iraq, the Middle East, Denmark, Ireland, Netherlands, Finland and Sweden. Despite the epic scope of his job, Tynan still had the friendly, straightforward manner that characterises the Irish and managed to remember a visit to the fishing communities of Peterhead and Fraserburgh with precision and some fondness.

Ok, the Irish have a habit of making difficult jobs look easy.

But Scots will have no chance to demonstrate or hone our own considerable negotiating skills within the EU until we find the confidence to leave huffy Britain behind.

Back in 2019, the Scottish press met another impressive Irishman, Daniel Ferrie. He was the Commission's Brexit spokesperson for three long years, working beside Chief Negotiator, Michel Barnier, before becoming spokesperson on banking and financial services, taxation and customs, helping EU politicians to decide if the City of London's big financial companies should be granted 'equivalence' post Brexit to let them keep trading in Europe. The fate of the City (sort of) lay in his hands. Don't you love to (finally) be in control?

Ferrie reminded us this much sought after 'equivalence' could be terminated by the EU with just 30 days' notice. Yet this is the uncertain future the City of London faces, as the EU develops capital markets in Frankfurt and Paris. If Scotland had voted Yes in 2014, Edinburgh would be on that list.

Not now. Not until we get weaving.

Finally, EU officials told us continuing access to Scotland's fishing grounds by European countries had indeed been discussed with British ministers during Brexit trade talks. And sure enough, Scotland's fishermen soon had egg on their collective faces, as Brexit failed to exclude EU vessels from Scottish waters. The trawlermen had been played. The shellfish industry has almost been decimated.

If Scotland had voted Yes in 2014, and applied for EU membership as an independent coastal state, some fishing access might still have been traded – that's true. But for something valuable to Scots, not passporting rights for London fat cats – which is what seems to have happened.

Coming across all these powerful Celts ten days before Scotland's enforced exit from the EU in 2019, was a profoundly bittersweet experience.

It was great to see so many top jobs held by confident, articulate Celts from a country smaller than Scotland with fewer people, energy resources, and an even more difficult history, right at the heart of the European project, mixing easily, charming effortlessly and talking with energy and authority about future plans that would (mostly) be a perfect fit for green-leaning, progressive Scotland.

If we'd taken the leap in 2014.

But we didn't. So now, we are out.

And the new, evolving, European world will soon be a foreign country for Scots.

No matter what polite sympathy these top EU bureaucrats showed to the dozen Scots journalists who made that final press trip, one thing was clear. Scotland doesn't figure in their future plans for one nanosecond – and that won't change until we vote for independence and apply to rejoin.

Scots were leaders in the team that created the Europol

database which helps police track people traffickers and terrorist movements across Europe. But neither Police Scotland nor any other British police force can access that vital database, or the even more useful Schengen Information Service now because of Brexit. In fact, even as we stood shaking hands, British data was being removed from the EU's 'interoperability' database of biometric information used to stop identity theft – and the data of EU citizens was being removed from databases here.

The contrast couldn't be starker.

While the genial Irish civil servants collected their briefing notes and hurried off to other top-level meetings, the Scots employed as non-permanent staff by the European Commission were clearing desks, leaving flats, and looking for new jobs – just like EU staff working in Scotland.

Leaving the EU may still feel like an abstraction for most Scots.

But our fate – being walled up with English Tories for the foreseeable future, minus the EU's steadying presence – is very real.

So what happens next?

Well, our Celtic cousins will keep planning the future of Europe.

EU members will keep developing big ambitious projects – a European Education Area by 2025, so that diplomas from neighbouring states will have mutual recognition; the first Carbon Neutral continent, introducing air pollution controls and investing in the circular economy; tackling cyber-crime by ensuring each user has a unique IP address and of course, concluding new trade deals across the world.

In all of this Ireland will lead, Northern Ireland will be protected and Scotland will be nowhere.

The Irish have exhibited solidarity, generosity and care towards their northern neighbours – old-fashioned values that have been all but wiped from public life in England by a succession of hard-nosed, hard-faced Tory governments. It's not beyond the bounds of possibility that Northern Ireland voters will demand a cross border poll on reunification with the South despite the NI protocol-solving, Windsor Framework. Maybe not immediately, but soon. When that happens, the radicalising effect on Scots will make a second indyref inevitable.

As Amanda Coakley put it:

> Our 'Oirish' identity is becoming a thing of the past, while little Englanders still force nostalgia for the British Empire on reluctant northern compatriots.

So how might Scotland fare as a small independent country in the EU?

In a massive turnaround from 2014, when the example of our nearest neighbour spoke only of grief and bloodshed, Ireland is now showing the way.

Our friends in the North

Scotland has reconnected with its go-ahead Celtic cousin.

But we have other valuable small country connections and comparators too – the whole of the Nordic region.

Genetically speaking, island Scots have more Norse DNA than any other Britons, Viking placenames and a Presbyterian share of the Nordic Lutheran aversion to pomp, bling, display and empty status. But more than helping re-energise old cultural connections, our Nordic neighbours can teach us how to make the most of independence.

When Alex Salmond described an Arc of Prosperity around Scotland based on Iceland, Norway and Ireland in 2006, he got it half-right. Within 18 months, Iceland and Ireland had succumbed to the financial crash and Scottish Labour leader Jim Murphy was joking about an independent Scotland joining the Arc of Insolvency. He mocked too soon.

Iceland had three main banks with accumulated debts ten times the size of the whole economy – it let them all go the wall. The state prosecuted and jailed bankers and compensated only domestic savers, sparking a legal wrangle between Reykjavik,

London and the Hague that took a decade – to be won by Iceland.

Meanwhile, as its currency tanked, the crafty bosses of Icelandair realised tourists might now flock to a country once so expensive that a large packet of crisps cost £13. I kid you not. So, in the midst of a recession so bad people were trapped with negative equity and couldn't afford to emigrate, the airline used government cash to buy new planes, build hotels in almost any gap site and start shovelling tourists in by the planeload. Iceland rapidly became a service/tourism-oriented economy – not perfect at all for citizens who're still paying a massive price for the greedy exploits of the buccaneering few and the near-complete failure of regulation.

But still, bankruptcy – both national and personal – has largely been averted. But the dry facts of economic recovery overlook the part played by Nordic solidarity. Icelanders are keen to tell you the first £30 million loan in the dark days of 2008 arrived from the 55 thousand inhabitants of the neighbouring Faroe Islands and represented 3 per cent of their entire GDP. British banks might have been 'too big to fail', but Iceland was too warmly-regarded by its Nordic neighbours to go under.

And too darned resilient.

Iceland kept going, adapted, picked itself up and pushed the marketing boat out even further after the Eyjafjallajökul eruption of 2010, which grounded planes across Europe. Outsiders saw only danger and disaster. The Icelanders saw the best possible advertisement of their weirdly powerful volcanic landscape and relative proximity to Europe. Visiting in 2011, slogan T-shirts were all the rage: 'Don't mess with Iceland – we may not have cash, but we got ash'; and 'What part of Eyjafjallajokull don't you understand?'

But behind this defiant exterior, Icelanders were determined to make sure their politicians learned a democratic lesson.

Iceland's constitution was pretty much a copy of the Danish constitution adopted hurriedly in 1944 after which a full overhaul was planned within years. Decades later, this 'crappy' constitution as lawyer and campaigner Katrin Oddsdottir memorably described it, was still in place, giving too much power and patronage to the country's President, along with other weaknesses highlighted by the financial crash. So, an Icelandic Assembly was set up to start a new constitution from scratch, composed of 475 men and 475 women demographically representative of the population but randomly chosen. It suggested a Commission elected by popular vote to draft a People's Constitution and the 15 men and 10 women chosen in a nationwide online vote – including a farmer, pastor, art museum director, radio presenter, trade union leader, a student, filmmaker but excluding professional politicians – devised this opening line:

> We the people of Iceland wish to create a just society
> with equal opportunities for everyone.

A modest but powerful statement of intent that would perfectly fit a new Scottish constitution.

The commission used social media to open the drafting process to all of Iceland's citizens and gathered feedback on 12 successive drafts that embedded human rights, democracy, transparency, equal access to health care and education, a more strongly regulated financial sector, and public ownership of Icelandic natural resources in a new constitution, backed by the majority of Icelanders but not yet ratified by politicians.

Katrin Oddsdottir is '100 per cent certain we'll get it over the line soon' – and in the meantime, Iceland has become the focus of world attention for its audacious use of people power to resolve a constitutional problem.

Icelanders bounced back from economic chaos with even greater democracy – just like Ireland – and with fresh confidence in the future. Now the country that was put on the Terrorism Register alongside Al Qaeda by Gordon Brown stands within a credit rating whisker of dear, special, old Britain.

So that's what they've been doing since 2008.

What've we been up to?

Britain – well England – whipped itself into a righteous froth about Brussels, voted to withdraw from the European Union on the basis of lies posted on the sides of buses and now finds itself with the worst performing economy in the OECD.[36]

And the point?

Iceland and Ireland have valuable lessons for Scotland. Not about prosperity – but about resilience. That's my quibble about Alex Salmond's Arc. He was in the right forest, barking up the wrong tree.

There's no point ogling the euros and kroner of our neighbours – prosperity waxes and wanes – but we should be mightily impressed by their ability to make the most of whatever happens, without once looking over their collective shoulders. And we should consider why we find such resilience, hard to emulate.

These are the smartest, healthiest and most successful countries on the planet by any measure, whether that's child wellbeing, happiness, democracy, literacy, income equality, or the triple A credit ratings enjoyed by Denmark, Norway and Sweden. Finland is ranked AA+, Iceland stands at A after recovering from near bankruptcy and Britain stands between these two on AA.

But it's resilience that's got them all there – with prosperity as a by-product of income equality. Indeed, in my experience as Director of Nordic Horizons for 12 years, bringing almost 70 experts over to speak in the Scottish Parliament, not one has ever asked for a fee, upmarket hotel or first-class travel. Every single one has made an attempt to relate their experience to Scotland – indeed Finnish educationalist Pasi Sahlberg amazed everyone by producing a new PowerPoint he'd worked on overnight to include comparative statistics on Scottish education. And then stunned parliamentary staff

---

36 https://www.bloomberg.com/news/articles/2023-03-17/uk-and-russia-alone-among-shrinking-major-economies-oecd-says#xj4y7vzkg

by plugging his European two-pin MacBook into a Scottish socket by skilfully inserting a biro into the missing third pin. Intellectual, practical and rule-bending. Generous with time, easy going, interested and relentlessly positive – the proof of the Nordic pudding is in the people.

And I know they'd happily share expertise from decades of dealing with pretty much every situation that could possibly face an independent Scotland.

Of course, there are many points of divergence. Scotland industrialised earlier and harder than the Nordics, retained feudal land tenure which created a large pool of landless labour and cannon fodder for the low paid, casual jobs of the industrialised central belt, then we failed to democratise, embrace co-ops and social enterprise, or retain truly 'local' government.

By contrast, the Nordic nations have relatively tiny but powerful municipal councils; high personal tax to equalise opportunity with comparatively low business taxes; excellent, universal welfare services, 'flat' organisational structures with little hierarchy; social contracts where unions are involved in everyday management; relatively cheap land prices; strong connections with nature and weekends spent in wooden cottages not street corners and shopping malls; greater gender equality; higher levels of investment in research and human capital; almost no private education; and universal, affordable kindergarten with a school-starting age of six, not four. Currently Scotland ticks only a couple of these boxes – but that's precisely why involvement with these advanced democracies could be so transformational. They could become Scotland's political life coaches. Not because any one country is Scotland's double. Not because they are always right. But because they are relatively serious people who place the rational calculation of national interest, far above party-political dogma.

Not the United States of Scandinavia

Take an imaginary conversation between EU members Finland and Iceland who are members of the EFTA 'halfway house.' Finns would no more dream of trying to persuade the fishing-dependent Icelanders to join the EU (and Common Fisheries Policy) than the Icelanders – so distant from the threat of Russian invasion – would encourage the Finns to quit the EU, their sole source of European solidarity. In short, when it comes to big policy decisions there is no three-line whip or bludgeoning attempts at pointless uniformity. Indeed, not a single Nordic country uses the same currency as its immediate neighbour. A recipe for chaos? No.

Each country respects the different interests of its neighbours and that permissiveness is the engine behind multilateral agreements like the Nordic Common Travel Area, collaboration on procurement, defence and the Nordic Council of Ministers. All this cooperation is possible precisely because there is no United States of Scandinavia with a single imposed solution – instead it's horses for courses.

Progress has been stronger amongst the five separate Nordic nations working together than within any large monolithic union in the world, precisely because each sovereign state respect the sovereignty of the others.

There's a model in there for a post-independence UK, though of course, Rule Britannia will be reluctant to even examine it – because it requires former colonising powers to get over themselves.

A case in point. On Sunday 3 September 1967, Sweden changed from driving on the left-hand side of the road to driving on the right. Not simple, but in classic Swedish fashion, well organised and accident-free. Why did they do it? Because all their Nordic neighbours drove on the right and Sweden – despite having the most powerful economy– realised it was odd one out. It just made more sense to change. And it enabled more Swedish Saabs and Volvos to be bought by neighbours.

Once you remove petulance, emotionalism and a preoccupation with status from international affairs it's astonishing how much more productive life can be.

Finns adopted a constitutional ban on NATO membership in the 1960s to persuade Russia there would never be an American base on Finnish soil. This lapsed, obviously with Russia's invasion of Ukraine. But that explains Finland's very keen membership of the European Union – the only Nordic country to have embraced the Euro. Sure, EU membership is not as strong or formal a source of armed defence in the event of Russian aggression as NATO – hence the application to join, arm-in-arm with former colonising power Sweden. But the EU will always be valued highly in Finland as the country's original link with Europe.

Iceland, meanwhile, considered EU and Euro membership in the immediate aftermath of the financial crash, but abandoned the application the minute their ship had steadied, largely because of the inevitable and unwelcome imposition of the Common Fisheries Policy. The only 'war' Icelanders ever fought was the Cod War against Britain to protect a 12-nautical-mile (22 km) exclusion zone around its shores and a 200-nautical-mile zone where other fleets need Iceland's permission. Why? Iceland is the 12th largest fishing nation in the world. Finland is not.

These are two Nordic nations with very different attitudes to EU membership, because their geopolitical interests are also very different.

And that's ok.

Nowhere in the Nordic world do you find one country trying to boss its neighbour or recapture lost imperial status.

That's why greater awareness of the Nordic nations since 2014 is so important for Scotland – they act in ways we can only imagine. They've spent a century creating the equality we can only talk about. And they've demonstrated how small independent countries can park old pecking orders, ditch old enmities, and work together.

But more than all that, they've shown how independence

creates progress by reflecting the outlooks of local citizens, not former colonial masters. This is utterly key.

Take Norway.

The pioneering Peasants' Parliament

The Norwegians' first bid for independence happened in 1814, when colonial rulers Denmark made the great mistake of backing Napoleon in war. He was beaten, Denmark was beaten and its possessions were taken away. One of them was Norway. For a short, tantalising period, the Norwegians were convinced they were heading for independence. So their relatively enlightened Prince Christian Frederik gathered 112 men in a village called Eidsvoll to write a constitution in five weeks flat. It gave the vote to all men over the age of 25 who owned land or were officials, and so many men owned land in Norway that 45 per cent got the vote overnight. The same landowning clause within the British 'Great' Reform Act of 1832 increased the male electorate to just 5.8 per cent in England and Wales and a pitiful 2.5 per cent in Scotland – such were the chronically low levels of land ownership, which in turn triggered the right to vote.

Norway gained the legal status of an independent state in 1814, with its own parliament, judiciary, legal system, armed forces, flag and currency, but was forced into a union of crowns with the King of Sweden. Its pioneering constitution survived intact, underpinning successful Norwegian challenges to Swedish royal prerogative over the next 70 years, and gradually creating a different, more equal kind of state.

In 1833, there were more peasant farmers than officials and civil servants in the Norwegian Parliament for the first time, earning it the nickname Bønde-Stortinget (Peasant Parliament). Now, to be clear *bønde* in Norwegian carries none of the Monty Python associations of the word 'peasant', in English.

Au contraire, Norwegian *bønde* 'filled the role of 'heroes' in the years leading up to 1814,' according to Professor John Bryden, because of their organised opposition to Danish rule.

And they were no pushovers in the country's new parliament either, passing a local self-government law in 1837, which meant Norwegians have the right to govern themselves in geographically limited areas via *kommuner* (elected municipal councils) and not from distant Oslo.

This Act provided a brake against centralisation in Norway for almost two centuries, and has supported a more dispersed rural population than any of Norway's neighbours. Keeping people on the land also turbo-charged the development of hydroelectricity and prompted the Størting to act when it realised the country's most precious resource – the hydro power of rivers – was quietly falling into the hands of English and Dutch industrialists. But the Concession Laws of 1906–9 – which essentially nationalised river ownership – put hydro power back into the hands of each local municipality, not central government, creating funds for all kinds of local improvement. The template of public ownership created by hydroelectricity was automatically applied again when oil was discovered in the 1970s, driving Norway's far-sighted decision to establish a Sovereign Wealth Fund to guarantee prosperity for unborn generations.

In short, the progressive, canny decisions of the Peasant Parliament shaped modern independent Norway, pretty well.

Would any of that have happened if Norway had remained under the control of a King who ruled Sweden like an autocrat until 1905?

Very doubtful.

Ditto Finland.

The cooperative Finns

Finland has a 1,300 km land border with Russia, fought two wars in the 1940s to defend its territory, and is now applying to join NATO. There, most knowledge of Finland ends.

Which is a shame.

Because a staple of Finnish life – developed during their

independence movement in the early 20th century – could help
solve the energy, price and supply-side crises facing Scotland
today. Using cooperatives not corporations to deliver.

I became aware of Finland's cooperative default during a
cycle round the Åland archipelago 12 years ago. Chatting to
farmers heading for the cooperatively owned abattoir on a
cooperatively owned ferry, it turned out we had been staying
in a cooperatively owned hotel and changed money in a
cooperatively owned bank.

What did cooperative ferry ownership do for them, I
wondered? 'In a good year, our dividend is a breakfast share
– enough for one fry-up in the ferry cafe.'

Cue much laughter.

But there is a greater reward for customer/owners than mere
cash – local control. A third of all car places are reserved for
locals, ferries are constantly maintained and quickly replaced
and tourists are required to break journeys across the ferry
chain with one overnight stop to boost small-island tourism.
As Hebridean islanders know, local priorities and local control
are valuable beyond measure.

But that snapshot of cooperative life on the Åland islands
is just a tiny part of the cooperative story.

Co-ops in Finland began in 1899 – a way to strengthen
society after a period of 'Russification' aimed at suppressing
Finland's burgeoning independence movement. They gave
people a 'non-political' way to unite, organise and avoid
trading monopolies that left customers overcharged and
farmers underpaid. The first Cooperative Act was passed in
1901 and co-op banks, dairies and shops opened immediately
almost everywhere.

Even though they operated within the capitalist system,
the workers' movement backed co-ops as a way to develop
civic abilities and rid people of 'subservient attitudes'. After
independence in 1917 and despite a terrible civil war and two
Russian invasions during the 1940s, cooperatives continued,
adapted, expanded and modernised to become a defining

aspect of the country today.

When Finnish scientist AI Virtanen won the Nobel Prize for chemistry in 1945 he said:

> We have no Rockefellers or Carnegies, but we have cooperatives.

So, Finland has become an economy based on mutuality. It is also the world's happiest country for the fifth year running, according to the UN Sustainable Development Network. Are the two connected? How could they not be?

There are over 4,000 cooperatives in Finland today and 7 million cooperative memberships (more than the human population of the country).

To be fair, cooperatives also operate in Russia. As reported by *Izvestiia*, their productivity is several times higher than equivalent state enterprises and their earnings are higher too. This has created some resentment and Russian citizens complain about the generally higher prices charged by cooperatives, their practice of siphoning off the best workers from state enterprises, and reliance on state supplies thereby exacerbating shortage in the state sector. Many cooperatives have been vulnerable to exorbitant taxation by local officials and protection rackets run by criminals. 'Kooperativshchiki' (cooperative owners) has thus became a term of abuse in ordinary Russian speech.

Combine that with corrupt, oligarch control of privatised former state monopolies, and I'm guessing that if Finland had remained under Moscow control, its cooperative revolution would not have happened and the country would be a very different place today.

As it is, Finland's water cooperatives avoid both the under-investment that plagues state operations in Russia and the crazy profits that bedevil privately owned water companies in England. There are seven electricity coops in Finland and even more companies which use the Mankala principle – whereby electricity is distributed at production cost instead of making a profit. Around two fifths of Finnish electricity is based on this principle, which means citizens of this sub-Arctic state don't freeze or rush to heat banks in winter.

That's the relatively benign corporate thinking a cooperative society can generate.

Similarly, the 100,000 members of the Metsäliitto Cooperative own about half of Finnish private forests and together form a cornerstone of the country's recent prosperity. When newspaper sales exploded in the early 20th century, Finnish wood pulp was in high demand. And since hundreds of thousands of Finns owned forests and land, wood pulp income was evenly spread across the whole population, not pocketed by a single Duke. (Looking at you, Richard.)

Today consumer cooperatives produce half of all daily goods – like the massive S-Group with 1,800 outlets including supermarkets, department, hardware and speciality stores, petrol stations, travel and hospitality outlets, car dealerships, dairies, and the S-Bank.

Its retail sales revenue last year totalled 12 billion euros – some paid out as bonuses to its 3 million cooperative 'client-owners', some paid to the government as tax, some used to hold prices steady and some re-invested to expand the company's renewable energy portfolio – S-Group wind turbines produce around 80 per cent of the group's entire electricity demand and it's also the country's biggest solar producer.

But despite its vast size, S-Group is no monolith, run instead as 19 independent regional cooperatives, six local coops and a central procurement company (SOK) that's owned by the regional cooperatives.

This is how Finland operates today. A relaxed, consensual society that's developed in a very different direction to its former colonial master – Russia.

There's another thing independence did for Finland. It gave the world Jean Sibelius. His music is the sound of winter, forests, nature and for Finns, the sound of their own hard-won independence – broody, powerful, emotional, vivid and northern.

Sibelius was an unlikely champion of Finnish culture, born into a Swedish-speaking family – common enough since the country was run as a Swedish province from 1323, till it became a Russian Grand Duchy in 1809. Sibelius was originally a violinist but found inspiration in Finland's myths, sagas, and folklore – particularly the *Kalevala*, a 19th-century work of poetry based on Finnish oral folklore which told a story about the creation of the Earth. An abridged version, published in 1862 – just three years before his birth – was thought to have inspired JRR Tolkien's Middle-Earth mythology. It certainly influenced Sibelius who honeymooned with his wife Aine in Karelia – where the *Kalevela* was set – and later produced music based on Kullervo (one hero from the epic poem) and four symphonic poems based on another called Lemminkainen – one of which is the famous Swan of Tuonela.

All this folklore-based work reminded Finns they inhabited a real nation, with its own distinctive language (denied by Russian-controlled officialdom) and traditions that were also different to the prevailing Norse mythology of Asgard.

Still, performing in public wasn't easy.

In 1899, under a renewed crackdown by Tsar Nicholas II, Sibelius was asked to compose music for a fundraiser supporting newspaper workers' pensions. But the concert's real purpose was to finance a free press. That work – the Symphony No. 1 in E minor – ended with the rousing finale 'Finland awakes', later revised by Sibelius as a standalone piece with the defiant title Finlandia.

Seriously, if you have never heard it, please go online and listen right to the end. If you aren't blown away by the optimism and soaring majesty of Finlandia, you probably gave up reading this book some time ago.

Anyway, when the Finnish Parliament declared independence from Russia after the October Revolution in 1917, Sibelius could finally acknowledge the part his music had played:

We fought 600 years for our freedom and I am part

of the generation that achieved it. My Finlandia is the story of this fight. This is the song of our battle, our hymn of victory.

But the song was nearly silenced again.

After a bloody civil war in Finland, Russia invaded the country twice during ww2. Despite offers of sanctuary abroad, Sibelius refused to leave, hunkering down at his forest home Ainola where he lived with his wife and five daughters until his death in 1957.

And that's when the modern battle to save Sibelius really began.

The composer had forbidden any performance of Kullervo or other early folklore-based work during his lifetime. According to Tuomas Kinberg, former manager of the Lahti Symphony Orchestra:

> It was partly because he didn't want to be dismissed as a local composer playing only 'nationalist' music and partly because he was a perfectionist. In the 1980s, his family gave the original sheet music to Helsinki University library and biographers were given permission to examine them. Sibelius was 91 when he died, so he controlled things for a very long time.

Bizzarely, that tight control also meant Finland had no concert hall bearing the name of its most famous composer until the Symphony Orchestra of Finland's seventh city, Lahti, decided to construct the country's first Sibelius Hall completely from wood. It was a master stroke. Tuomas recalls:

> In 1996, with 28 per cent unemployment, it was politically hard to justify a new concert hall. But the government wanted a prestigious building for its 'Year of Wood.' They had failed with other big projects – a promised wooden ice hockey hall was finally built from steel. And although the city of Lahti

was not keen – voting seven times before success by
a single vote – the government needed this project.
The Orchestra also had sponsorship from the huge
Metsa cooperative – which needed to advertise more
sophisticated uses for wood than just sawn timber.

So finally, with the country's first Sibelius Hall in a
pioneering wooden building, Lahti Symphony sought and won
the family's permission to record everything Sibelius had ever
written. In 2000 they announced an annual Sibelius Festival –
four days playing nothing but Sibelius and majoring on those
early, unperformed works.

Critics predicted the event would be repetitive and
parochial. But 22 years later the festival is still going strong
and the Sibelius Hall is in the world's top ten for acoustics.

The Hall has also changed the city. It was built in an old
industrial area, two kilometres from the centre, but once
complete, a marina, housing, restaurants and paths sprung
up in the reclaimed stunning lakeside location, which is now
the 'living room' of Lahti.

The orchestra has continued to innovate, becoming the first
in the world to livestream concerts in 2007 – and therefore
coping with lockdown better than most.

All of which gave the Symphony Orchestra in Finland's
seventh city the confidence to welcome international rising
star Dalia Stasevska as its first female chief conductor. Why
did she take the post?

Jean Sibelius created the idea of what Finland sounds
like. You can hear his enthusiasm for discovering the
Finnish sagas – folklore that's ours alone – even as he
was becoming a universal composer. Finland doesn't
have a history of Kings and castles. We have always
been occupied. When we finally became free it was
built on language, literature, paintings and music.
This is so true.

Finland celebrated its centenary by opening a new national library in a coveted space opposite its parliament. Why? Because half of all Finns visit a library every month. Why? Because spending time in libraries is encouraged in an education system that is simply the best in the world, thanks to its emphasis on local schools, autonomy for teachers, an absence of external exams till the age of 15 and a language once banned by colonial powers.

Self-belief works. But it takes self-knowledge, sisu (determination) and equality. All of which are wrapped together in Finland's unique cooperative tradition.

So what did they get from a century of independence – they got themselves.

And when little Estonia finally broke free from the Soviet Union in 1991, a Big Sister was waiting across the Baltic to help with investment and alternative ways to run services – especially education. Finland and Estonia share the same language, forest, bog and lochan landscape and memory of guerrilla resistance to Russian occupation. So within a decade, Estonia had pivoted away from the Russian approach to education, adopting the world-beating Finnish system and ousting their mentor from top spot for basic education in the PISA charts.

This ability to jettison old, limiting frameworks is the biggest gain possible from Scottish independence. Even though we have our own systems, their generally egalitarian outlook is half-buried. And the British mania for judgement, comparison and grading – something Pasi Sahlberg calls 'testing children to destruction' – is a virus operating inside the Scottish system too. Successful countries like Finland and Estonia trust their teachers to deliver and the teachers trust the children to take responsibility for learning. All teachers in Finland have a Masters Degree (including primary teachers) – a decision taken by the profession itself. Teachers spend the lowest amount of time face-to-face with pupils and the longest time discussing ideas with colleagues, reading up and preparing for classes, where their aim is to improve average attainment – not just the performance of the most talented. Indeed, the high-flying Estonians almost dispensed with exams altogether in the aftermath of Covid.

These successful outlooks depend on many things – but uppermost is trust. And trust is not helped by testing kids at the age of five.

How easy will it be for Scotland to complete its slow pivot away from the destructive preoccupation with testing, rote-learning and exams which – according to traditionalists – once made Scottish education the envy of the world? I'm no expert, but perhaps it was the early and universal nature of parish schools in Scotland that let all ships rise.

Whatever, in the shape of our experienced Nordic neighbours, we have fellow travellers who can act as models for the new Scotland, just as they did for the new Estonia. And does anyone think the Baltic Tiger would be better off remaining a forgotten bit of a resentful, expansionist but under-performing Soviet empire? No they don't.

So that's how the 'breakaways' of Norway, Finland, Iceland and Estonia have done. But how did their departure affect the former 'colony' powers of Denmark and Sweden?

Quite evidently, they also survived. Pretty well.

Losing colonies – gaining focus

Many Nordic historians think the loss of distant, hard-to-control territory helped focus Danish and Swedish minds – on themselves.

The Danes lost Norway in 1814 and therefore the chance to 'borrow' hydro-electric energy from Norway's vigorous rivers and later its oil and gas income. (Looking at you Westminster)

But the loss of that easy option – nicking Norway's resources – has also been the making of Denmark, because it encouraged the bold move towards wind power after the OPEC crisis of 1973. Without Norwegian oil and hydro, Denmark had no other long-term alternative. In the 1970s, 92 per cent of Denmark's energy came from oil imports and OPEC had demonstrated how very unwise such dependence could be. It took courage, cooperation and the absence of home-grown fossil fuel stopgaps for Danish politicians to turn wholesale and cross-party towards a different green strategy. But fortune favours the bold – and the early adopters.

Independent of Norway and its vast oil reserves, Denmark had to deal with its own future using its own reserves. It turned out their greatest national asset has been their own human ability to reach radical, grown-up, long-term energy decisions which have stuck for generations, despite changing constellations of party-political control. As a result, a Danish company is world leader in wind turbine manufacture and Denmark has become a world leader in the Green Transition with the island of Samsøe winning the UN Climate Champions Award at COP26 and Copenhagen named the world's most liveable city – for the seventh year running. Their secret is local control.

Søren Hermansen – one of *Time Life*'s Heroes of the Environment – is a pivotal part of Denmark's community-based, local energy approach. In 1997 his small, tight-knit, conservative, farming island of Samsøe, nestled in the Kattegat Strait, won a contest sponsored by the Danish Government to become Denmark's showcase for sustainable power, going carbon-free without any long-term state funding, tax breaks or technical expertise.

In the '90s almost all Samsøe's power came from oil and coal and although farmers had small district heating schemes, most of the island's 4,300 residents didn't know a wind turbine from a grain silo. Søren, though, saw an opportunity. Today Samsøe isn't just carbon-neutral — it produces 10 per cent more clean electricity than it uses through a battery of offshore wind turbines, and feeds that extra power back into the grid at a profit.

The transformation of Copenhagen into one of the world's top cycling cities follows similar lines. 40 years ago, cycling rates in the Danish capital were as poor as Scotland today. Then the oil crisis of 1974 happened and the Danes changed tack. Today the Danish capital is a near ideal cycling system – more than 60 per cent of residents commute to work or school by bike. Copenhagen also guarantees a swimming opportunity within 15 minutes of every resident. That exacting promise was delivered, thanks to one dedicated council employee who masterminded conversion of the city's harbour into a giant, outdoors swimming pool, with material used in moon landings to cover and block dozens of waste water pipes. Now Copenhagen Harbour is a clean, swimming mecca and the same technique has created swimming opportunities in other canals across the city.

How did they manage that transformation in just 40 years?

Well, it helped to have a preceding century of the horse-trading and compromise that comes with proportional representation (see *Borgen*), the Nordic tradition of powerful, quasi-sovereign local government and a meaningful 'social contract' between state and citizens. For Danes the welfare state operates like a cushion to cope with difficult times or like a personal bank – with deposits and withdrawals throughout the different stages of a lifetime. Professor Jon Kvist gave Nordic Horizons an account of this Nordic 'welfairytale' – characterising welfare as a way to redistribute income across the lifetime of each individual as well as between people and described the social investment of the Nordic countries as 'policies that not only mitigate social ills but also prevent deep social cleavages'.

Sighs.

And what about Sweden?

Well, losing Finland in 1809 and being rebuffed by the Norwegians in 1905 were just the most recent territorial losses experienced by Sweden – the only Nordic country to have been a major military power. In 1648, after the Thirty Years' War, Sweden actually controlled the third-largest land mass in Europe, surpassed only by Russia and Spain. But defending this empire was expensive and draining, especially for a country of just 1 million people struggling to survive in a sub-Arctic climate on thin soils. Sweden's King Charles x Gustav for example, attacked Poland in 1654, gained some territory and promptly died of exhaustion. But in a country famed for producing extremely capable warrior kings, the wars went on. Swedish generals consistently outperformed their opponents, and the military system devised by Swedish kings used the most advanced tactics in Europe at the time. As a result, Swedish armies routinely defeated far greater forces until Russian victory finally halted Sweden's eastbound expansion. When Charles XII died in 1718 only a weakened, smaller territory remained. His biographer wrote:

> A whole new age began, better suited to the stature
> of ordinary men than the era that had ended.

But perhaps that was no bad thing.

Sweden had been a fighting machine for centuries – but as territory disappeared, its focus changed. Trading and manufacturing became important – and much was pioneered by Scots, who'd already been through the industrialisation process back home. Arbroath-born William Gibson founded Sweden's first textile factory in 1834 at Jonsered, near Gothenburg. Since the site was totally undeveloped, beside a powerful waterfall, Gibson had to build a mini-town for workers with housing, a school, basic sick pay, medical care and a tiny old folks home. It was a self-sufficient industrial community - a first for Sweden and a bit like Robert Owen's New Lanark. Some say Jonsered even inspired the creation of the 'cradle to grave' Swedish Welfare State, since the influential Gibson became a Swedish MP. But he was a hard taskmaster with no time for trade unions or any talk of socialism. Today his paternalistic legacy is still as hotly debated in Sweden as Robert Owen's legacy is in Scotland.

Meanwhile another son of a Scot, William Chalmers Junior,

founded Gothenburg's Chalmers University in 1829 – one of the best engineering universities in Europe today. And those are just two of a clutch of Scots who helped expand Swedish trade. Swedish industry grew thanks to its status as a neutral country during both World Wars (though it supplied the Nazi regime with steel and ball-bearings and allowed passage to German troops travelling to occupy Norway). Avoiding occupation in both wars, Sweden's industrial base expanded and so did its prosperity. But the Swedes did something fairly dramatic with that cash. In 1932, its socialist leaders created the Folkhemmet (People's Home) – one of the most successful social democratic systems in the world, and the carefully constructed deal between labour, capital and all the parties and classes represented in the Riksdag, led to 44 years of Social Democrat government (1932–76) and 20 years deepening and broadening the welfare provisions in the People's Home.

This is an almost offensively abbreviated history. But the question remains. Would Sweden have become world-renowned for the care of its citizens, in the world's most extensive welfare state if its people were still regarded as useful cannon fodder in the defence of an impossibly large kingdom?

Of course, we are all changed by the choices taken or forced upon us, so history doesn't work in hindsight. But let's just put it this way.

After Swedish rulers stopped trying to take over Europe, their world-renowned capacity for military planning was applied to a welfare state instead. Was this a bad thing?

Where beer costs an arm and a leg

Now, I'll grant you this towering Nordic success is slightly intimidating for innocent bystanders. Indeed, all this achievement can make Scots feel unworthy, rather than inspired. The higher the pedestal, the more Nordic nations appear unreachable and slightly alien to earth-bound Scots who create flies in the Nordic ointment to justify why we're absolutely fine as we are.

Thus, they've no sense of humour.

A pint of beer costs £700 (joke).

And they may be slim, healthier and better off than us – but they're all depressed.

Straw-clutching should really become a new Olympic sport.

Seven years ago, the humourless Swedish deputy Prime Minister posted a picture of herself signing a new Climate Change Act surrounded by female ministers – eloquently taking the mickey out of Donald Trump's much circulated photograph signing an anti-abortion order, surrounded by men.

Isabella Lovin said her Swedish government – 'the first feminist government in the world' – was urging European countries to lead the climate change challenge as 'the US is not there anymore'.

Not laugh out loud funny, I'll grant you, but sharp. And brave.

In fact, Sweden has taken pelters from the Americans after adopting a totally different post-war path, with a peaceful redistribution of political power and wealth creating the world's most generous, effective and enduring welfare state. For this, the Swedes were criticised by successive American Presidents including President Eisenhower who declared that Sweden was a hotbed of 'sin, suicide, socialism and smörgåsbord'. That pronouncement was largely responsible for creating the unsubstantiated belief that Scandinavians are somehow morbid and depressed – along with the Swedes early habit of counting suicide victims because the Lutheran Church didn't exclude them from graveyards, unlike most other Christian denominations.

But the Swedes real crime in a post-war world was simple – its 'middle-way' of social democracy or caring capitalism produced a higher post-war GDP than the nakedly competitive and capitalist USA. But under fire, the Swedes held firm.

Can Scotland catch up?

Absolutely, once we get these countries off the pedestal, stop envying their current prosperity and examine the decisions they made over the last century about equality land ownership and local control – which laid the groundwork for their success today.

It's also time to get real about ourselves.

Truly remote is what Nordic neighbours experience – we don't.

They have taken steps to distribute power, control, energy production, top jobs and government departments – we haven't.

In return, their remote areas produce geothermal power (Iceland) along with the world's most successful fisheries and largest supplies of hydro electricity (Norway) whilst protecting the livelihoods of their indigenous Sami people.

With independence we can do the same – indeed that's the only way Scotland will ever gain control over vital resources and shrug off the deep-seated belief that our land is too poor and our people too unimaginative or lethargic to sustain new ways of working. It isn't and we aren't.

Scotland's population was 70 per cent greater than Norway in 1800. It was 50 per cent bigger in 1900. Today the two populations are almost the same – one vivid measure of our rural stagnation.

'Sparsely populated areas' in Scotland are defined as having 10,000 people or less within 30 minutes of travel.

But 30 minutes travel has a different significance in remote Norway. It's the maximum distance anyone should travel to reach their local council headquarters. If that was applied in Scotland, Highland Council would stop at the Black Isle.

Looked at the other way, if our councils (average population 170k) were Norwegian sized (average 15k) and they collected all standard rate income tax (like Sweden), we'd have sizeable, vigorous towns across the country and a very different kind of democracy.

Meanwhile the top four places in the UN's Happiness Index this year are occupied by Nordic nations – Finland followed by Norway, Denmark and Iceland. All countries score highly on income, healthy life expectancy, social support and trust as well as perceptions of generosity, freedom and the absence of corruption. According to Meik Wiking of the Happiness Research Institute in Denmark,

> GDP per capita in Finland is lower than its neighbouring Nordic countries but the Finns are better at converting wealth into wellbeing.

As the most remote economic region in the EU they have had to become creative and self-reliant.

We can learn from that.

But only when we've decided that Scotland means business.

When we've decided to thrive and not just keep ticking over.

And that means all of us – not just politicians.

What's most needed is not guarantees of prosperity but resilience – 'a feeling that demands are challenges worthy of our investment and engagement'. That definition was produced by researcher Aaron Antonovsky, looking at survivors of war. How does it apply to Scotland?

Independence is undoubtedly a challenge, worthy of our investment and engagement and big enough to demand our all.

Independence won't be easy but the effort involved will be worthy of our time, investment and emotional engagement. That will only be possible if the political class can see the importance of everyone getting a touch of the ball, everyone's skills being called upon to devise pathways and solutions, everyone being allowed to jointly own this national project.

If the Nordics are willing to tolerate a keen understudy, the Scottish Government could apply for the equivalent of observer status the day after a Yes vote. Joining the Nordic

Council would give an independent Scotland the same catch-up challenge facing Greece, Italy and Portugal in the Eurozone. But it's the right sort of challenge for Scotland. And the right sort of company.

It's hard ploughing a new furrow on ground ploughed the British way for centuries. So many under-scrutinised, harmful defaults are baked into traditions, habits, expectations and behaviour. We desperately need other templates – other ways of doing things that still chime with our deeper selves. Other outlooks we could have been shared if Scotland had escaped the twin yokes of feudalism and deep involvement in Britain's imperial project.

The Nordic nations have those alternatives – in spades. It's as if they have large chunks of our early promise, held in deep freeze.

So, will we, won't we? Should we, shouldn't we? If we want to unpick the stuck problems of centuries, we need the power and the elbow room. If we're scared the fabric of society will collapse without the hierarchy and second place we've tholed for centuries, let's not bother.

But answer this question – and be honest.

What will keep our children living and thriving in Scotland?

Whatever your answer – vote that way next time.

Postscript

Ten years after indy

Indulge me.

It's ten years after independence.

Let's not speculate about the eventual date of Independence Day or the means by which the Scots finally exercised self-determination and voted to leave the UK, except that a majority of English residents also voted Yes, which blew everyone away.

So, what happened?

Ten years after independence, Trident was finally relocated to King's Bay in Georgia, USA, where the submarines have always gone pick up missiles.

The peace camp campaigners who put their own lives on hold for more than 40 years received Scotland's first Medals of Honour outside the Hermless Hoose in Edinburgh Castle, which contains ten volumes naming all those who campaigned for an independent Scotland, they didn't live to see.

Scotland has rejoined the EU after launching our own currency in parallel with the independence negotiations, joined the Nordic Council as a full member and the Council of the Isles, along with the newly reunited Federal Republic of Ireland. Scotland is the only country to be a full member of both the Nordic and Isles Councils and Aberdeen University has a new North Atlantic Research Hub, housed beside its Institute of Irish and Scottish studies.

Three years ago, we voted by a 70 per cent majority to ratify our new, crowd-sourced constitution and interim President Andy Murray, handed over to Karine Polwart, the first head of state elected in accordance with Scotland's written constitution.

Land reform was enacted after recommendations by a Citizens Assembly set up by the first Social Democratic coalition government – it recommended a Land Tax, Norway's system of boplikt so 'first' homes buyers must be on the local electoral register a Succession Act has given all children the right to equally inherit land, already breaking up several massive 'sporting' estates and there's a new maximum acreage per person. It's busy at last in the straths and glens of Scotland, with plots staked out along rivers, primary schools re-opening and expanded as community hubs, powered by off-grid renewable energy systems based on Eigg's blend of solar, wind and hydro power. Community-sized 'mini' councils have control over all grants relating to land use, which has encouraged 90 per cent election turnouts and ensured locals aren't completely priced off the land by the tens of thousands of 'New Scots' heading north to escape the rat race.

Scots is finally recognised as a language.

Meanwhile, the Welsh Senedd has been given tax-raising powers and control over energy by a Westminster government desperate to keep its last Celtic colony and both governments are finally building a Severn barrage that will renewably power Wales, Devon, Cornwall and Somerset.

What have I got?

I've got a hut, an old age pension twice as generous as Blighty and a weight off my mind.

What has Scotland got?

The world's most sought-after passport.

And our children, staying, building, hoping, arguing and digging where they stand. At last.

Has it been worth waiting for?

Yes.

Crossing the Forth by train, that familiar echoey rumble says we are crossing the bridge. I cease work, take off my glasses and survey one of the most stunning maritime landscapes in the world.

A silent act of awestruck admiration.

Like everyone else in the carriage.

And the train.

And all the other trains.

And all the buses.

This is a beautiful country and it was always ours.

Waiting for the day we finally plucked up the courage to step up... and claim it.

Also published by **LUATH PRESS**

McSmörgåsbord
What post-Brexit Scotland can learn from the Nordics
Lesley Riddoch and Eberhard Bort

ISBN 978-1-912147-00-7 PBK £7.99

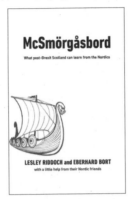

Of course, the majority of Nordic nations are EU *members. But perhaps the* EEA *is a closer fit for Scotland? Perhaps, too, a viable halfway house option would boost support for Scottish independence? Especially since Holyrood may not automatically retrieve powers from Europe post Brexit.*
PADDY BORT

Inside or outside the UK, Scotland wants to keep trade and cultural links with Europe – that much is clear. But is the EU really the best club in town for an independent Scotland?

These tough questions have already been faced and resolved by five Nordic nations and their autonomous territories within the last 40 years. Perhaps there's something for Scotland to learn? The unique combination of personal experience and experts' insights give this book its hands-on character: pragmatic and thought-provoking, challenging and instructive, full of amazing stories and useful comparisons, enriching the debates about Scotland's post-Brexit future as a Nordic neighbour.

Blossom
What Scotland Needs to Flourish
Lesley Riddoch

ISBN 978-1-912147-52-6 PBK £11.99

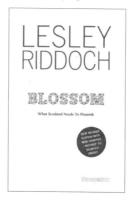

A brilliant, moving, well-written, informative, important and valuable piece of work.
ELAINE C SMITH

Not so much an intervention in the independence debate as a heartfelt manifesto for a better democracy.
ESTHER BREITENBACH, THE SCOTSMAN

Weeding out vital components of Scottish identity from decades of political and social tangle is no mean task, but it's one journalist Lesley Riddoch has undertaken.

Dispensing with the tired, yo-yoing jousts over fiscal commissions, Devo Something and EU in-or-out, *Blossom* pinpoints both the buds of growth and the blight that's holding Scotland back. Drawing from its people and history as well as the experience of the Nordic countries, and the author's own passionate and outspoken perspective, this is a plain-speaking but incisive call to restore equality and control to local communities and let Scotland flourish.

Huts, a Place Beyond
How to End Our Exile from Nature
Lesley Riddoch

ISBN 978-1-913025-63-2 PBK £9.99

*...a clarion call for a revolution in the way that we understand
home, leisure and our relationship with the natural world*
THE GUARDIAN

*Lesley Riddoch uses her new book to explain why our country
is perfect to find a bolt hole away from the stresses and strains
of modern city life.*
THE TIMES

Why have the inhabitants of one of Europe's prime tourist
destinations been elbowed off the land and exiled from nature
for so long?

Lesley Riddoch relives her own bothy experience, rediscovers lost
hutting communities, travels through hytte-covered Norway and
suggests that thousands of humble woodland huts would give
Scots a vital post-Covid connection with nature and affordable,
low-impact holidays in their own beautiful land – at last.

Riddoch on the Outer Hebrides
Lesley Riddoch

ISBN 978-1-80425-011-2 PBK £12.99

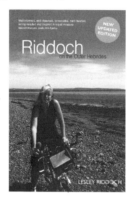

*Let's be proud of standing on the outer edge of a crazy
mainstream world – when the centre collapses, the
periphery becomes central.*
ALISTAIR MCINTOSH

*Chatty without being oppressive and informed without
being lecturing, Riddoch's style nicely brings home the
beauty of the islands and the charm of those who live there.*
THE HERALD

Riddoch on the Outer Hebrides is a thought-provoking
commentary based on broadcaster Lesley Riddoch's cycle
journey through a beautiful island chain facing seismic cultural
and economic change.

Her experience is described in a typically affectionate but hard-
hitting style; with humour, anecdote and a growing sympathy
for islanders tired of living at the margins but fearful of closer
contact with mainland Scotland.

Details of books published by Luath Press can be found at:
www.luath.co.uk

Luath Press Limited

committed to publishing well written books worth reading

LUATH PRESS takes its name from Robert Burns, whose little collie Luath (*Gael.*, swift or nimble) tripped up Jean Armour at a wedding and gave him the chance to speak to the woman who was to be his wife and the abiding love of his life. Burns called one of the 'Twa Dogs' Luath after Cuchullin's hunting dog in Ossian's *Fingal*. Luath Press was established in 1981 in the heart of Burns country, and is now based a few steps up the road from Burns' first lodgings on Edinburgh's Royal Mile. Luath offers you distinctive writing with a hint of unexpected pleasures.

Most bookshops in the UK, the US, Canada, Australia, New Zealand and parts of Europe, either carry our books in stock or can order them for you. To order direct from us, please send a £sterling cheque, postal order, international money order or your credit card details (number, address of cardholder and expiry date) to us at the address below. Please add post and packing as follows: UK – £1.00 per delivery address; overseas surface mail – £2.50 per delivery address; overseas airmail – £3.50 for the first book to each delivery address, plus £1.00 for each additional book by airmail to the same address. If your order is a gift, we will happily enclose your card or message at no extra charge.

Luath Press Limited
543/2 Castlehill
The Royal Mile
Edinburgh EH1 2ND
Scotland
Telephone: 0131 225 4326 (24 hours)
Email: sales@luath.co.uk
Website: www.luath.co.uk